HERE'S THE PITCH

HERE'S THE PITCH

The Amazing, True, New, and Improved Story of Baseball and Advertising

ROBERTA J. NEWMAN

University of Nebraska Press
Lincoln & London

Acknowledgments for the use of copyrighted material appear on page xii, which constitutes an extension of the copyright page.

Library of Congress Cataloging-in-Publication Data
Names: Newman, Roberta J., author.
Title: Here's the pitch: the amazing, true, new, and improved story of baseball and advertising / Roberta J. Newman.
Description: Lincoln: University of Nebraska Press, 2019. | Includes bibliographical references and index.
Identifiers: LCCN 2018023752
ISBN 9780803278479 (cloth: alk. paper)
ISBN 9781496213655 (epub)
ISBN 9781496213662 (mobi)
ISBN 9781496213679 (pdf)
Subjects: LCSH: Baseball—Economic aspects—United States. | Baseball—Social aspects—United States. | Advertising—Social aspects—United States. | Mass media and sports—United States.
Classification: LCC GV880 .N48 2019 | DDC 331.8811796357—dc23 LC record available at https://lccn.loc.gov/2018023752

Set in Minion Pro by E. Cuddy.

For Eddie, Evan, Marya, Clark, and Ada

Contents

Illustrations

Acknowledgments

This project began in 2000 as a response to an off-handed, general suggestion by former Baseball Hall of Fame librarian Tom Heitz that someone (not necessarily me) ought to write a book about baseball and advertising. Thanks to him for throwing the idea out into the wind for me to latch onto. I'd also like to offer my sincere gratitude to my friends and colleagues at the NINE Spring Training Conference (an annual event bringing together baseball historians, scholars, and writers), most particularly Jean Hastings Ardell, Dan Ardell, Trey Strecker, Geri Strecker, Steve Gietschier, James Brunson, Steve Treder, George Gmelch, Anna Newton, Bill Ressler, Noa Ressler, Maureen Smith, Stephanie Licio, Lisa Doris Alexander, Gary Gershman, Scott Peterson, Lee Lowenfish, Larry Gerlach, Dick Crepeau, David Pegram, Lee Kluck, John Leonoudakis, and the late, great Bill Kirwin, NINE's founder. I am especially indebted to James Walker and Rob Bellamy, whose superb work on baseball and broadcasting was invaluable to this project, and whose guidance and good humor made my task all the easier. Had it not been for the sage advice of Helen Churko, I would never have become a baseball researcher. I cannot thank her enough. Thanks, too, to Margaret Plotkin, who gave me valuable feedback on early chapter drafts, and to Emily Bauman, who never failed to respond to my requests for writing help, even when she had a class to prepare.

For supporting this project on its trip from embryonic proposal to published book, I thank Rob Taylor, Courtney Ochsner, Joeth Zucco, and everyone else at the University of Nebraska Press who touched this work in any way. Thanks, too, to copyeditor Karen H.

Brown. I'd also like to acknowledge those company archivists and legal representatives who aided me in securing image permissions.

Ed Grupsmith, Evan Grupsmith, Marya Fisher, Clark Fisher, Jamie Newman, and the whole Newman clan, I cannot begin to express how grateful I am for your love and support, even when you were sick of me going on about baseball and constantly pointing out product placements and insidious advertising. Finally, special thanks to Ada Frances Fisher, who has already learned the words to the chorus of "Take Me Out to the Ball Game," and is about to start on the verses.

I wish to thank the following publications for their support of my work as it developed. Parts of chapter 2 first appeared as "It Pays to Be Personal" in NINE: A Journal of Baseball History and Culture 12, no. 1 (Fall 2003): 25–42. Parts of chapter 4 appeared as "Pitching Behind the Color Lines: Baseball, Advertising, and Race" in Baseball Research Journal 11, no. 36 (January 2007): 81–90. Parts of chapter 6 appeared as "Let's Just Say It Works for Me: Rafael Palmeiro, Major League Baseball, and the Marketing of Viagra" in NINE 14, no. 2 (Spring 2006): 1–14. And parts of chapter 8 originally appeared as "Driven: Branding Derek Jeter, Redefining Race" in NINE 17, no. 2 (Spring 2009): 70–79.

Introduction

Here's the Pitch!

"Baseball," writes Roger Angell, "is a commercial venture, but it is one of such perfect equipoise that millions of us every year can still unembarrassedly surrender ourselves to its unique and absorbing joys. The ability to find beauty and involvement in artificial commercial constructions is essential to most of us in the modern world; it is the life-giving naïveté."[1] It is a twenty-first-century commonplace to complain that baseball was better, purer, more authentic back in the days when it was just a game. Predating Ken Burns's *Baseball* by three years, HBO's documentary series featuring amateur footage shot by fans and players borrowed this evocative phrase for its title. According to Amazon.com, *When It Was a Game* "captures the full magic of America's National Pastime as you've always imagined it—the way it really was."[2] Angell, writing in the *New Yorker* in 1964, knew better. Professional baseball is a business, and it always has been. The real focus of Angell's essay is relocation, expansion, television's stranglehold on the sport, and that year's World Series. Yet his observation about the commercial nature of the professional sport applies to virtually every aspect of our national pastime. Advertising is just one part of the wider baseball industry. But every time we hear the "AT&T Call to the Bullpen," every time we enter Guaranteed Rate Field—once U.S. Cellular Field—or Minute Maid Park—once Enron Field, every time we engage in the annual ritual of voting, now online, for our favorite All-Stars, brought to us by MasterCard or Camping World, or we wait on tenterhooks to see who, if any, of our team's players will win this year's Esurance MLB Awards, we are reminded that advertising has become inseparable from the Major League Baseball experience.

Since its inception in the mid-nineteenth century, baseball has grown up alongside its longtime companion, its nearly conjoined twin, the advertising industry. Indeed, were the two not so connected, generations of adults would have been spared the pain of their mothers disposing of the precious baseball cards; millions of Americans would not know that nothing goes together like baseball, hotdogs, apple pie, and Chevrolet; and Wheaties would not be the Breakfast of Champions, as it has been since the waning years of the Great Depression.

It is a common assertion that advertising reflects culture. In fact, it is almost as cliché as the suggestion that Major League Baseball was once just a game. The former, however, is far more accurate than the latter. Advertising does reflect culture. Paired with baseball, the reflection is refined, perfected, doubled. But advertising also creates culture. It influences patterns of consumption and introduces consumers to new sets of ideas. As media critic Grant McCracken observes, "Advertising puts at the disposal of modern culture an area of play, experimentation and innovation with which to fashion new cultural meanings and reorganize and reassign old ones. It is where culture does its diecasting."[3] It forms the backbone of the "artificial commercial construction" to which Angell and many of the rest of us "unembarrassedly surrender ourselves" with joy. Like Major League Baseball, advertising is a fundamentally American enterprise. Together, these industries have contributed to crafting American identity, from their paired inception in the mid-nineteenth century to their continued healthy relationship in the twenty-first. Just look at those cards, that Chevy, that bowl of cereal.

The Project

The marriage between baseball and advertising in its twinned roles as reflectors and creators of American culture, of American identity, is the subject of this book. Although this project has strong historical underpinnings, it is not strictly a history. It is by no means a complete chronicle of the relationship between the two industries, nor is it a catalogue of baseball-related advertising.

And while it draws upon media and representation theory, neither is it strictly a work of media studies. Rather, *Here's the Pitch* is an amalgam of these and ideas from other disciplines, including cultural studies, sociology, art criticism, and even marketing theory. In writing it, I have tried to paint a picture of the ongoing liaison between these two fundamentally American enterprises and, in small part, what their partnership may mean.

Rather than provide an overview of the marriage between baseball and advertising, I have chosen to focus on a series of occasions when, to misquote another common adage, the whole—the relationship, itself—is worth more than the sum of its parts. As such, I examine various instances in which baseball and advertising have come together to create a clear lens through which to view certain aspects of American culture. Among other things, I foreground the creation and uses of new technology, from chromolithography and high-speed rotary printing in the nineteenth century through to the introduction of radio and television in the twentieth. These are the tools with which the twinned industries were disseminated, and without them, both would have remained small and relatively unimportant. Together, professional baseball and advertising used these tools in new and innovative ways, occasionally pushing boundaries, but also from time to time implementing them to retreat from innovation, promoting a fundamentally conservative world view.

Major League Baseball and the advertising surrounding it would be nothing without their stars. After all, MLB is a reliable supplier of celebrities, and advertising has found any number of ways to use them. Central to this project is the changing nature of celebrity. Following McCracken's lead, I explore the ways in which celebrities harness culturally constituted meanings, making them easily available for consumption via product endorsements.[4] From Ty Cobb to Babe Ruth, in the 1920s and '30s, to Mickey Mantle, Yogi Berra, and Willie Mays, in the postwar years, to Derek Jeter, Rafael Palmeiro, and David Ortiz in the twenty-first century, I look at baseball's celebrities and attempt to determine what qualities make the perfect pitchmen for specific products at specific historical moments, considering the ways in which variations of those qualities—the culturally constituted meanings—shine a light on the zeitgeist, the spirit of the times.

Inextricable from any study of baseball or advertising, especially as expressions of American identity, are the implications of race and ethnicity. Historically, baseball played as equally an important part in upholding the segregated status quo as it did in America's desegregation narrative. For sixty years, the Major Leagues barred players of African ancestry from competition, the result of an unofficial, unwritten, but carefully enforced rule. In response, another professional baseball industry developed on the other side of the color line. The same is true of advertising. But even after Jackie Robinson took the field on April 15, 1947, with the Brooklyn Dodgers, followed by a slow but steady stream of African American players onto Major League rosters, African American faces were conspicuously absent from advertising in major mainstream media. The world of baseball and advertising behind the color line, the ways in which the paired enterprises answered segregation with ads of their own, is another focus of my study.

With growing numbers of Latinos entering the Major Leagues, baseball has been central to the ways in which Afro-Latinos are perceived by the largely white, Anglophone majority. Since many Americans first encounter what they perceive to be "the other" in advertising, I also look at the representation of Afro-Latino ballplayers in English-language advertising. Looking back to *Saturday Night Live*'s Chico Escuela, the fictional Dominican New York Met whose catchphrase "Beisbol been berra, berra good to me" became shorthand for the stereotype of the bumbling Afro-Latino player, I also examine the perpetuation of the Chico Escuela image in advertising well beyond its cultural shelf life.

In 1964 media guru Marshall McLuhan predicted that baseball would become irrelevant, a victim of new forms of communication, most notably television. While in most things media-related, McLuhan has proven prophetic, his assertion here was off the mark. Baseball has remained healthy, despite incurring a few bumps and bruises along the way, some more serious than others. Setbacks notwithstanding, baseball's relationship with advertising in the new age of new media is stronger than ever. A book about baseball and advertising would not be complete without a look at how Major League Baseball has embraced digital media in its many permutations and combinations.

Ultimately, *Here's the Pitch* is a book about American identity, writ both large and small. It represents my attempt to draw many strains of American cultural history together in order to offer a portrait, however incomplete, of the ways in which the artificial "commercial construction" to which we "unembarrassedly surrender ourselves," and the techniques by which it sells itself, help convey and constitute the various meanings of American identity.

HERE'S THE PITCH

CHAPTER ONE

Hustlers, Hucksters, and Snake-Oil Salesmen

Two Industries Emerge

I n the mid-nineteenth century two industries emerged upon the American scene. One was strictly a business, yet it helped create, define, and disseminate American culture. The other was a game, yet it soon became emblematic for what it meant to be American, a potent signifier of national identity as well as a successful enterprise in its own right. Each—the business of advertising and professional baseball—had a transformative effect on American consumers. And though neither enterprise was of purely American origin, both were revolutionized by America's hustlers, hucksters, and snake-oil salesmen, who molded them into central cultural and economic institutions.

Baseball as a participatory sport and advertising as a nascent American industry both date from the decades prior to the Civil War. The first professional agency dealing in print advertising, Volney Palmer, opened in Philadelphia in 1843, just two years before Alexander Cartwright founded the Knickerbocker Base Ball Club, and three years before the first officially recorded game (though certainly not the first game) was played on Hoboken's Elysian Fields. And just as the rules of the Knickerbocker Club's game differed from baseball as it came to be played in the early twentieth-century Deadball Era, so, too, were Volney Palmer's advertisements a far cry from the professionally written and illustrated work that was produced at the century's turn. With neither art nor copy departments, the pre–Civil War agency's only function was to sell advertising space in print publications to companies and individuals promoting their goods and services. Generating content, such as it was, was up to the advertisers.[1] It was not until the decades that followed the war that advertising, like baseball, was fully professionalized.

Of course, the simultaneous professionalization and commercialization of baseball and the astronomical growth of the advertising industry in post–Civil War America did not happen simply by chance. Nor did the intimate relationship between the two enterprises develop in a vacuum. A combination of factors led to the rapid expansion of the businesses of baseball and advertising. Arguably the most important factor in both cases was a veritable explosion in the number of potential fans and consumers. During the last three decades of the nineteenth century, America's Gilded Age, the nation's population nearly doubled, from 39,818,449 in 1870 to 76,212,168 in 1900.[2] A major demographic shift was also underway. More and more Americans relocated from rural areas to the nation's cities, especially cities in the Northeast, Mid-Atlantic, and Upper Midwest. Americans, including the new urban dwellers, were also growing richer. Over the same period, average annual per capita income increased from $174 to $236, representing an increase of more than 100 percent in actual purchasing power.[3]

Not to be overlooked was the fact that America was also becoming a nation of readers. By the turn of the twentieth century, mass literacy was a reality, and not just for the new white, urban, middle classes. According to James D. Norris, "Literacy, which had always been high by comparison with Europe, increased from 80 percent in 1870 to 94 per cent by 1920. Most striking were the gains in literacy of the Black population, from 80 percent illiteracy to nearly 80 percent literacy in the same period. The United States enjoyed a rapidly growing population at the height of its producing and consuming age, with the education necessary for an industrializing economy."[4] Clearly, the conditions were right for the development of the advertising industry. A new urban population with increased buying power represented a new consumer base, potentially receptive to advertising messages. The same factors also led to the growth of baseball both as a spectator sport and as an amusement that could be marketed by means similar to those used to sell other forms of professional entertainment. And baseball was so much more than a product. With its immense popularity and potentially marketable stars, baseball could also be used as a vehicle by which to sell other products to consumers.

Inside the Park

Baseball's first consumers were live spectators, so it stands to reason that one of the first forms of baseball-related advertising would be found inside ballparks. Ballpark signage, designed to market consumer goods to baseball fans, or "cranks," as they were often called in the late nineteenth century, was close to ubiquitous in venues where professional teams played. Outdoor advertising was not a novelty at the time. It was, in essence, one of the first forms of commercial mass communication, one of the first ways in which large groups of potential consumers might be reached at once with information about products and services. In fact, outdoor advertising was already in wide use in the Roman Empire. There is even evidence of outdoor signage from ancient Mesopotamia.[5] Nevertheless, "standardized off-premise advertising"—organized, coordinated campaigns featuring standard images, slogans, or messages, reproduced in a number of outdoor locations—was not introduced until 1835, when the first giant bill or poster for the Great Wallace Shows Circus was displayed in New York City.[6] The first leased billboard, erected specifically for the purpose of advertising, went up in 1865. By the 1870s this modern iteration of advertising had become a regular feature of the American landscape.[7]

Ballpark signage was unique in that it was simultaneously both outdoor and indoor advertising, given the fact that baseball venues were without exception "open air," although the grounds were surrounded by fences. Spectators represented a captive audience who could not help but see ads plastered or painted around them as they watched games or milled about ballparks. Fans of professional baseball were the perfect demographic to which to pitch the many types of products conventionally advertised in ballparks— consumer goods such as sports equipment, tobacco products, alcohol, and men's wear. Early twentieth-century spectators at Brooklyn's Washington Park, home of the team that would become the Dodgers, for example, saw signs pitching Old Bushmill's Irish Whiskey, Coronet Dry Gin, Green River Rye Whiskey, and Perfection Scotch Whiskey, as well as Turkish Trophy and Fatima Cigarettes. They were also pegged as potential consumers by the Adams Chewing Gum Company, a local Brooklyn enterprise that was represented in Washington Park with an ad for its Pepsin Tutti-Frutti gum. But this was not all. Along with their baseball, Brooklyn fans were treated to an especially large ad for BVD Loose Fitting Men's Underwear as well as signs for Hanes and the Ullman Shop, a local haberdashery.[8] Judging by this sampling, the majority of Brooklyn's spectators were whiskey-drinking, cigarette-smoking, gum-chewing, underwear-wearing men. Ladies' Days promotions notwithstanding, this image of Brooklyn fans constructed solely upon the outdoor advertising at Washington Park is, in fact, fairly accurate.[9] In this way, ballpark signage truly reflected this segment of consumer culture.

Smoke 'Em If You Got 'Em

Brooklyn fans were not alone. Baseball spectators were deemed to be a desirable demographic by tobacco advertisers almost from the outset. Perhaps no other enterprise so benefited from the connection between baseball and advertising as did the tobacco industry, a connection that was already evident by the 1880s.[10] But pre-rolled cigarettes like the Turkish Trophies and Fatimas advertised on Washington Park's fences were not mass-produced or mass-marketed until the very last years of the nineteenth century. Prior to that, cigarettes were hand-rolled. The widespread popularity of cigarettes can be traced back to British involvement in the Crimean War (1853–56), where they were introduced to English officers by the Turks. Shortly thereafter, cigarette smoking spread from the battlefield to England and from there to the United States. Cigarette makings were initially sold in bulk by tobacconists, whose establishments were often indicated by the presence of "cigar-store Indians" outside the door. By the 1880s, cigar-store baseball players also marked the location of tobacconists' shops. In some locations, like New York City, carved wooden baseball-player "show figures," as they were known in the industry, became the dominant form of on-site advertising for tobacconists, owing to the local popularity of the professional sport.[11]

Cigarette tobacco was first "branded" during the Civil War. In the late 1850s John Green, of Durham, North Carolina, began marketing packaged bright-leaf tobacco, the most common variety used in cigarettes, under the brand name "genuine Durham Smoking Tobacco." W. T. Blackwell took over Green's company after the founder's death, changing the product's name to one suggested by its widely recognizable bull logo. Bull Durham, the first nationally advertised tobacco brand, quickly became the best-selling cigarette tobacco in America. Named by way of tribute, the Durham Bulls of the North Carolina State Professional Baseball League were established in 1902. Although it may not have been an intentional marketing ploy, naming the city's team for the local tobacco manufacturer further contributed to the establishment of the brand. The team's name inextricably linked the product—bright-leaf tobacco—with qualities extrinsic to it, in this case, those associated with professional baseball. That the Durham Bull was so often copied was a testament to the strength of the product's brand image on the market.[12]

Not limited to display in the Bulls' own Durham ballpark, the brand's easily recognizable emblem was placed in baseball venues around the country. While it may be apocryphal, it has been suggested that the term "bullpen" derives from the fact that relief pitchers often warmed up in the shadow of giant Bull Durham billboards.[13] Whether or not this is true, it is certain that the Durham Bull was regularly featured in ballpark signage throughout the country by the early twentieth century, as evidenced by the many photographs and ads of the time. For example, a full-page ad in the 1911 *Bull Durham Baseball Guide* includes a large reproduction of the trademark image beneath large display type reading "Hit the 'Bull.'" In smaller type beneath the art, the copy reads:

Hit the "Bull"

This "Bull" Durham sign is a facsimile of the cut-out Bulls located in the majority of the baseball parks throughout the country.

Any player who hits the bull with a fairly-batted fly ball, during a regular scheduled league game on any of the grounds where these "Bull" Durham signs are located on the field, will receive

$50.00 IN CASH

Any player making a home run in a regular scheduled league game on any of these parks where the "Bull" cut-out signs are located will receive

A Carton containing 72 Five-cent Packages of
"BULL" DURHAM SMOKING TOBACCO

BLACKWELL'S DURHAM TOBACCO COMPANY
111 Fifth Avenue, New York

1. Ad for Genuine "Bull" Durham Smoking Tobacco, published in the *Bull Durham Baseball Guide* of 1911. Legend has it that the "bullpen" derived its name from strategically placed "Bull" Durham ballpark billboards.

This "Bull" Durham sign is a facsimile of the cut-out Bulls located in the majority of the baseball parks throughout the country.

Any player who hits the bull with a fairly-batted fly ball, during a regular [*sic*] scheduled game on any of the grounds where these "Bull" Durham signs are located on the field, will receive

$50.00 IN CASH

Any player making a home run in a regular [*sic*] scheduled league game on any of these parks where the "Bull" cut-out signs are located will receive

A cartoon containing 72 Five-cent Packages of
"BULL" DURHAM SMOKING TOBACCO[14]

That this baseball guide was produced as a promotion for the cigarette tobacco only serves to emphasize the connection between baseball and Bull Durham advertising.

Durham, North Carolina, which acquired the nickname Bull City based on its most famous product—itself an early example of the now common practice of city branding—was also the home of the American Tobacco Company (ATC), which would go on to make its name manufacturing and marketing factory-rolled cigarettes. Interestingly, the ATC's cigarette business was born not in North Carolina but in New York City, where James Buchanan "Buck" Duke established his first factory in a loft on Rivington Street on Manhattan's Lower East Side. There he installed one of Virginian James Bonsack's newly patented, mechanical cigarette-rolling machines, capable of increasing the company's daily output a hundredfold, establishing the beginning of what would truly become "big tobacco."[15] First listed on the New York Stock Exchange in 1890, Duke's American Tobacco was already well on its way to dominating the cigarette market. By then it had swallowed up most of the nation's small producers, eventually acquiring as many as 250 other manufacturers.[16] Even though the ATC effectively eliminated the competition in the cigarette and loose-tobacco market, the company continued to advertise heavily, differentiating its numerous brands by drawing on baseball imagery. The ATC would continue to control the market until 1911, when the United

States Supreme Court declared it a monopoly engaged in restraint of trade and ordered it broken up into five smaller companies. These firms followed in the ATC's footsteps, continuing to rely on baseball-related imagery in their advertising, as well.

Billboards in Your Pockets

Arguably, trade cards—baseball "trading" cards to twenty-first-century children, attic-cleaning mothers, and collectors alike—were the single most significant baseball-related tool for advertising tobacco in the late nineteenth and early twentieth centuries. Although off-site outdoor signage provided an excellent means for tobacco advertisers to reach baseball fans, the form had its limitations. In order to communicate clearly, the content of ball-park ads, like all large-scale signage, had to be read quickly. As such, ballpark ads were restricted to the use of display text featuring large, clear letters that announced the product name and perhaps a slogan. There was little room for explication or elaboration on the wonders of a given product. More importantly, the advertisers' messages were site specific: they could only be conveyed to those in attendance. Billboards and ballpark signage are, moreover, one-sided. But what if billboards could be made portable, perhaps pocket-sized? And what if there were two times the space on which to print? Then advertisers' messages might reach a wider group of consumers with a more emphatic message. In fact, the trade card is basically a pocket-sized, two-sided, portable billboard.

The production of trade cards was made possible by a nineteenth-century technological innovation, chromolithography, or four-color printing. First patented in Germany in 1837, the chromolithographic process, which allowed for the reproduction of a full range of colors and tones, was soon adapted for use on the steam-driven rotary press. "From 1840 to 1900," writes Meredith Eliassen, "Europe and North America increasingly experienced what has been called 'chromo civilization'—an era when original paintings were reproduced lithographically in color and sold by the millions."[17] Trade cards first became an important retail advertising medium following the 1876 Centennial Exhibition in Philadelphia, at which they were widely distributed. According to Jennifer M. Black:

> Exhibitors traveled from every corner of the country and abroad to present their information and products to fairgoers. Many of them clamored for fairgoers' attention and trust, promoting unfamiliar brand name products such as Fleischmann's yeast and Libby's canned meats. These exhibitors distributed pocket-sized advertisements called trade cards—3x5 in. lithographed cards with colorful images and descriptive text that authenticated the wares for sale with testimonials and expert advice. Visitors moved through the Exposition collecting their portable lithographs along with holiday greeting cards, calling cards (similar to today's business cards), and other printed material from the fair.[18]

The practice by retailers of distributing loose trade cards to customers along with the purchase of products like soap and patent medicines declined by the 1890s.[19] At the same time, Duke and his soon-to-be-neutralized competitors pioneered the inclusion of trade cards into cigarette packs. Cards depicting exotic locales, pure-bred dogs, and flags of many nations were packaged with a variety of cigarette brands. So, too, were "bachelor cards," pictures of scantily clad women. But by far, the most popular trade cards were embellished with pictures of baseball players. These were the first baseball cards. Informally called pack stiffeners by the tobacco industry, trade cards were released in numbered sets in order to provide incentive for the repeat purchase of a given brand of smokes.[20] Writes Black, "Printing trade cards in series encouraged consumers to become invested in the story and seek out other cards in the series itself—with the added benefit of increased consumption. Consumers often received trade cards as free 'gifts' packaged with other items they purchased. Thus, the desire to receive additional trade cards could be an incentive to purchase more goods."[21] Given the fact that all cigarettes were made from the same bright-leaf tobacco and were manufactured, for the most part, by the same company, consumer decisions about which brand to smoke were based largely on factors extrinsic to the product, such as the pictures on the enclosed trade cards.

Unlike product endorsement advertising, baseball trade cards with players' pictures were often produced without the consent of or payment to the players themselves. Legend has it that the famously rare Honus Wagner card, the holy grail of twenty-first-century card collectors, originally packaged with the ATC's Sweet Caporal and Piedmont–brand cigarettes in 1909, was pulled from the market almost immediately after issue owing to the fact that Wagner had a moral objection to marketing tobacco, especially to children. But like so many other baseball myths, this one may be apocryphal. Wagner's moral outrage may very well have stemmed from the fact that the Pittsburgh shortstop's image was used without his permission and without compensation. This notion is reinforced by the fact that Wagner's name and image had long been associated with other tobacco products, most notably Hans [*sic*] Wagner Cigars.[22] After all, children were not the only target market for baseball trade cards. Adults were also avid collectors, then as now. Indeed, trade-card production and distribution fueled a late nineteenth-century scrapbooking craze.[23] Nevertheless, it is impossible to ignore the fact that pack stiffeners featuring pictures of ballplayers were attractive to young boys as well as to men and their scrapbooking wives. In this context, the Wagner card was, in fact, used to market cigarettes to children, whether or not marketing tobacco to children really fueled Wagner's outrage.

In addition to baseball trade cards, the American Tobacco Company packaged baseball silks, felts, and flannels—the fabric equivalents of trade cards, meant for piecing together in order to create quilts—along with cigarettes. While the first standardized cigarette advertising campaign aimed explicitly at women did not appear until the 1920s, given that smoking in public by women was taboo in polite company in prior years, trade silks and flannels appear to have been designed to appeal to female consumers. That women may not have actually smoked the cigarettes that were packaged with baseball trade blankets is immaterial, as long as they were the purchasers or influenced the purchasers. The American Tobacco

Company seems to have recognized early on that women represented a previously untapped market and used trade blankets to widen their consumer base.

The American Tobacco Company, or what was left of it after the breakup of the monopoly, was eventually forced to rely more heavily on trade cards as a promotional tactic. Faced with stiff competition for the first time after the 1911 antitrust decision, the much smaller ATC ramped up its production of baseball trade cards and blankets. So, too, did the competition. Thus, cigarette trade premiums became even more important as marketing tools. By the time the United States entered World War I, trade cards had begun to fall out of favor as premiums aimed at adults. Still, advertisers continued to bank on the appeal of trade cards to children. As their use in cigarette packaging waned, trade cards appeared at an increasing rate in packages of candy and chewing gum. So began the transition from the trade cards of the nineteenth century to the trading cards of the twentieth.

Official Base Ball Guides

An increasingly literate population meant an expanding readership for baseball news that went beyond box scores and game recaps, especially as the sport professionalized. By the last years of the nineteenth century, a market developed for dedicated baseball publications such as the aforementioned *Bull Durham Guide*. Like the *Bull Durham Guide*, the new baseball pamphlets served as advertising vehicles for their publishers at the same time that they met consumer demand for specialized information about the game. Of course, the mass-production of baseball guides, not to mention newspapers and magazines, would not have been possible without further technological advances in the printing industry. Stereotype printing—a process by which multipage forms are cast into solid metal, thereby creating a plate capable of standing up to multiple pressings—was introduced in 1725. In 1865 stereotype printing plates proved to be durable enough to be used with the Bullock rotary press, a machine that printed simultaneously on both sides of continuous rolls of paper and then cut the pages automatically with a serrated knife, producing twelve thousand pages or more per hour.[24] The linotype machine, a hot-metal type compositor, was introduced in 1886, providing a means by which type might be set with ease and speed.[25]

Among the baseball guides published using this new technology were *Beadle's Dime Base-Ball Player*, *DeWitt's Base-Ball Guide*, and the *Players' National League Base Ball Guide*, all of which carried advertising for sporting goods. Several also carried ads for other products, including tobacco and beer, as well as ads for haberdasheries and similar business establishments targeting the guides' predominately male readers. Originally predating the introduction of linotype, the most widely circulated and certainly the longest-lived of these guides was *Spalding's Official Base Ball Guide*, which commenced publication in 1877, just a year after Spalding's first sporting-goods store opened. The *Spalding Guide* was followed by the competing *Reach's Official Base Ball Guide*, marketed by fellow sporting-goods entrepreneur A. J. Reach in 1883.

As a pitcher, Alfred Goodwill Spalding was a man of firsts. He was the first two-hundred-game winner, the first pitcher to toss a shutout, and the first baseball man to understand the commercial value of his name. The very title *Spalding Guide* is proof positive of its publisher's commercial savvy, as each copy bore the name not only of its celebrity founder, but of his sporting-goods business as well. Taking a page from other large retail firms—such as America's first grocery-store chain, the Great Atlantic and Pacific Tea Company, A&P, which sold popular novels on cheap paper stock with store advertising before and after the body of the text—Spalding's guides also contained pages of ads for his company's products, bracketing the content. This arrangement helped maintain the fiction that the true purpose of the *Spalding Official Base Ball Guide* was the dissemination of information rather than advertising, though advertise it did.

In addition to ads for their publisher's products, the Chicago-based baseball guides carried advertising for other enterprises, most notably for travel-related businesses. The 1889 *Spalding Guide*, for example, included ads for the Pennsylvania Lines railway, the

Pitts[b]urgh, Fort Wayne and Chicago Railway, and the Chicago, St. Louis and Pittsburgh Railway, as well as for the Michigan Central, the Milwaukee, Lake Shore and Western Railway, the Chicago and North-Western Railway, the Burlington route of the Chicago, Burlington and Quincy Railway, the Chicago and Alton Railway, Chicago, Milwaukee and St. Paul Railway, and the Monon route of the Louisville, New Albany and Chicago Railway. That so many rail lines, especially those serving the Chicago area, should have advertised in the *Spalding Guide* stands to reason. After all, teams playing competitive baseball depended upon reliable means of transportation to reach their opponents. Perhaps more importantly, these ads also targeted readers of the *Spalding Guide* who played only on a local level or who did not play at all. By associating railroad lines with the sport, the transportation companies attempted to add a specific type of value to their companies in the minds of the guide's readers. In a sense, the baseball expertise conferred by the text of the *Spalding Guide* transferred to the railroads. If the Michigan Central, the Chicago, Burlington and Quincy Railways, and the other lines were good enough to be stamped with the imprimatur of the *Spalding Guide*, then they were certainly good enough for baseball aficionados seeking a means of transport in and out of Chicago, even when that travel was not related to baseball. The same may be said for Chicago's Tremont House Hotel, another advertiser in the 1889 *Spalding Official Base Ball Guide*. Unlike the railroads, which spoke directly to a broad consumer base and only indirectly targeted baseball teams by association, the Tremont House outwardly solicited the patronage of ball clubs that presumably read the guide. By extension, the ad was also aimed at nonplaying readers; it clearly implies that by staying at the Tremont House, fans might somehow become more like the players they admired.[26]

Reach's Guide, like the *Spalding Guide*, also served as an advertising vehicle for its sporting-goods manufacturing and retailing publisher. A. J. Reach, who, like Spalding, had been a player and was a team owner, having founded the Philadelphia Phillies, appears to have been less shy than his competitor about including advertising for products not his own. The *Reach's Official Base Ball Guide* of 1900 includes on its first page an ad for the Syracuse Gun, available in both twelve and sixteen gauge, in a variety of barrel lengths. The Syracuse Gun was produced and sold by another sporting-goods retailer, Simmons Hardware of St. Louis, Missouri. While no rate card is available to provide hard evidence, Simmons, "The Great Sporting Goods House of America," no doubt paid well for its ad's privileged placement at the beginning of the guide.[27] This is reinforced by the placement of ads for Reach's own sporting goods, which appeared only in the back of the guide.

Licensing, Trademarks, and the Art of Branding

Of all advertisements in both *Reach's* and the *Spalding Guide*, one in particular stands out. The entirety of the 1889 *Spalding Guide*'s back cover is taken up with an ad for "The Official Spalding League Ball," complete with a color illustration of the product. Although it is partially obscured by its packaging in the rendering, clear lettering on the ball proudly states the product's status as the Official League Ball (of) the National League. As one of the National League's founders in 1876, not so coincidentally the same year he went into the sporting-goods business, Spalding was in a unique position to capitalize on the demand for his products. By paying the National League one dollar for every dozen balls it ordered in order to make his the league's first official ball, Spalding and the league were the first to engage in an innovative form of sports sponsorship now known as licensing, whereby an institution sells the rights to use its name to an advertiser.[28] When it came to licensing, Reach followed Spalding's example, yet again. Immediately after the birth of the American League in 1901, Reach's baseballs began to bear the stamp "Official American League Ball," while the 1902 guide bore the title, *Reach's Official American League Base Ball Guide*.

In order for Reach and Spalding to preserve their claims to the title "official," it was essential that the respective companies protect their names and logos legally. That an advertising image should be protected by law was not that unusual, even in the last years of the nineteenth century. The process of registering trademarks, by which specific advertising imagery, product names, logos, and slogans are reserved for the exclusive use of a single company, was initiated in 1870.[29] Clearly legible on the Spalding balls pictured in the 1890 guide is the label "Trade Mark," indicating that the logo and slogan were so registered. By 1905 the Spalding Company had registered several variations of its logo.[30] The Reach Company, too, registered its trademarks. Sometimes, however, issues regarding trademarks became complicated. Such was the case with the dispute between A. J. Reach and Company and Simmons Hardware that ended their commercial relationship. In 1910 Reach filed a lawsuit charging Simmons with trademark infringement, claiming that the competing sporting-goods manufacturer had no right to the use of "American" (as in Official American League) on its balls.[31] Following a long legal battle, the Missouri Supreme Court held that "geographical or descriptive words cannot be appropriated as trademarks."[32] By then, as would be expected, Reach no longer carried Simmons advertising.

Why was it so vitally important that Reach prevent Simmons from calling their balls the "official balls" of the American League when, in fact, the American League actually used Reach balls? The reasoning behind the suit is that A. J. Reach desired to protect the company brand. Indeed, this is the reasoning behind trademark law, in general. On a basic level, the Reach ball, like the Spalding Official National League Ball, bore its literal brand—its mark—on its surface. But labeling alone did not effectively "brand" Reach and Spalding balls. There was more to it. According to Mark Batey, "A product becomes a brand when the physical product is augmented by something else—images, symbols, perceptions, feelings—to produce an integral idea greater than the sum of its parts. A brand might be composed of a single product, or it might be made up of multiple products that span many categories. But at its core there remains a soul, a distinctive identity and image that resonates with its consumers and transcends its physical representation in terms of product format."[33]

The souls of the Reach and Spalding balls lay neither in their labels nor their hard rubber hearts. The balls derived their core identities from their respective leagues. To be designated the Official League Ball, even if the title was acquired by a purely financial licensing arrangement, suggests that a given product is of an extraordinarily high quality, good enough to be used exclusively and officially by the given league. As such, the ball itself carries with it all the meanings of the league. It suggests the highest level of professional accomplishment in the field of baseball. Following this logic, fans of teams in the respectable, professional "senior circuit," the National League, looking to purchase baseballs for their own use, would have been likely attracted to the Spalding brand, while fans of teams in the upstart "junior circuit," the American League, would likely have reached for a Reach. By extension, the very qualities of respectability and professionalism associated with the National League may have been linked in the minds of consumers, however unconsciously, with the Spalding product, while the Reach product may have connoted a certain youthful exuberance associated with the American League. In reality, there was no difference between the Spalding and Reach balls, as a statement by both manufacturers in the *New York Tribune* on October 14, 1911, clearly asserts.[34] But in this case, the lack of actual differentiation made the necessity of branding all the more important.

All the Advertising That's Fit to Print

Dedicated baseball guides like those published by Spalding and Reach served but a small niche market compared to circulation of daily and weekly newspapers. As early as 1870, there were 542 daily newspapers and 4,425 weeklies published in the thirty-seven United States.[35] But while newspaper coverage of baseball grew with the popularity of the game as a spectator sport, it took print advertising some time to reach its potential as a vehicle for commercial speech. According to *Printers' Ink*, a pre-1870s ad campaign "was likely to consist of two-inch, one-column space in three or four publications one time, although a plunger might take two inches in two columns for three insertions in a half dozen papers. A quarter or half page was a sensation, indulged mainly by an occasional patent medicine manufacturer."[36] Art was virtually nonexistent. And where there were illustrations, they tended to be decorative, having little or nothing to do with the ad's message.[37]

Small game announcements were among the limited advertising placed in newspapers prior to the 1870s. Most of these were in keeping with other print advertisements of the time. Baseball game ads were, for the most part, purely utilitarian, giving only the name of the venue, the start time, and the home cities and nicknames of participating teams. By the 1880s, however, things had begun to change. Baseball-related advertising proliferated in the pages of America's newspapers. Although simple game announcements continued to dominate baseball-related print advertising, much as they had in the previous decade, some told more nuanced stories. A two-inch spot in the *Chicago Daily Tribune* of July 18, 1882, for example, promoted a contest between the "Buffalos" and the "Chicagos," noting that this would be the "last opportunity to see the celebrated Buffalos in Chicago." It also included some vital information: "The one-armed pitcher, Dailey [*sic*] will pitch for Buffalo." The ad goes on to suggest that fans "avoid the push at the gate by securing tickets" in advance at one of several locations including Spalding's Sporting Goods.[38] By emphasizing that the main attraction would be a pitcher with one arm, the ad clearly suggests that this would be no ordinary baseball game, but rather a theatrical spectacle of sorts, a must-see event. Creating demand with the threat of shortage, noting none too subtly that it would be wise to secure advance tickets, serves to reinforce the unique nature of the contest. Moreover, event promotions of the period, whether theatrical, sporting, or otherwise, often relied upon the sensational, bordering on the freakish, to draw spectators. Observes cultural historian Jackson Lears, "In the chaotic economy of the emerging United States, carnivalesque subversions were unmoored from traditional ritual, left free to float along the margins of settled society, promoted by picaresque rogues. . . . In the traditions of hucksters on both sides of the Atlantic, they mingled entertainment and moneymaking, provoking an ambiguous response of titillation, laughter, and suspicion among the populace at large."[39]

While the prospect of seeing a one-armed pitcher dominate the opposition is hardly subversive, the fact that this ad singles Daily out as a selling point situates it firmly in the carnivalesque tradition, much like events promoted by P.T. Barnum and other traveling showmen of the era. By the 1880s, the age of the itinerant snake-oil salesman and the mountebank was on the wane. Still, traveling circuses and sideshows were a constant on the American scene. This ad is certainly blatant about the theatrical appeal of the event it promotes. Like it, many late nineteenth-century baseball ads made no bones about selling the sport as part of the larger entertainment industry. Game advertisements, even those that did not rely on the carnivalesque to draw spectators, routinely appeared in newspapers along with theatrical announcements and ads for circuses, historical re-creations, and other forms of live entertainment under the heading "Amusements." Professional baseball would evolve to consider itself an industry separate and distinct from the wider world of amusement. But the very fact that these well-established National League teams, one of which was Spalding's own pennant-winning Chicago club, advertised by stressing the carnivalesque says a great deal about the status of both the advertising and baseball industries in the late nineteenth century.

Baseball Sells, Selling with Baseball

Of course, all baseball-related advertising, carnivalesque or otherwise, sold the game itself. The expanding number of column inches devoted to baseball coverage, a response to increased demand, also offered new opportunities for advertisers to pitch a whole range of products to enthusiastic consumers. Not surprisingly, tobacco companies—already reliant on baseball imagery on trade cards to sell their products—also advertised heavily in newspapers. Tobacco manufacturers and merchants went beyond simply placing print ads in proximity to baseball coverage. Rather, they reinforced the baseball connection by tying their merchandise directly to the national pastime via promotional language. The most frequent examples of the baseball-tobacco nexus in the print advertising of the era were to be found in tie-ins and cross-promotions. These were game announcements that included the name of the business handling ticket sales, more often than not a tobacconist. Of course, it stands to reason that a consumer entering a shop to buy game tickets might very well purchase his cigars at the same time, were they readily available.

Less common, though hardly unheard of, were newspaper ads that appeared to be selling baseball, but were, in fact, selling other products, more frequently than not, tobacco. Appearing in the spring of 1888, an ad for Yellow Label Cigars ran, bearing a headline common to game announcements—"BASEBALL! This is to be one of the best years for baseball ever known." The copy continues, "It behooves everyone to lay in a supply of the 'Yellow Label Cigars,' as many of the distinguished players will have no other." It concludes, "Truth is mighty."[40] Not only does this ad capitalize on the growing popularity of the professional game to capture the much-desired attention of newspaper readers, but it does something far more important. It uses the growing celebrity of ballplayers to convince consumers to buy Yellow Label Cigars. Noting that their product is the only acceptable cigars for the "distinguished" few, the advertisers thereby transfer the quality onto the product. By extension, the cigars, themselves, serve as a conduit of "distinguished-ness" to the smoker. The ad goes one step further, asserting its authority as a teller of the mighty truth. At a time when there was no expectation that advertising was accurate or truthful in any way, the assertion itself was powerful. What the ad fails to do, however, is to name specific distinguished players or their teams. It contains neither a testimonial nor an endorsement. Although there were rare instances of tobacco endorsements and testimonials as early as the 1880s—for example, in a cigarette ad from 1888 that makes the claim, "Van Haltren, California Baseball Pitcher, smokes Old Judge in preference to all others"—such ads by athletes were still few and far between.[41]

Beer advertising also regularly appeared both in and around baseball coverage in local newspapers. Unlike the splashy, quarter-page beer ads that would dominate sports pages in the decade before the enactment of Prohibition, the earliest beer advertising was often printed in and among a given newspaper's baseball coverage in small type, occupying only one or two agate lines in a single column, touting the products of local breweries. Although the majority of brewing and the majority of brewery advertising remained local, larger, national brewers also came on the scene in the late nineteenth century. Larger producers also meant larger advertising budgets. St. Louis's Anheuser-Busch was the first on the national market with Budweiser in 1876.[42] By the end of the new century's first decade, ads linking Budweiser with baseball were nearly ubiquitous in America's newspapers. Because it promoted a national product, Budweiser advertising was most often standardized—the same ad ran in newspapers nationally. One visually striking, unusually ornate, standardized Budweiser ad features a tall, handsome, generic ballplayer with a *C* on his chest, waiting for his turn at bat. Behind him, a fielder applies a tag to a base runner as an umpire signals "out." In the distance, a presumably cheering crowd fills a grandstand. The copy reads, "BASEBALL— The Favorite Sport of Millions. Its [*sic*] hard to find an American who does not declare baseball to be the *best* of out-door sports, and its [*sic*] harder to find one who does not declare Budweiser the *best* of all bottled beers."[43] The strategy used in this ad is clear. By associating the product with baseball, the national game, and placing emphasis on the opinion of the majority, the ad elevates the status of Budweiser to that of the "national" beer. To argue with this assessment would be downright undemocratic. That this strategy proved successful for Anheuser-Busch is clear, given the fact that Budweiser advertising continues to be heavy on Americana into the twenty-first century—in 2016, it even rebranded itself as "America" beer—though it is owned by a multinational corporation based in Belgium.

But not all nineteenth-century Budweiser advertising relied upon claiming national consensus. In an unusual step, Anheuser-Busch hedged its bets by running a different print campaign in the same newspapers at the same time the standardized ad ran. An ad in the *Washington Post* of April 15, 1910, was placed directly under a long article about pitcher Walter Johnson. The spot, a cartoon, depicts a group of flashily garbed, smiling men with money clenched in their fists accompanied by a terrier and a bird, racing to a box office, having been spurred on by a large sign reading "BALL GAME TODAY." Above the drawing, the headline reads "EVERY-BODY IS IN A HURRY TODAY," while the copy underneath asks "Ever hurry and wear yourself plumb out?—at such a time nothing invigorates one as a cold bottle of BUDWEISER. Because of its *Quality* and *Purity* it's in a class by itself."[44] A similar ad appeared in the same newspaper, just five days later. Another cartoon, it features a maniacally grinning batter, standing on top of a giant globelike baseball labeled "WORLD OF SPORTS." Its slogan reads "Budweiser is always on top," followed by similar claims about its quality and purity.[45]

At first glance, there is nothing remarkable about these ads. They neither make outrageous claims, nor do they represent the product as something it is not. Rather, it is the cartoon format that sets them apart from the other baseball-related ads of this period. Although comic-strip advertising became common during the Great Depression, it was not a regular feature of newspaper advertising in 1910.[46] But like later comic-strip ads that might easily be mistaken for content by the casual viewer, the Budweiser spots mimicked the single-panel baseball cartoons that appeared with some regularity on sports pages. These ads, which were only distinguishable from baseball cartoons under close scrutiny, essentially served to get the attention of readers who might otherwise pay little or no mind to advertising, in the same way the Yellow Label Cigar ad aimed to lead readers into thinking it was a game announcement.

In addition to tobacconists and breweries, men's clothiers regularly invoked baseball to call attention to their haberdasheries. One such ad appeared on a daily basis in the *Washington Post* in the summer of 1887, praising the quality of E. B. Barnum and Co. clothing shop. Although the proprietor does not appear to have been related to P.T. Barnum, the copy and art used in his advertising displays a certain quality of Barnum-esque humbug. Half the piece is dedicated to art; it features a crudely rendered cartoon image of a ballplayer with oversized hands, reaching out as if to make a catch. In order to emphasize the importance of the image, it bares the parenthetical note "(Copyrighted)."[47] Both Spalding and Reach trademarked their brands as a means of protection, so why shouldn't E. B Barnum have done the same thing? While he certainly could have, he did not. Copyright law does not protect commercial logos. They are protected by trademark law.[48] This was as true in 1910 as it is in the twenty-first century. Had it been legally registered, the image would have been labeled "Trademark," as were the Reach and Spalding balls. The addition of the parenthetical notation on Barnum's ad is legally meaningless. Nevertheless "(Copyrighted)" is meaningful from an advertising standpoint. The parenthetical label may have served to protect the image from poaching, at least to some extent, without either the bother or legal costs involved in registering it. More importantly, the label calls attention to the image as something unique and worthy of legal protection, and thereby implies that the store has the same unique quality.

The other half of Barnum's ad features copy reading, "A Champion is one who meets and overcomes all competitors. We lay the claim to the championship in the Clothing business. Not that we carry the most goods or make the most show, but that in quality, styles and prices we have overcome all competitors in Washington. Where can you find a stock so clean, so free from old goods, so stylish in cut (taken as a whole) or so many fine grades? For anything so nice in this line, come to us."[49] Like the "Champion" himself, Barnum seems to suggest that he—or at least his haberdashery—is a fierce competitor, able to dominate the clothing-store business by merit alone. That the store's merit appears to be based not only on the stylishness but also on the cleanliness and newness of the stock is particularly telling. The ad appears to say that the quality of Barnum's product lies in its novelty, its modernity. Thus, by extension, Barnum ties his business to the novel, modern, and presumably thoroughly clean, not to mention wildly popular and stylish, professional sport. Without an endorsement or testimonial from a baseball "Champion," the connection between the sport and the store is tenuous at best. But the art and the copy tell a different story. Together, they effectively single the ad—and the business—out from all the other old-fashioned, non-championship-level, unprotected ads on the same page.

"The Finest and the Most Active and Thorough and Pain Killing and Healing Oil or Lineament We Have Ever Used"

With few exceptions, baseball-related advertising, both in print and on ballpark fences, was aimed at a male consumer base. Katie Casey, the narrator of Jack Norworth and Albert von Tilzer's 1901 anthem "Take Me Out to the Ball Game," and the occasional scrapbooking trade-card collector or tobacco-blanket quilter notwithstanding, the baseball-related advertising of the time did not actively target women. This would seem to exclude patent-medicine advertising— one of the earliest and certainly one of the most conspicuous categories of advertising in the burgeoning print media—from this investigation. After all, ads for patent medicines, with their exaggerated claims that proclaimed the efficacy of a variety of ingredients ranging from herbal folk preparations to opium and alcohol, were aimed at female consumers, though the nostrums had their fans among Civil War veterans who returned from battle addicted to morphine as well as to those in need of a drink in "dry" areas under control by temperance supporters.[50] But this is not the case. Male baseball cranks were not spared pitches for patent medicines.[51]

Patent-medicine advertising, more than any advertising for any other product, baseball-connected or otherwise, has deep American roots. In fact, it is intimately connected to the American evangelical tradition. Prior to the advent of print advertising, prior even to the distribution of trade cards or the introduction of standardized outdoor advertising, patent nostrums were peddled around the country by itinerant salesmen. While some sold their often-suspect wares on an individual basis, door to door, a significant number used spectacles to market their miracle cures.[52] These spectacles, commonly referred to as medicine shows, were often remarkably similar to the evangelical tent revivals and camp meetings that spread like wildfire during the Second Great Awak-

ening of the earlier nineteenth century, a movement characterized by growing religious and spiritual enthusiasm in America.
Writes Roger Brun:

> The advent of the camp meeting at the turn of the century enabled
> folks from many towns to travel to the revival service and camp
> for the night, sometimes several days. At the meetings minis-
> ters mounted large platforms and exhorted the people to repent;
> moans and cries and tears of anguish and victory swept up the
> crowds in religious fervor as people gave themselves to God,
> faced their sins, and changed their lives. This was religious frenzy
> played out in moth-filled tents and ramshackle buildings. Some
> people fell so violently under the revivalists' preaching that they
> lay on the ground rigid, as if frozen in a trance, uncommuni-
> cative, barely breathing; others sang and prayed and confessed
> and cried. There were scenes, observers reported, of mass psy-
> chological torment and joy.[53]

Like the spiritual salvation sold at camp revivals, medicine shows
marketed a form of salvation—salvation from a world of physical
ills. And like the traveling preachers who ministered to the enthusiastic faithful, the itinerant charlatans and mountebanks who
peddled patent nostrums offered their products to their own set
of believers. Medicine shows, too, were elaborate affairs, with origins dating back to medieval Europe. Promoted by advance men
who distributed handbills and trade cards, nineteenth-century
American medicine shows often featured sideshow attractions
and carnival acts such as "freaks," talking birds, performing animals, and fortune tellers of various stripes.[54] The aim, of course,
was to draw in spectators in order to sell them a particular medicine with a branded proprietary formula.[55]

It is no surprise that patent-medicine manufacturers, early
adopters of both organized word-of-mouth and outdoor advertising, were also early adopters of newspaper print advertising.[56]
Because there were so many nostrums on the market, patent-
medicine advertisers depended heavily on branding, differentiating their products from all the others on the market. A typical

patent-medicine newspaper or magazine ad might celebrate the powers of a given nostrum to aid "ladies suffering from 'internal fever,' congestion or ulceration," like Dr. Pierce's "Favorite Prescription."[57] Lydia Pinkham's Vegetable Compound was touted as a cure for more general "female complaints."[58] In contrast, many of the patent-medicine ads that invoked baseball targeted men— primarily players who might be suffering from aches and pains resulting from active participation in the game. A "Special Notice" to "All Baseball Players" in the *San Francisco Chronicle* offered testimonials from a long list of professionals, stating that "We the undersigned, members of the Louisville Baseball Combination, have used Dr. Barlow J. Smith's CALORIC VITA OIL for the various accidental ailments to which the profession are subject, namely bruised, strained and sore muscles, sprained joints and contracted cords of the elbow," while members of the California Baseball League found "DR. BARLOW J. SMITH'S CALORIC VITA OIL . . . the finest and the most active and thorough PAIN CURING and HEALING OIL or LINIMENT we have ever used."[59] While the language of the ad appeals directly to players, naming any number of professionals enthusiastically recommending the product, it does not necessarily target the pros. The ad implies that by using Caloric Vita Oil, amateur players will be magically transformed into better athletes, becoming more like their professional idols. In a rudimentary fashion, this ad relies upon the same technique as more sophisticated endorsement and testimonial advertising would in the future.

Despite this ad's inflated rhetoric, Dr. Barlow J. Smith's Caloric Vita Oil appears not to be a typical patent nostrum, but rather a potentially useful topical anesthetic. There is nothing in this ad suggesting that sickly women, opium addicts, or anyone suffering from anything but the minor aches and pains associated with physical activity might find salvation or even temporary relief in this product. But other, non-baseball-specific ads for Caloric Vita Oil belie this assumption. Various print promotions claim the product's efficacy in treating "Congestion of the Heart, Liver and Kidneys, Lame Back," and "Dropsy" as well as "Tumors or Glandular Swellings," not to mention having the benefit of "cleansing the blood of scrofulous drugs or virus poisons."[60] So why does the baseball endorsement ad embrace a different advertising strategy? Rather than gathering baseball players and cranks into the sickly patent-medicine fold, the baseball testimonial ad functions as a kind of brand extension. Viewed in the context of the larger campaign, the ad represents an attempt on the manufacturer's part to expand his product's target demographic beyond conventional patent-medicine users to otherwise healthy men, those who might be either directly engaged in playing baseball or devoted to the sport as fans.

In addition to using testimonials like the putative Dr. Barlow J. Smith, some patent-medicine manufacturers embraced another important advertising tactic—the placement of advertising copy designed resembled editorial content, known as "reading notices," in newspapers.[61] In fact, the earliest reading notice promoted a nostrum, Warner's Safe Cure, "a remedy for kidney and liver disease as well as Malaria, Dyspepsia, Blood Impurities, and Rheumatism," among other ailments.[62] Baseball-related reading notices were frequently placed in newspapers around the country by the manufacturers of Benson's Porous Plasters. With the headline, "That Great Game of Baseball at the Park Today," one Benson's Plaster ad states, "Hundreds of leading players say they find more prompt relief from strains, sprains, bruises, rheumatism, stiff and enlarged joints, lameness, etc., but using Benson's Plasters for such troubles than any other external remedy known to the profession. All athletes as well as those in the ordinary avocations of life unite with baseball players in certifying to the value of this plaster in such accidents. . . . Owing to its popularity, many worthless substitutions are offered. Buyers should always ask for Benson's, firmly refusing all other plasters."[63]

Compared to ads for other patent remedies and nostrums that made outrageous claims, Dr. Smith's Caloric Vita Oil among them, the Benson's reading notice is fairly tame. Benson's Plasters were, in fact, topical anesthetics. As such, they would probably have been reasonably useful to athletes. In this regard, neither Benson's Plasters nor its claims were especially remarkable. It is the form rather than the content of this ad that sets it apart. Placed on a page along with an actual article, this ad, unlike the other two, was intended to dupe unsuspecting readers into accepting this praise for the product as the genuine endorsement of the newspaper's editors. By the time the reader arrived at the admonition to accept no substitutes, it was too late to ignore the ad's message. Although it might seem obvious that the content of this piece is, in fact, paid advertising, this technique was extremely common and often effective.

Patent-medicine advertising targeting baseball's faithful was not limited to newspapers and occasional magazines like the *National Police Gazette*, the prototype for contemporary men's magazines. Nostrum advertising could be found in the pages of the nascent sporting press. The first sports newspaper, the *Sporting Life*, which identified itself as "The Representative B.B. Paper of America," was, according to its own promotional material, "Recognized by all Organizations, all Players, and the entire Base Ball loving public as the BEST BASEBALL JOURNAL PUBLISHED. . . . To Read It Once Is to Swear by It Forever."[64] Founder and editor in chief Francis E. Richter introduced the dedicated sports paper, which covered boxing and horse and dog sports, as well as baseball, in 1883, three years before Alfred Spink published the first edition of the *Sporting News*. Richter's paper did nothing if not promote its own modernity. By its own account, it was "the only sporting paper in America which has all the mechanical work performed under its own roof, and which is printed on its own Web Perfecting Press, with a capacity of 15,000 printed, cut, and folded complete, papers per hour."[65] It appeared on a weekly basis until 1917, resuming publication in 1922, only to fold in 1924.

During the first few years of its existence, the eight-page *Sporting Life* carried but one page of advertising. Included on it were the requisite promotions for sporting goods, most particularly baseball equipment, and also ads for local Philadelphia theatricals, spectacles, and other sorts of performances. But as the paper's circulation grew and with it, its size and the space devoted to advertising, ads for retailers and theatrical promotions were joined by those for patent medicines. Although, like the conventional ads and reading notices for Caloric Vita Oil and Benson's Plasters, respectively, the patent-medicine advertising in the *Sporting Life* targeted male consumers, the products promoted therein claimed to cure entirely different types of complaints. Sharing a page with baseball news of November 9, 1895, an ad for a descriptive book available from the Erie Medical Company of Buffalo, New York, explained how the company's patented products could positively reverse "Failing Manhood" and "General Nervous Disability," as well as "Weakness of Body and Mind, Effects of Errors or Excesses in Old or Young," and strengthen "Weak, Underdeveloped Portions of the Body." At least at first glance, the Erie Company's products appear to be positioned as treatments for what is now referred to in direct-to-consumer drug marketing as erectile dysfunction. Erie's products were sold as the Viagra or, at the very least, the Enzyte, of their day. Certainly, the product claimed to achieve the same results as those more contemporary products. But buried, though not too deeply, in the ad's language are promises of treatment for mental weakness and other presumably undesired symptoms resulting from Errors or Excesses, suggesting that what the Erie Medical Company really sold was a cure for sexually transmitted diseases.[66] Similar were ads for Old Hallock's famous Electric Pills, offering to cure users of "Lost Manhood, Nervous Disability, Lost Power, Dimness of Sight, and Defective Memory," having already "saved thousands from death or the mad-house by their timely use."[67] The reader could also find the Dinsmoor Remedy, a treatment for Blood Poison of the "Primary, Secondary or Tertiary" variety.[68] Other patent-nostrum advertising was far more direct. In a single column in the *Sporting Life*, directly below the Erie Medical Company's ad, no fewer than four print promotions claim in clear language to provide relief from syphilis, diseases of the blood, gonorrhea, gleet (a constant discharge from various orifices resulting from an STD), spermatorrhoea, and other inflammations, irritations, and ulcerations of mucus membranes.[69]

What do these ads say about the overwhelmingly male readership of the *Sporting Life*? While it would be overgeneralizing to suggest that all of the publication's readers were STD sufferers, ads for Swaim's Panacea, Brou's Permanent Cure, Santal-midy, and Big C as well as Old Dr. Hallock's nostrum and the others seem to indicate that the *Sporting Life*'s readers were baseball fans who liked to engage in the "sporting life" of a different type altogether, or at least fancied that they did. By extension, the content of these ads implies that this publication's demographic might also include those who frequented prostitutes. As such, the charlatans and mountebanks who advertised in the *Sporting Life* preyed on men looking for salvation of a very serious type.

When You See an Arrow

Dr. Barlow J. Smith's Caloric Vita Oil, Swaim's Panacea, and the like ceased production by the early decades of the twentieth century, the manufacturers of these and similar patent medicines having been investigated and heavily fined by the United States Department of Agriculture, the agency tasked with enforcing the Pure Food and Drugs Act of 1906.[70] While baseball-related, patent-medicine ads did not entirely disappear from the pages of the general interest or sporting press, their numbers were greatly reduced following the law's institution. There was one notable exception. Tied inextricably to baseball by its advertising was an extremely popular patent-medicine, a "nerve tonic" originally introduced to consumers in Atlanta, Georgia, in 1885, and an imitation of the extremely popular Vin Mariani.[71] Pemberton's French Wine Cola, as its name suggests, contained wine, cola nut, and, like a number of patent medicines, extract of coca leaf containing cocaine alkaloids.[72] But in 1886, amid valid concerns that Atlanta was to become the first major city in the United States to go "dry," banning nonmedical sales of alcoholic beverages, Pemberton concocted another nostrum, substituting carbonated water and caffeine for the wine, naming it Coca-Cola.[73] Plagued by financial difficulties, Pemberton sold shares of his company to a series of partners, eventually ceding control to another Atlanta drugstore owner, Asa Briggs Candler, in 1888.[74] It was Candler, a marketing whiz, who registered the Coca-Cola Spenserian script logo with the U.S. Patent

Office four years later.[75] Over the first decade of the twentieth century, Coca-Cola became the best advertised product in America. Among the 100 million premiums and other novelties to reach consumers in 1913 were twenty-five million baseball trade cards.[76]

In reality, the coca alkaloids were removed from Coca-Cola by 1905, replaced by spent coca leaves, stripped of their active ingredient.[77] Nevertheless, the drink was still marketed as a nerve tonic, a cure for headaches, and an excellent choice for a quick pick-me-up. Around the same time, the Coca-Cola Company's advertising agency, William d'Arcy, introduced an especially successful standardized campaign, placing spots in newspapers and magazines. The ads, which featured a large arrow encircling drawings and text, were emblazoned with the slogan, "Whenever you see an arrow, think of Coca-Cola." Taking a page out of Dr. Barlow J. Smith's playbook, many of the Coke arrow ads involved testimonials by star baseball players. Miller Huggins, Eddie Collins, Frank Chance, and Ty Cobb—a major investor in the Coca-Cola Company—all praised the product for its ability to restore even the weariest ballplayers.[78] One arrow ad of particular note features Napoleon Lajoie and Rube Waddell, the latter stating, "More than once a bottle of your Coca-Cola has pulled me through a tight game. There is nothing better for pitchers in hot weather. I find Coca-Cola stimulating to both body and mind. And is the only beverage of the kind that does not leave an after effect."[79] Whether or not Coca-Cola actually helped Waddell, who was reputed to have been extremely distractible, is unclear. After all, truth-in-advertising laws aimed at preventing athletes and other celebrities from endorsing products that they, themselves, did not use, or for making false claims, were several decades away. Nevertheless, the language of Waddell's endorsement places the arrow ad firmly in the patent-medicine category.

"To the Patriotic and Baseball Public of Brooklyn"

Baseball-related advertising in the print media was not limited to pitching patent medicine, cigars, or appearances by one-armed players. The professional sport even played a role in early twentieth-century political advertising. Baseball took center stage in a particularly contentious advertising war surrounding the Democratic nomination for Brooklyn Borough president in 1917, fought in the pages of the *Brooklyn Daily Eagle*. The seeming focus of the dispute was the blue law prohibiting Sunday baseball. A Dodgers game intended to benefit dependents of soldiers fighting in World War I and members of the Red Cross ran counter to the law, which, in New York, was by then enforced only sporadically.[80] Of course, as is so often true of political advertising, the subtext is more important than the text.

On one side were Dodger's owner Charles Ebbets and his partner Edward J. McKeever; on the other was Brooklyn's powerful sheriff Edward Riegelmann, the candidate of the borough's Democratic machine. Backed by staunch blue-law supporters, Riegelmann vocally opposed the game and arrested Ebbets at his eponymous ballpark for disturbing the peace.[81] Ebbets and McKeever responded by placing a number of quarter-column ads in the *Eagle* in support of Bird S. Coler, Riegelmann's opponent. But this was not enough. One day before the primary, a half-page "open letter" appealing "TO THE PATRIOTIC AND BASEBALL PUBLIC OF BROOKLYN" ran in the *Eagle*, paid for by Ebbets and McKeever. Although, at first glance, it resembled an actual letter, in the same way a reading notice resembles an editorial, it made no bones about being a paid political ad. In large type, the "letter" begins, "During the past week a controversy has arisen between Sheriff Riegelmann and the undersigned relative to a Patriotic Concert, followed by a baseball game at Ebbets Field on July 1, for the benefit of the Militia of Mercy; We therefore deem it a duty to the public and ourselves that we should explain in an advertisement and detail our position on the matter; the public can thus judge whether or not we are in error." What follows are four columns of tiny, agate type accusing Riegelmann of terrible, unpatriotic behavior in service of his own political career. Ebbets and McKeever write, "We submit to you that this procedure, justifiable in the detection of a heinous crime, was utterly discreditable to the intelligence and motive of its author in his effort to bring a patriotically conceived enterprise of unquestioned philanthropic purpose under the prohibition of a blue law (enacted in 1787, 130 years ago) which is a dead letter with every respect except professional baseball games at Ebbets Field."[82] Ebbets and McKeever go so far as to accuse Riegelmann of forging letters from former president William Howard Taft to the sheriff in support of the arrests.

Taft's incursion into the discussion, whether real or forged, would suggest that this particular controversy had national implications. On the contrary, it was fundamentally local, speaking specifically to the Brooklyn political scene as well as to the economics of running a baseball team in the borough. At its heart was the collision between the ball club's ethnically diverse fan base, which included a significant number of Irish, Italian, and Jewish Americans, individuals for whom the Anglo-American Sabbath, which the blue laws were meant to protect, had little meaning, and the Brooklyn Heights power structure, which was largely Protestant. As the letter notes, Riegelmann's purpose in arresting Ebbets was totally self-serving.[83] If Coler, with the backing of Ebbets and McKeever, backed Sunday baseball, then Riegelmann would necessarily oppose it. Ultimately, Riegelmann won the primary and the subsequent election, but not without the seemingly requisite accusations of ballot-box stuffing and other forms of election fraud.[84]

While the results of a local political race contested in 1917 had little bearing on national affairs, the fact that Sunday baseball was one of the central issues and, more importantly, that professional baseball figured prominently in paid political advertising speaks to the power of the relationship between politics, the game, and the industry in the early decades of the twentieth century. Indeed, baseball-related advertising would continue to play a role in political campaigns in the decades to come, not only in Brooklyn, but nationally.

A Bright Future

From the last decades of the nineteenth century to the end of the First World War, both baseball and advertising matured into sophisticated businesses. As America moved from the Gilded Age through the war years and into the Roaring Twenties, both industries experienced unprecedented growth. Although the business of Major League Baseball experienced a short downturn in the aftermath of the 1919 Black Sox scandal, it boomed again in the 1920s. The demise of the Deadball Era, ushered in by the introduction of a livelier ball in 1920, may have been partially responsible. But even more important were the celebrity ballplayers who hit the new, lively balls high and far, not least among them, Babe Ruth. The growth of American celebrity culture, which fed on the game, as it did the new moving-picture and radio industries, would change the way in which Americans consumed baseball and baseball-related advertising. It would also usher in the golden age of product endorsements.

CHAPTER TWO

"It Pays to Be Personal"

Baseball and Endorsement Advertising in the First Golden Age

I n 1930 a short verse written by an anonymous contributor to the advertising trade publication *Printers' Ink* opened with the line, "It pays to be personal now." The writer, according to the editors, was "lashed into poetic frenzy" by the power of testimonial and endorsement advertising. It's claim was that to sell everything from "Baluchistan rugs" and "revolvers to thugs," celebrity endorsements were the way to go.[1] In the 1920s, with the ascent of the Hollywood film industry, bolstered by the advent of tabloid newspapers, movie gossip magazines, not to mention the rise of radio, American celebrity culture found its full commercial expression in endorsement advertising. Of course, Hollywood alone was not responsible for minting celebrity endorsers. Professional baseball also produced its share of formidable stars, as adept at advertising as they were on the diamond. They, too, proved it paid to be personal.

In the mid-1920s, Stanley Resor, president of the J. Walter Thompson agency, noted that celebrity testimonial advertising succeeded because consumers participate in "the spirit of emulation," the desire to "copy those who we deem superior in taste or knowledge or experience."[2] Note celebritologists Irving Rein, Philip Kotler, and Martin Stoller, "Celebrities provide stories, entertainment, diversions, uplifts, moral instruction. Through them we enjoy vicarious emotions and experiences rarely found in our daily lives."[3] Then as now, advertisers regularly banked on consumers' vicarious participation in emotions and experiences when they selected individuals to pitch their products. Fans certainly looked to baseball's professionals, as they looked to the spectator sport itself, to provide them with narratives, entertainment, diversion, uplift, and even moral instruction. Some baseball-loving consumers were also influenced by players' good looks, excellent taste, fashion sense, and their presumed wealth. But unlike Hollywood starlets who used their beauty to sell cold creams, or leading men who used their suave sophistication to sell cigarettes, athletes brought another skill set to the table. By virtue of the sheer physicality of the acts they performed, baseball players provided almost visceral heightened experiences and emotions, arguably more extreme than those provided by movie stars and other celebrities to whom consumers looked for vicarious pleasure.

Professional baseball's first golden age extended from the early years of the twentieth century through its second decade.[4] It dovetailed with the first golden age of endorsement advertising, the "high tide and green grass" of the Roaring Twenties.[5] Bookending baseball's first golden age and that of advertising, no two players exemplified the shifting zeitgeist, the spirit of the times, as did the Georgia Peach, Tyrus Raymond "Ty" Cobb, and George Herman Ruth, the Bambino, the Sultan of Swat, the Caliph of Clout, or quite simply, the Babe. Famous rivals, Cobb and Ruth stand as exemplars of the athlete-endorser, their testimonials serving as illustrations of the increasingly sophisticated advertising industry.

Ty Cobb

To identify a period as a "golden age" is to imbue it with certain qualities, especially in retrospect. According to Donald J. Mrozek, "The rhetoric of a golden age in sport, in a literal sense, gave attention to excellence and the pursuit of the ideal in sports performance. But the enthusiasm that spawned and bolstered the rhetoric was rooted in something broader and older—an underlying faith that human perfectibility was not only a possibility, but an obligation."[6] That very same faith in the possibility of human perfectibility, a radical, Pietistic Protestant notion that humanity had the capacity to rise above the necessity to sin, also gave birth to the physical culture movement, which amounted to a religion of the body. Physical culture's doctrine, as expressed by its creator and high priest, Bernarr Macfadden, was "Sickness is a sin; don't be a sinner. Weakness is a crime; don't be a criminal."[7] If any early twentieth-century ballplayer may be regarded as the public embodiment of this statement, it was Ty Cobb. Despite at least one unpublicized bout in a sanitarium and frequent injuries, Cobb rarely showed weakness, and he kept his sickness to himself. From this standpoint, though certainly not as later represented by Al Stump and other Cobb biographers, Cobb was neither sinner nor criminal. Succumbing to neither physical nor what was publicly perceived as moral weakness, he was close to perfection. Of course, perception and reality often differ. By all accounts, Cobb was no paragon of virtue. But in the world of celebrity product endorsement, perception is reality.

Cobb began his big league career with the Detroit Tigers in 1905, and he was first immortalized on a tobacco trade card in 1909, having already won two batting titles. A year later, the American Tobacco Company also marketed Ty Cobb Smoking Tobacco, "King of the Smoking World," according to the copy on its trade cards. With deliberately vague syntax, this slogan effectively suggested that this particular throne had two monarchs. Both the player and the brand were king, and thus were inextricably linked. Despite the appearance to the contrary, the use of Cobb's name and image on these cards constituted neither testimonial nor endorsement on the player's part. The same may be said for the majority of late nineteenth- and early twentieth-century tobacco trade cards. Although it was hardly unknown for players who did not smoke to offer paid testimonials touting the benefits of specific cigarette brands, Cobb was not among them. Unlike Honus Wagner, whose name was linked to several tobacco products even after his famous objection to the use of his image on trade cards, Cobb did not endorse the use of any tobacco products at this point in his career.

In fact, Cobb was emphatically opposed to tobacco consumption. If a short piece in Henry Ford's antismoking missive, *The Case Against the Little White Slaver*, titled "What Ty Cobb Thinks of Cigarettes," is to be believed, the "foremost ball-player of his time, and probably the greatest exponent [*sic*] the game has ever

2. Ty Cobb cigarette trade card, issued by the American Tobacco Company in 1909. The back reads "King of the Smoking World." Cobb virulently opposed tobacco use.

known . . . the idol of every youthful fan," objected vehemently to the habit. Cobb reputedly claimed:

> Too much cannot be said against the evils of cigarette smoking. It stupefies the brain, saps vitality, undermines one's health, and lessens the moral fiber of the man. *No boy who hopes to be success-ful in any line can afford to contract a habit that is so detrimental to his physical and moral development.*
>
> The alert brain, the strong body, and the moral stamina neces-sary for success in any line of endeavor are weakened and destroyed by the cigarette habit; and young men should realize its disas-trous effects.[8]

So why this disconnect between Cobb's published opinion and the message on the trade cards and branded tobacco? Prior to 1953, when players were granted the legal "right to publicity"—the right to control the use of their own likenesses—makers of cigarettes, gum, and other consumer goods were not by constrained by law and so were essentially free to appropriate images without the permission of or remuneration to the individuals whose names and pictures were used.[9] It is possible that some players may have been compensated for the use of their images on cigarette cards, but such compensation was not common practice. In this regard, the fact that Cobb publicly objected to smoking while simultane-ously appearing to promote tobacco use was the rule rather than the exception. Wagner, the tobacco user now more famous for his vocal objections to the use of his image on a trade card than for his actions on the field, was the outlier.

Although names and images of ballplayers were often used in advertising without permission or remuneration, paid player endorsements were far from unknown, even prior to the first golden age. A handful of nineteenth-century baseball players offered tes-timonials for patent medicines—Dr. Barlow Smith's Caloric Vita Oil, for example—as well as lending their names to a variety of sporting goods. Still, nineteenth-century baseball player endorse-ment ads were few and far between. In contrast, the first decades of the twentieth century saw their share of early adopters in the endorsement game. Ty Cobb may not have been paid for the use of his likeness on trade cards, and he certainly did not offer his testimonial to the putative Dr. Smith, but the same cannot be said for his endorsement of another early "performance-enhancing drug," a nutritional supplement called Nuxated Iron. Of the nostrum, which was widely advertised in reading notices in newspapers between 1915 and 1917, Cobb enthused:

> Hundreds of people write to me to know how I train and what I do to keep up that force and vitality which enables me to play practically every day of the entire baseball season. They wonder why I can play a better game today than when I was younger. . . .
>
> At the beginning of the present season, I was nervous and run down from a bad attack of tonsillitis, but soon the papers began to state "Ty Cobb has come back. He is hitting up to the old stride." The secret was iron—Nuxated Iron filled me with renewed life.[10]

What qualities did the "50,000 Ty Cobb" regain from this marvelous product, presumably responsible for his rebirth?[11] What made him a "Super-Man, World's Greatest Baseball Player," as the Nuxated Iron ads attest?[12] They were force and vitality, the very elements of human perfectibility touted by physical culture. While Cobb was hardly a practicing physical culturist—Macfadden's system placed an emphasis on clean living, temperance, and vegetarianism at the same time that it labeled patent medicines like Nuxated Iron one of the world's great evils—Cobb was profiled in Macfadden's *Physical Culture* magazine. In a 1910 article, looking ahead to the upcoming baseball season, *Physical Culture* held him up as the embodiment of the benefits conferred by conditioning. According to the publication, Cobb's success was entirely the result of "well-chosen exercise and under a proper system of training."[13] But Cobb's Nuxated Iron testimonial clearly claimed that the nostrum deserved all the credit. And if Nuxated Iron could do all that for Cobb, what would it do for others?

In order to answer this question, it is helpful to look at the way endorsement advertising works. What happens when an athlete like Cobb endorses a product? This ad—really, all endorsement and testimonial advertising—serves to transfer meaning from the culturally constituted image of the celebrity to consumers.[14] Writes media critic Grant McCracken, "Celebrities create a self out of elements put at their disposal in dramatic roles, fashioning cultural meanings into a practicable form. When they enter the endorsement process, they make these meanings available in material for the consumer. Consumers are grateful for these meanings and are keen to build a self from them. The celebrity is supplying not just an example of self-creation, but the very stuff with which this difficult act is undertaken."[15] In other words, celebrities, by their very nature, dramatically embody specific qualities and meanings with which consumers wish to associate. It is the stuff of which individual consumers, whether consciously or unconsciously, wish to compose themselves. The endorsement ad serves as a conduit through which the meanings of these qualities are transferred from the celebrity to the consumer via the product. First, meanings, be they personal qualities or social roles, are associated with specific celebrities. In Cobb's case, these would be athletic talent and toughness. Added to these would also be the meanings derived, however indirectly, from notions associated with physical culture, strength and health. Next, these qualities and meanings transfer through the endorsement to the product: Cobb uses Nuxated Iron, therefore Nuxated Iron means athletic talent, toughness, strength, and health. Finally, the consumer uses the product, absorbing these meanings and qualities along with it. In these terms, a healthy dose of Nuxated Iron contained all the qualities and meanings embodied by Ty Cobb in addition to the actual chemicals from which it was made.[16]

By following Cobb's lead, Nuxated Iron users did more than just improve their health—consumers added important elements to their own notions of selfhood. Celebrities, McCracken notes, "are 'super consumers' of a kind. They are exemplary figures because they seem to have created the coherent and powerful selves that everyone seeks. They are compelling partners to the meaning transfer process by which these meanings can be assembled and some of the novel shapes into which they can be assembled."[17] Thereby, celebrity endorsements and testimonials essentially help consumers create their own identities as they draw meaning from the ads. Taking Nuxated Iron, consumers—presumably young and middle-aged men, the demographic most commonly targeted by the celebrity testimonials of ballplayers—participated in Cobb's near perfection, his renewed life. As Cobb stated emphatically in his memoir, *My Life in Baseball*, the game "is a red-blooded sport for red-blooded men. It's no pink tea, and mollycoddles had better stay out. It's a contest and everything that implies, a struggle for supremacy, a survival of the fittest."[18] With help from Nuxated Iron, the consumer presumably became that red-blooded man—no mollycoddle, he. Strong, tough, athletic, with nerves of steel, he was ready to engage successfully in whatever Darwinian struggle came his way.

Ultimately, symbolic meaning transfer proved to be the only benefit conferred by taking Nuxated Iron. Citing Cobb's endorsement in its own testimony, a 1916 article in the *Journal of the American Medical Association* found that the nostrum contained "but Little Iron and Practically No Nux."[19] The authors concluded, "It is sold under claims that are directly and inferentially false and misleading, not only in regard to its composition, but also as to its alleged therapeutic effects. As for the claim that 'Nuxated Iron' is the responsible agent for Jess Willard's victory over Jack Johnson or Ty Cobb's 'come back,' it would be just as reasonable to and true to give this nostrum credit for the success of Samson's historical escapade with the jaw-bone of an ass."[20]

As *JAMA* rightfully asserts, Cobb's offensive rebirth had no connection to the restorative powers of Nuxated Iron. In fact, it is far from a given that Cobb even used the nostrum. Active in the fight against patent-medicine advertising, the American Medical Association regularly warned its members not to make false claims for payment and to avoid becoming involved in testimonial advertising. The American League, however, issued no such warning. Although the Associated Advertising Clubs of America, the industry's professional organization, adopted "Truth in Advertising" as its slogan in 1911, "Truth in Advertising" was relative.[21]

Not until the 1960s was the practice of publishing false testimonials policed with any regularity. Up to that point, it was common for celebrities to endorse products they had never used and would never use. The words attributed to Cobb in the Nuxated Iron ad were, in all probability, the stylings of an advertising copywriter. This is not to suggest that Cobb did not profit from Nuxated Iron. The Georgia Peach was paid the not insignificant sum of $1,000 (more than $23,000 in twenty-first-century buying power) for his endorsement of the patent medicine.[22]

Cobb was one of the highest-paid players of his era for his work on the diamond. And as his relationship with Nuxated Iron demonstrates, he also made a tidy sum from endorsements. But neither his salary nor his fees for endorsing Nuxated Iron came close to the rewards he reaped from his commercial connection to Coca-Cola. Following World War I, Coca-Cola executive Robert Woodruff, who in 1923 would become president of the company his father bought in 1918 from Asa Griggs Candler, convinced Cobb, his hunting buddy, to invest in the Georgia-made beverage. And invest, Cobb did. His Coca-Cola stocks were reportedly worth $1.7 million at the time of his death in 1961.[23] Cobb's commercial Coca-Cola connections actually extended back to the early days of his baseball career. He was one of the first players to be featured in Coca-Cola's iconic "arrow" ads in 1907, claiming, "On days when we are playing a doubleheader I always find that a drink of Coca-Cola between the games refreshes me to such an extent that I can start the second game feeling as if I had not been exercising at all, in spite of my exertions in the first."[24] Here, once again, this ad transfers meaning from Cobb, in this case his effortless performance, to the product, and on to the consumer.

Cobb's commercial activity was not limited to nostrum testimonials. He also endorsed General Motors vehicles.[25] Beginning in 1924, Cobb was paid the hefty sum of $25,000 a year to promote GM, making personal appearances up and down the Eastern Seaboard. But this was hardly his first foray into automobile advertising. He had already inked a one-year deal worth $15,000 to hawk Hupmobile as early as 1909. As Augusta, Georgia's Hup-

3. Iconic Coca-Cola arrow ad. Cobb profited handsomely from his relationship with Coca-Cola, both as an endorser and an investor. Courtesy of the Coca-Cola Company.

mobile official sales agent, Cobb flew a banner outside his dealership reading, "Ty Cobb Drives One, the Georgia Peach Says So Should You."[26] While personal appearances and individual banners could not possibly reach as many consumers as newspaper ads, they still functioned as potent forms of advertising in the early twentieth century. What clearer testimony to the quality of a product could there be than to be sold the item directly by the endorser himself? Not only might the purchaser of a Hupmobile transfer the qualities and meanings of the player onto himself by driving a Cobb-endorsed vehicle, the consumer could skip the middleman, acquiring those meanings and qualities, along with the car keys, directly from Cobb. This is not to suggest that Cobb personally participated in individual sales. But to buy a Hupmobile from Cobb still suggested a direct transaction.

Cobb's prowess at pitching automobiles became evident early in his career. In 1909 the trade publication *Automotive Industries* noted that Cobb had expressed his intent to go into the automobile business full time following his eventual retirement from baseball.[27] And his participation in the industry was not limited to endorsements and sales. Cobb was also a race car driver, competing in a number of events including an early endurance rally, the New York–Atlanta Good Roads Tour, sponsored by the *New York Journal-Herald*, in which he drove a Chalmers-Detroit automobile over one thousand miles.[28] That Cobb selected this particular car for the road race made sense, given the fact that he also owned a Chalmers dealership in Atlanta. Cobb also raced on a track, once competing against fellow ballplayer Napoleon Rucker at the Atlanta Automobile Association's Speedway. Again, he drove a Chalmers, while Rucker piloted a Buick.[29] As a race car driver, Cobb provided yet another meaning to transfer to the consumer by means of the product—speed. According to ghostwriter John N. Wheeler in his preface to the reputedly Cobb-authored *Busting 'Em: And Other Big League Stories*, "Cobb is the greatest base runner that baseball has ever produced. He makes lightening look slow, for he is a speed flash. He is the fastest thinker in the game, too, and the fans delight to see him make some rival player, who is not as fast as Cobb intellectually, look foolish."[30] This was the public image of Cobb—tough, smart, and above all else, fast. By buying a Cobb-endorsed auto, be it a Chalmers, a Hupmobile, or a General Motors vehicle, the consumer, too, could be made to make lightning look slow, if not on the base paths, then behind the wheel of a new car.

Cobb's effectiveness as a celebrity endorser was due, in no small part, to what Rein, Kotler, and Stoller, call "memory lock." Indeed, Cobb certainly earned his place in the collective "memory channel, the ultimate sign of celebrity success," during his career.[31] As Wheeler claimed, it was never in question that Cobb was "the most sensational player the game has ever produced," and "an institution in baseball like the Presidency of the United States is in politics," or at least one of the greatest players of his era.[32] Cobb's stature as well as his financial acumen made him an ideal endorser for a whole host of products, including Bevo, a beer-flavored Prohibition-era soft drink produced by Anheuser-Busch—which Cobb unofficially claimed was popular in his native Georgia because it mixed well with moonshine—as well as Duplex razors, autographed Louisville Slugger bats, baseball gloves, California Oranges, Florida Spas, Elastica Floor Finish, and Cracker Jack, not least among them.

Although Cobb's claim to memory lock was and remains solid, his place in the collective memory channel is not necessarily prime real estate. Tales of Cobb's bad behavior are legion. Although, as biographer Dan Holmes has suggested, Cobb may not have been quite as unsavory a character as Al Stump had previously claimed, at the very least Cobb was responsible for jumping into the stands and attacking a loud-mouth heckler missing one hand and a few fingers on the other, as well as committing a number of additional less-than-exemplary acts.[33] Writes Holmes, "Throughout his life, Cobb carried with him prejudices and character flaws that resulted in broken friendships, failed marriages, and violent episodes." He was, moreover, a "short-tempered, high strung, impulsive man."[34] Yet, for all his bad behavior and lack of "likability," Cobb's earning potential, his celebrity capital, did not diminish. Where Cobb differed from generations of unpleasant ballplayers was in his continued success in endorsement and testimonial advertising.

So why was he so successful when others were not? Playing and endorsing in the early twentieth century, Cobb emerged when the celebrity-making machine was still in its infancy. Rather than rely on a staff of image consultants, agents, and publicists, Cobb was primarily responsible for managing his own brand. Mass media was, at the beginning of Cobb's career, limited to print. While Cobb's attack on the heckler and its aftermath—his subsequent suspension by Ban Johnson, president of the American League, and the strike by his teammates in reaction to the penalty he received—was certainly covered by the sporting press, it did not receive even a fraction of the media attention a considerably less antisocial act by a player of his status would have received several decades later. While radio emerged as an important source of news and information in the early 1920s during the second half of Cobb's career, America's obsession with celebrities and celebrity behavior was still in its infancy. As such, the public Ty Cobb and Ty Cobb the person were not one and the same. While Cobb may not have been represented as entirely likeable, his overall public reputation was that of a rugged, athletic star of the diamond.

Cobb, moreover, exhibited several important qualities that may have overridden his lack of likability. Rein, Kotler, and Stoller write, "As part of our cultural heritage, we are taught to gravitate toward people in whom we perceive such qualities as competence, ability, assertiveness, friendliness, intelligence, and empathy. We're also subject to captivation by negative qualities such as arrogance, rudeness, and disdain for authority."[35] Though friendliness and empathy are not qualities usually associated with the Georgia Peach, nor were they in his lifetime, the others by which we are subject to captivation were certainly associated with Cobb. His competence, assertiveness, ability, and intelligence, all of which he publically exhibited, as well as his arrogance, rudeness, and disdain for authority, may have helped make him an ideal celebrity endorser. That he answered his own fan mail may have also aided in his cause.[36]

To a great extent, the advertising industry helped craft celebrity images as much as it banked on them. Of this, Cobb is a prime example. The public Ty Cobb was the sum of his baseball prowess, his ghostwritten articles, and his product endorsements. In this regard, Ty Cobb may have actually derived some of his strength from Nuxated Iron, some of his fortitude from Coca-Cola, and some of his speed from Chalmers-Detroit motor cars. Advertising may have contributed as much to the public perception of Cobb as Cobb lent his meaning to consumer goods through advertising.

Ty Cobb died in 1961. While his endorsement and testimonial activity had fallen off after his retirement from professional baseball in 1928, his career as a pitchman outlived him. Following the devastating baseball strike of 1994, ESPN, in an attempt to improve ratings for its coverage of the game, launched an ad campaign called "Back to Basics." At the time, ESPN's marketing people were wary of linking the network's product, televised baseball, to contemporary players, who were perceived by the public as greedy. The sports network instead chose Cobb as a representative of the "good old days," when, as their viewers believed, professional baseball—which was, in fact, always a business—was not about money. The cable sports network banked upon Cobb's reputation as a fierce competitor, harking back to the ideals of Bernarr Macfadden and the physical culture movement, flashing Cobb quotes—"Baseball is something like war" and "The base paths belong to the runner"—during its promos. That Cobb, baseball's first multimillionaire, was notoriously interested in making and keeping money, does not seem to have been important to ESPN or its target audience, nor does the fact that Cobb was one of the founders of the comparatively impotent, but historically important, Base Ball Players Federation, an early predecessor to the Professional Baseball Players Association. In 1995, as in the early part of the century, there seems to have been a disconnect between the historical Cobb and Cobb the celebrity, Cobb the brand.

Babe Ruth

Given Cobb's talents at bat, his play on the field, his savvy as an investor, and his earnings from paid testimonial advertising, it is not at all surprising that he was, by 1923, the highest-paid player in the Major Leagues. Reports that Babe Ruth had surpassed him in earnings inspired Cobb to exclaim, "Ruth endorsed whorehouses by word of mouth. He talked a lot. I advertised milk and Cobb candy."[37] Although Ruth may have given his private stamp of approval to certain houses of ill repute, his earnings from more public product endorsements and testimonials would soon eclipse Cobb's. So, too, would his celebrity. By all accounts, Babe Ruth was one of the first, if not the first, modern sports celebrities. Cobb and other baseball players—Honus Wagner, Walter Johnson, and Eddie Collins, for example—were certainly famous enough to warrant immortalization on cigarette trade cards. Their feats on the field of play and their advertising presence made their names recognizable even to those who did not follow the sport. Ruth, however, was something altogether different. His outsize swing and his outsize personality made him the perfect object for adoration in an age of new media. Jules Tygiel observes:

> In the 1920s people across the nation could see Babe Ruth in pictures and newsreels, they could hear Babe Ruth (or at least descriptions of him) on radio, and they could experience the drama of Babe Ruth at the moment that it unfolded. In an age in which the modern ideal of celebrity was virtually invented, Ruth, along with a handful of Hollywood stars, personified the concept. Others might briefly eclipse his fame—Jack Dempsey on the eve of one of his infrequent heavyweight championship fights or Charles Lindbergh after his transatlantic flight in 1927—but from 1919 until his retirement in 1935 the omnipresent Ruth alone appealed to the popular imagination on a day-in, day-out basis.[38]

As has been well documented, Ruth began his career as a pitcher with the Boston Red Sox in 1914. Despite his obvious ability and early success on the mound, his ascent to baseball's pantheon of product endorsers took a few seasons. The 1919 season, Ruth's final one with Boston, marked his emergence as a slugger, one in which he set a home-run record at an astonishing twenty-nine. A pivotal year in Ruth's career, it also saw his sale to the New York Yankees.

But Ruth's remarkable performance alone did not catapult him past Cobb and other contemporary ballplayers in terms of commercial power; success on the diamond, no matter how remarkable, meant little without the means with which to communicate it to a mass consumer base. It was, therefore, no coincidence that 1919 also marked a sea change in the print media. America's first tabloid newspaper, the *New York Illustrated Daily News*, later the *New York Daily News*, commenced publication on June 26. Inspired by England's already popular tabloids, the *Daily Mail* and the *Daily Mirror*, the *Daily News* adopted their half-page format and sensationalist style, focusing on crime-scene reporting and photographs, all with financial backing from its parent publication, the *Chicago Tribune*. But the *Daily News* was far from an immediate success. Something was missing. Crime alone did not sell papers. Though the *Daily News* continued to adhere to the credo "If it bleeds, it leads," the paper soon added a healthy dose of celebrity gossip and photographic coverage of sports to its up-to-the-minute reports of death and destruction. In 1920, as Babe Ruth amassed his fifty-four home runs for the New York Yankees, *Daily News* readers could easily access pictures of Ruth in action. Given its success, the *Daily News* soon inspired a host of new tabloids. Between 1919 and 1924, fifteen new newspapers using the half-page tabloid layout coupled with the sensationalist tabloid formula appeared on the newsstands of the nation's major cities. Rather than rely on the old subscription model common to more traditional publications, tabloids, with their many editions, depended largely on advertising dollars to be profitable. And nothing sold advertising like the tabloid recipe of sensationalism, sports, and celebrity. The new tabloids devoted many column inches to advertising of all types. Indeed, the tabloids provided a perfect vehicle for endorsement and testimonial advertising by Ruth and his cohort. More traditional newspapers, like the *New York Times* and the *Hartford Courant*, needing to boost their own earnings, followed suit, also increasing the number of column inches of advertising, a significant portion of it testimonials and endorsements, as well.

With increased space devoted to celebrity, sports, and testimonial advertising came an increase in ads that looked like endorsements but were not. As was true of Cobb-branded tobacco products, there was no guarantee that Babe Ruth–branded products were actually paid endorsements, especially in the early years of his celebrity. Tobacco companies were once again culprits in the uncompensated use of names and images, but they were not the only guilty parties in Ruth's case. Haberdasheries, in particular, seem to have specialized in the practice of invoking Ruth in print advertising. Title & Rich, a local Hartford, Connecticut, menswear store advertised its clothes with a small illustration of a rather big-headed, rotund ballplayer with an oversized bat slung over his shoulder, identified as "Babe" Ruth. "This fellow thrives on home runs, and he expects to hit the ball hard this Summer!" the copy reads, continuing, "We made the best hit of the season so far and hung up a new clothing record in Hartford!" The ad goes on to claim Title & Rich's astonishing sale of 415 suits in three days, a Hartford record, asserting, "This Is A Different Clothing Sale From All Others. And men folks [sic] know it. . . . It Must Be True."[39]

Clearly, Title & Rich aimed to capitalize on Ruth's home-run record the previous season, comparing its own record with the player's hitting prowess. The focus on numbers seems to separate this ad from earlier examples of menswear ads that invoked baseball in more general terms. While earlier haberdasheries used baseball comparisons to emphasize the quality and modernity of their products, and thereby their shops, the Title & Rich ad emphasizes quantity. Like Ruth, a standout among all baseball players, Title & Rich represents itself as a standout among haberdasheries, with the statistics to prove it. But numbers mean nothing by themselves. Knowing their meaning was central to understanding the prowess both of Ruth and Title & Rich. Those "men folks [sic]" who recognized Ruth's greatness, even in 1920, also possessed the superior knowledge that led them to shop at Title & Rich.

At first glance, this ad appears to be little more than a poorly worded attempt to exploit Ruth's celebrity to sell cheap suits. Yet it actually speaks to another major shift in mass media, and by extension, in advertising. Just a few weeks before the tabloidization of American newspapers commenced, *True Story* magazine published its first issue. *True Story*, also the brainchild of physical culture guru Bernarr Macfadden, featured tales told by ordinary people, "common people," in Macfadden's terms. Notes Roland Marchand, the publication "touted its contents as the first folk-literature since the days of the Bible—a literature written *by* the people themselves and responded to by the people," its pages filled with tales of "girls gone astray, of jealous husbands intent on revenge, and of sublime love transformed into hatred."[40] With the slogan "Truth is stranger than fiction," *True Story* provided a winning formula and sired a stable of Macfadden publications, *True Romances*, *True Experiences*, and *True Detective* among them. It also spawned imitators like *True Confessions*.

At face value, the message of *True Story* and its ilk appears to be that stories told by regular folk bear as much weight, perhaps even more, than those told by professional writers. This trend would seem to run counter to the simultaneous explosion of celebrity testimonial advertising. But this is not necessarily the case. The introduction of *True Story* magazine represented a move toward the confessional in mass media. Truth is what is important here, no matter whose truth it may be. And who better to tell the truth than one who knows? Thus, many Macfadden publications, including *Photoplay* and, of course, *Physical Culture*, included "true" testimonials of celebrities, Cobb and Ruth among them. Covering all bases, the Title & Rich ad relied on these twinned strategies, simultaneously invoking Ruth as celebrity and the notion that the "truth" comes from real people like him and the "men folks" who already knew of his greatness.

The Title & Rich ad and those of its kind, like print advertising for Truly Warner Hats, another menswear retailer that capitalized on Ruth's name without actually securing an endorsement, were but small potatoes in comparison to the contested use of Ruth's identity by the Curtiss Candy Company. In 1919, just as Ruth's star was on the rise, the Chicago confectioner began to use the name Baby Ruth for one of its products, originally marketed as Kandy Kake, though the all-out marketing push for Baby Ruth did not occur until 1921.[41] Unlike Title & Rich or Truly Warner Hats, Curtiss did not merely invoke the slugger in its advertising but branded its product with an iteration of his name. In all fairness, Curtiss did not market Baby Ruth with Ruth's image, nor did it mention him in its advertising, nevertheless, the relationship was obvious. That Ruth was occasionally referred to as Baby in the press—

especially in humor columns poking fun at uninformed baseball fans, usually women or recent immigrants with heavy accents—served to reinforce the connection between the branded product and the celebrity.[42] Even without specific, baseball-related advertising, the fan who purchased a Baby Ruth bar participated in the meaning transfer process, though perhaps not as directly as those who took Nuxated Iron to consume the meanings of Cobb. The case of Baby Ruth might have ended there, another instance of image appropriation in which the celebrity was not protected by law, had not Ruth decided to produce his own branded candy, "Babe Ruth's Home Run" bar, applying for trademark protection. But the Curtiss Company had already received a protected trademark in 1924.[43] Ruth's competing claim led to a series of lawsuits in which Curtiss insisted that its product was named after Ruth, the popular daughter of President Grover Cleveland, who was not, in fact, referred to as Baby Ruth by the press.[44] Unlikely as this may have been—Ruth Cleveland died in 1906—the appellate courts upheld Curtiss's right to the name.[45] Baby Ruth stayed on the market. Ruth's Home Run bars did not.

Spurious endorsements notwithstanding, Ruth certainly offered more than his fair share of testimonials. Even before he became a full-fledged celebrity, and well before the introduction of his failed candy-marketing venture, Ruth lent his name and image to a few select consumer goods. Just weeks after his sale to the Yankees, at approximately the same time as Baby Ruth hit the market, an ad ran in the *Boston Daily Globe* announcing, "New York Paid $130,000 for Babe Ruth—3 for 35c in Boston, BABE RUTH CIGAR."[46] At first glance this appears to have been just another appropriation of his name by an opportunistic tobacco company. But this was not the case. Ruth actually owned the small Boston factory that manufactured the cigars bearing his name and packaged with his image on each wrapper. The company began production in 1919 and, as the ad indirectly notes, continued to do so after Ruth's departure for the New York.[47] Using humor, not yet a common advertising strategy in 1920, Babe Ruth Cigars managed to buck the serious advertising trend. The ad suggests that although Ruth might have become too expensive for Boston, his cigars were not. Though they'd lost their star, Bostonians might still partake in Ruth's athletic prowess, which was worth a great deal, but certainly not as much as the Yankees paid. By extension, it implies that Bostonians smoking Babe Ruth Cigars were somehow savvier consumers than New Yorkers. After all, they could ingest all of Ruth's meanings at a bargain price, while New Yorkers, apt to pay too much for everything, were fleeced.

Although Ruth's celebrity star truly began to rise 1919, his career as a product endorser did not really take off until 1921. Babe Ruth Cigars notwithstanding, actual testimonials and endorsements by the pitcher-turned-slugger were far fewer before 1921 than after, when Ruth made the acquaintance of an associate who would change the course of his career as a celebrity. On May 1 of that year, a small item appeared in the bimonthly *Motor West* magazine, the self-proclaimed "Motoring Authority of the Pacific." Under the heading "Christy Walsh Starts Syndicate," it states, "Christy Walsh, newspaper writer, publicity man par excellence, cartoonist of note and recently connected with the Van Patten agency in New York, has formed the Christy Walsh Syndicate, to put out the writings of notables like Mary Garden, 'Babe' Ruth, Capt. Eddie V. Rickenbacker, D.W. Griffith, F. Kane Conwell, Gene Burck, Harry Carr, Ray McNamara, DeWitt Van Court, Jack Kearns, Hendrik Van Loon, and others."[48] Christy Walsh, essentially Ruth's manager and business representative as well as the guiding force behind a stable of ghostwriters that produced reams of text for Ruth and other sports celebrities, Cobb included, began his relationship with the player that winter. Trained as a lawyer, which no doubt proved extremely useful in handling Ruth's affairs, Walsh had previously worked as a newspaper cartoonist and an automobile correspondent in California. Far more important than his direct experience creating content for print media was his experience in the advertising industry and the brand new field of public relations. As advertising manager for Chalmers automobile distributor L. H. Rose, Walsh handled the company's publicity. Five years prior to initiating his business relationship with Ruth, Walsh became an early "Mad Man," joining the Van Patten advertising agency on New York's Madison Avenue, where he handled Chalmers's house newsletter.[49]

Walsh had already signed a celebrity client, World War I flying ace and automobile racer Rickenbacker, when he worked his way into Ruth's life by posing as a deliveryman from a local delicatessen from which Ruth purchased contraband beer. Writes Walsh in his short memoir, *Adios to Ghosts*, "I'm showing my proposed contract to the pleasant old delicatessen man, as his telephone rings. The conversation ends abruptly; the old man hangs up, much discouraged. 'Baby Root vants a case of beer. Right avay, right avay and mine boy is gone. Yoi. Yoi. Yoi.' Here is my lucky break and in less than ten minutes I am in the Ruth kitchenette, actually counting bottles with the Babe."[50]

Ruth, until making Walsh's acquaintance, had been rather haphazard about accepting and rejecting business opportunities. Among the side jobs Ruth had undertaken was that of sports reporter, at least nominally. In return for each use of his byline—he sent the United Press syndicate a telegram with details, each time he hit a home run—Ruth was paid five dollars.[51] Walsh convinced Ruth that he was being exploited, assuring the player that he would parlay the name Ruth into $1000 within two months of the season opener. Walsh subsequently appeared at spring training with a check for Ruth, money which Walsh had actually borrowed. The ploy worked.[52] So began a relationship that vaulted Ruth to the top, not only of the baseball world but of the celebrity stratosphere, complete with product endorsements befitting a star of his status. With Walsh, the gifted storyteller, directing his publicity, Ruth was in good hands.

Christy Walsh's value to Ruth cannot be measured in ghostwritten articles alone. In many ways, Babe Ruth, the Bambino, the Sultan of Swat, the fun-loving, larger-than-life, sometimes naughty but always nice commodity was a Christy Walsh production. Walsh created what amounted to the Babe Ruth industry, understanding, above all else, how being personal paid. Through the articles Walsh occasionally ghostwrote for Ruth, or more often farmed out to others employed by his syndicate, Walsh carefully crafted Ruth's public image.[53] Walsh also arranged Ruth's barnstorming tours, personal appearances, and occasional turns on the vaudeville circuit. And he handled Ruth's endorsements. Ruth is estimated to have made as much as $1.5 million on baseball alone over the course of his career. But he may have made even more, perhaps as much as $2 million. "Ruth's personality fit the new game and the new era. In fact, he helped create both," write Elliott J. Gorn and Warren Jay Goldstein. "As the new advertising industry sought to undermine people's fears of spending too much, to encourage them to buy on credit, and to urge consumers to seek status symbols, it could not have found a better walking billboard."[54]

Given Walsh's connection to the automobile industry, it is no wonder that Ruth had a stake in automobile advertising. His first major foray into the business was the purchase of a Rickenbacker distributorship, showing Walsh's hand at work. According to a small item in a September 1921 issue of *Automobile Topics*, another in a series of automotive industry trade publications that seemed to multiply at breakneck speed:

> Though territorial franchises for the new car which is to be put out under the name of Capt. E.V. Rickenbacker have been withheld from the public eye so far, the popular appetite is being whetted through the tentative mention of names which carry their own guaranty [*sic*] of attention . . . publicity has been given to the intention of that popular baseball attraction, Babe Ruth, to enter the automobile business this Winter, provided that he can prevail upon Rick to grant him a franchise. Ruth admits that he has not seen the car as yet, but wants it nevertheless, simply because he knows it will be good.[55]

Technically, this was not a paid endorsement. Ruth's purchase of a Rickenbacker distributorship appears to have been a personal investment rather than "personal" advertising. But for all intents and purposes, it worked both ways. As the spot notes, connecting celebrity names to distributorships was big news, the subject of rumor, innuendo, and deliberate publicity. Since Rickenbacker was also Walsh's client, there is no doubt from whence the whispering originated.

The connection between Ruth's image and the Rickenbacker-branded car worked on a number of levels. In a broad sense, it operated in the same way Cobb's distributorships did. It linked Ruth's name to a quality product, representing modernity in motion. With the addition of Ruth's imprimatur to the automobile, by means of his very public willingness to invest in a product sight unseen, based entirely on its presumed superiority, the product assumed the meanings already associated with Ruth as well as those of Walsh client Rickenbacker. In this case, the central meaning transferred to the product was power. By the time *Automobile Topics* printed this notice on September 17, Ruth had already hit his fifty-fifth home run of the season, surpassing his astonishing total of fifty-four from the previous year. No run-of-the-mill batsman was he. And the Rickenbacker was no assembly-line Model T. It was a vehicle for those in-the-know, those wishing not just to drive a mechanically powerful vehicle but to project the type of strength and superior ability associated with Ruth and Rickenbacker.

It is easy to see how the meanings of Babe Ruth transferred easily onto cigars and automobiles. Not so easy is to understand how a celebrity athlete generally associated with the mass consumption of booze, hotdogs, tobacco, and women might be a valuable endorser of health-related products. But endorse them he did. Ruth's testimonial in support of Blue-jay corn plasters is not actually as out of character as it might at first seem. The 1926 ad—featuring a closeup photograph of a set of uniformed feet with a caption identifying them as Ruth's—reads, "It isn't always the length of the hit that scores the run. Sometimes it's the speed in getting around the bases. So I have to keep my feet in prime shape."[56] Given the copy, virtually any athlete might have endorsed the product. But a testimonial from Ruth, conferring his expertise, his knowledge, his ability, elevated Blue-jay plasters above all others.

This ad, which includes a photograph of Ruth, post-swing, placed directly next to the copy, also serves as an example of the ways in which the impetus toward "truth" telling, combined with the tab-

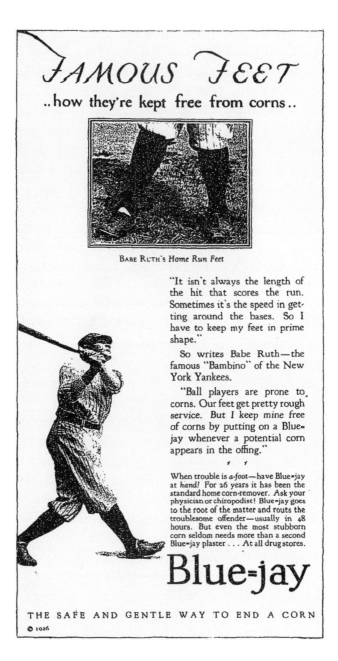
4. Possibly the first truly modern sports celebrity, Babe Ruth endorsed a vast array of products, from cigarettes and cigars to life insurance companies, from candy to a gym. His 1926 Blue-jay Corn Plasters ad focused on his superior knowledge of foot care.

loidization of the media, affected endorsement advertising. Prior to the 1920s, advertising photographs were few and far between. Toward the decade's end, however, the reproduction of photos in ads became common. According to Marchand:

> One obvious contribution of the photograph to the selling argument was the connotation of authentic "news." The tabloids and rotogravure sections educated the public to expect the latest news in photographic form. . . . An even more striking attribute of the photograph as a selling tool, art directors never tired of repeating, was its "sincerity." For understandable reasons, they used the word "sincerity" to denote effect rather than intention: the photograph was "sincere" because it is showing the literal truth. "Buyers do not question *photographic* evidence of merit," the Photographers' Association of America reminded advertisers. "They *believe* what the camera tells them because they know that nothing tells the truth so well."[57]

Thus, the photograph of Ruth tells the "true story" about Blue-jay plasters, far truer, far more sincere, and far more personal than the illustrations accompanying the questionable menswear ads of just a few years earlier. For consumers accustomed to seeing photographic evidence of Ruth's majestic swing in the daily sports pages, photographic evidence of his endorsement certainly helped. This is not to say that all of Ruth's testimonial ads included photos, but rather, that photos were an increasingly effective sales tool, especially for companies relying upon Ruth and other celebrities to tell the true story.

Less expected than Ruth's Blue-jay plaster endorsement or his testimonials as to the healing power of Absorbine Jr., a liniment, was his endorsement of McGovern's Gymnasium in New York City. A print ad advertising a Ruth-endorsed booklet, *Twelve Weeks to Health*, written by gym owner Artie McGovern, touting the "McGovern System of Health Building," first appeared in the *Wall Street Journal*, the *Brooklyn Daily Eagle*, the *New York Times*, and other area newspapers in 1927. Once again, this ad seems to be another capitalizing on the slugger's name without permission or payment, this time promoting a quack cure rather than a haber-dashery or a tobacco retailer. But this could not be farther from the truth. Artie McGovern was a respected early twentieth century fitness guru in the mold of Bernarr Macfadden. McGovern, a physical culturist, was not as big a celebrity as Macfadden, but his clients most certainly were. And none was bigger than Ruth. According to McGovern, Christy Walsh, whose fingerprints were all over this testimonial, brought Ruth to the gym in 1925. As a piece in the *Boston Globe*—which incidentally praised Harry Frazee for selling Ruth to the Yankees—claimed, Ruth was poised to have his best season, but instead, "he catches cold. Eats too much and sits in bed to read all about what the doctors have to say of his condition."[58] The condition was an ulcer; the treatment was surgery. In his own account of Ruth's recovery in his later self-help book, *The Secret of Keeping Fit*, McGovern reports, "During that winter Ruth weighed 254 pounds. His muscles were flabby. He panted at the slightest physical exertion. He suffered from severe indigestion and insomnia." Thanks to McGovern's guidance and a "rigid system of diet and exercise," "next spring he came on the playing field at 210 pounds. He was sound and solid. His waistline was off 11¾ inches from his 'new high,' and his chest, unexpanded, was off 3 inches. But his chest *expansion* had increased from 2½ to 7 inches!"[59] Ruth attested to the remarkable success of McGovern's system in the 1927 ad, specifying that his own weight loss and return to "perfect" health was the result of complete obedience to McGovern's instructions, testifying, "I ate only WHAT and WHEN he permitted."[60] The ad for McGovern's Gymnasium, referring to Ruth, calls the fitness expert, "the man who brought him back."[61] McGovern may have treated any number of celebrity athletes, Babe Didrikson and Johnny Farrell among them, but it was Ruth's success alone that he foregrounded in his ads.

It is clear that McGovern benefited from Ruth's testimonial as much as Ruth presumably benefited from McGovern's regimen. As *The Secret of Keeping Fit*, the language in the endorsement ads, and a profile in *Physical Culture* magazine make evident, McGovern's reputation soared as a result of his work with the often overweight slugger. In this case, the process of meaning transfer worked in more than one direction. In addition to his expanding chest capacity and his contracting waistline, Ruth's reputation may very well have received a lift from his association with McGovern, transferring the meanings and qualities of hard work, fortitude, and even self-discipline to his own image. While it would have taken a great deal more than a series of gym and fitness book endorsements to counter Ruth's public image as something of a hedonist, albeit a loveable hedonist, the testimonial did help to temper this image, if only in a minor way.

Ruth's endorsement of McGovern's Gym, though prominent, was not necessarily characteristic of his commercial work in the way that his Old Gold cigarette testimonial ads were. Like so many baseball players before and after him, Ruth placed his seal of approval on more than one tobacco product. Ruth, unlike Cobb, was an avid cigar smoker, endorsing White Owls and his own branded cigars as well as Old Golds.[62] Ruth's 1928 Old Gold endorsement is noteworthy specifically because it utilizes an unusual advertising strategy. Decades before the 1981 national rollout of the Pepsi Challenge, which invited Coca-Cola drinkers to participate in blind taste tests to determine which soft drink was, in fact, superior, Lorillard, Old Gold's producer, used the concept of the "blindfold cigarette testing" to challenge the supremacy of Lucky Strike, then the top-selling brand, and two others, as well.[63] Unlike the Pepsi Challenge, which charged presumptive drinkers of the competitor's product—men and women on the street—to determine which soft drink they preferred, the Old Gold test relied upon Ruth's superior taste and knowledge alone to select the best cigarette out of four. Since comparative advertising that actually mentioned the competition by name would not be an accepted practice until the 1970s, Old Gold's competitors were identified only by number. Moreover, since the Wheeler-Lea amendment to the Federal Trade Commission Act prohibiting false or deceptive advertising specifically related to ads for food, drugs, medical devices, and cosmetics was not enacted until 1938, Old Gold was under no real legal obligation to have actually conducted the test, despite the fact that it is depicted in the ad.[64] Nevertheless, a picture, especially a photograph, was worth a thousand words, and the Old Gold ad included photographic evidence not only of the test but of Ruth's participation in it.

Five columns wide and three-quarters of a page deep, the ad, which appeared in daily newspapers nationwide, asked, "What is this superiority that wins so many famous people?" The copy provides a specific answer regarding the product's "*honey-like smoothness.*" It is Ruth's endorsement that sells the product. It reads:

> Yes, I am well over 21 . . . so I could see no reason why I shouldn't make the blindfold test. As I tried the four leading cigarettes I kept this box score on the results:
> No. 1 . . . . out at first
> No. 2 . . . . . . this one "fanned"
> No. 3 . . . . . out on a pop fly
> No. 4 (Old Gold), *a home run hit!*[65]

This ad's appeal to the consumer is based directly on the notion that famous people possess superior knowledge that is not available to the average smoker. As such, it does more than support Stanley Resor's assertion that endorsement advertising works specifically because celebrities are presumed to possess such superiority, it explicitly states Resor's case. Not so coincidentally, Resor's agency, J. Walter Thompson, was responsible for the Old Gold account. That the agency had actually conducted a study several years earlier, the results of which strongly indicated that smokers were no more likely to select their own brands than any other when tested, does not seem to have mattered.[66] The Babe's testimonial was far more valuable than truth in advertising.

Along with Ruth's expert approval of Old Gold's quality, his endorsement offers some important information. Couched in the language of his testimonial is the assurance that Ruth is of legal age, "well over 21," in fact. But why was this necessary? There were, after all, no national regulations restricting tobacco consumption, and though many states had laws on the books forbidding sale of tobacco to minors, eighteen was generally considered the age of majority when it came to buying cigarettes. By the beginning of the 1920s, tobacco consumption in the United States was at an all-time high, doubling from the previous decade. This spike was partially the result of a decision made by General Pershing and his advisers to include cigarettes in military rations during World War I.[67] But even before the mass distribution of tobacco to the troops, the tobacco industry promoted its product heavily and persistently, as is exemplified by the proliferation of cigarette trade cards.

In 1928, when this ad appeared, cigarette smoking, though extremely popular, was not without its very vocal critics. And the cry against smoking grew all the louder when children and adolescents were involved. Among those naturally concerned were assorted parents groups. According to Allen Brandt, "Many parents noted that the fact that they smoked incited intergenerational conflict. Adolescent boys came under intense peer pressure to smoke. 'To refrain from smoking,' noted one author, 'would be the same as joining the 'sissy' group of boys.'"[68]

The language of "peer pressure" may have been new, but concerns about smoking by children were not. Honus Wagner's public objection to the use of his image to sell cigarettes to boys in 1909, no matter what the real motivation, certainly bore this out. So, too, did Henry Ford's publication of *The Case Against the Little White Slaver*, including its contribution by Cobb, in 1916. In 1918 a group of antismoking advocates, Ford among them, formed a Committee to Study the Tobacco Problem. The committee, however, had a public relations problem. The public perception of cigarettes was that they represented modernity, as Brand notes, "offering pleasure, solace, and relief from the stresses of contemporary life."[69] Additionally, antismoking groups were popularly associated with the extreme moralism of the Women's Christian Temperance Union (WCTU), which took up the antismoking crusade once the Volstead Act became law in 1919, ushering in Prohibition. By then the work of the committee fell on deaf ears. Still, the committee was not alone in its concern about the effects of tobacco, especially on children. Not all antismoking rhetoric was as extreme as the

WCTU's or the hell-fire-and-brimstone sermons against demon tobacco preached by baseball-player-turned-evangelist, Billy Sunday. Some relied on scientific evidence. In a 1928 *Atlanta Constitution* Health Talks column subtitled "Lady Nic versus Goddess Hygeia," for example, Dr. William Brady invoked several studies of the effect of smoking on children to support his plea: "In the interest of good health, manhood and womanhood, I urge all parents to extract from all children a pledge that he or she will never use tobacco while under 21 years of age."[70]

That neither the health-related argument nor the moralistic one had much effect on the rate of smoking among adults or children is a matter of record. Nevertheless, in light of concerns about children smoking, Ruth's Old Gold endorsement seems to take a defensive position. It clearly argues that Ruth, well into his majority, is entitled to express his paid opinion regarding Old Gold's superiority. After all, even Atlanta's Dr. Brady approved of "temperate" tobacco use, "an occasional indulgence, or not to exceed two or three smokes after your day's work is done," so long as those indulging were adults.[71] Given Ruth's appeal to children, such a preemptory statement was prudent on the part of Lorillard.

Central to celebrity product endorsement, whether by Ruth, Cobb, or any other public figure, is the notion of trust. Any number of meanings and values may be transferred from a given celebrity to consumers via advertising and consumption, but all others pale in comparison to trustworthiness. As a rule, it only pays to be personal if the person in question is perceived to be credible beyond a reasonable doubt. Never before was this truer than in the early 1930s when disposable income plummeted, and never before was it more necessary than in testimonial advertising for financial institutions. In early January 1931, an ad appeared in newspapers large and small, for the Equitable Life Assurance Society of the United States, pitching retirement annuity policies. With a crude line drawing of Ruth and a headline proclaiming "Babe Ruth says," the ad is an overt endorsement. It reads, "Everyone has to look out for the future no matter what business or profession he may follow. A few years ago Christy Walsh, my business adviser, told me about the Retirement Annuity policy. He explained how it would enable a fellow to invest a few hundred or a few thousand a year with a guarantee of a life-long income when retirement age comes. So I signed up for enough to keep me comfortable when the balls and strikes and home runs will be but pleasant memories."[72]

By the end of 1930, it was just beginning to become clear that what would come to be known as the Great Depression was more than a normal downturn in the business cycle. On December 11, just a few weeks before this ad was published, the Bank of the United States, the fourth-largest bank in New York with over 400,000 depositors, suspended business following minor runs on several of its branches, suggesting that a major run was in the making.[73] The failure of the Bank of the United States naturally attracted the attention of the national news media, leading to a banking panic. This and the failures of other large institutions caused a chain reaction, resulting in further runs on smaller banks and their subsequent collapses.[74]

So why, only two weeks after this major bank collapse, in the middle of the growing crisis, was Ruth urging those who still had a modest income to invest it in the Equitable's annuity policies? What did the Equitable offer those consumers who tore off, filled out, and mailed in the coupon at the bottom of the ad, telling the company's president, "Your Retirement Annuity adopted by Babe Ruth may interest me," that other financial institutions did not? The Equitable was essentially selling retirement insurance. In return for paying relatively small annual premiums, the policies assured a fixed income to policyholders upon retirement. As banks began to fail, investments in annuity policies grew exponentially.[75] The Equitable's financial prospects soared. Just a day after the Ruth endorsement ad first appeared in the *New York Times*, a short item in the same newspaper announced, "Total new ordinary life insurance and annuity business of the Equitable Life Assurance Society of the United States, on an agency production basis, was $887,895,171 in 1930, an increase of $6,596,402 over 1929."[76]

In a very real way, Ruth was the perfect endorser for the Equitable's policies. The ad's timing, too, was perfect, as it appeared on the heels of a protracted and very public salary dispute between Ruth and Yankees owner Jacob Ruppert leading up to the 1930 season. Following a battle that was covered relentlessly by newspapers across the country, Ruth signed a two-year contract for $160,000, famously paying him $5,000 more annually than President Herbert Hoover made. So much a part of the public conversation was the dispute that no less than Will Rogers offered his opinion on it, writing, "They offered Babe Ruth the same salary that Mr. Hoover gets. Babe claims he should have more. He can't appoint a commission to go up and knock the home runs. He has to do it all himself."[77] Of course, the target consumer for this endorsement ad was not wealthy like Ruth. Rather, the Equitable aimed to attract the "man on the street," one of the "common people"—albeit one fortunate enough to have a job amid skyrocketing unemployment rates—desperate to save a few dollars for the future in an environment where hiding money in a mattress was more secure than depositing it in the bank.

Merely being rich and famous did not necessarily make Ruth an expert on financial matters. Ruth, after all, was not necessarily known for his prudence. But he had something else his fans and the Equitable's target demographic did not have—a business adviser, someone trusted, someone who explained to him how his investment in the Equitable's annuity policy would enable him to have a secure future, and most importantly, someone not connected in any way to the sponsor. In this case, Ruth's testimonial was backed up by the superior knowledge of an expert, someone so well-informed, so credible, that no less a figure than the Sultan of Swat trusted him for advice on investments at a time when neither the banks nor the market were to be trusted—Christy Walsh. If the consumer could not believe the word of the one person Ruth put his faith in when it came to financial matters, then who might they believe? By buying the Equitable's retirement annuity policies, consumers participated in meanings and qualities newly associated with Ruth and reinforced by means of this ad—well-protected wealth and the promise a comfortable, secure future—both things that were in short supply in 1931.

The Equitable Life Assurance Society's financial growth not-withstanding, 1931 was hardly a banner year for the economy. As the Depression deepened, consumer confidence plummeted. Those still employed opted to save rather than spend, a trend that assured the success of the Equitable and other insurance companies that marketed annuity policies. But hard economic times had an understandably negative effect upon manufacturing and retail, and, hence, on the advertising industry. Not only did Madison Avenue face financial pressures, it was subject to growing criticism by a developing consumer protection movement. Advertising, consumer advocates argued, encouraged unnecessary consumption at a time when Americans had little expendable income.[78]

During the decades leading up to the economy's collapse, technological advances made mass-manufacturing possible, and advertising created demand. According to *Printer's Ink*, "Retail sales dropped off 47.7 per cent in four years. In the midst of plentiful supplies of most necessities and many luxuries of living, a large share of the total population was reduced to the level of bare subsistence." The remedy, according to the advertising trade publication, was that "some fundamental means must be found of distributing wealth in such a way as to insure an even, expanded flow of buying power through the hands of consumers, to make incomes go further and to put an end to under consumption."[79] Without consumption, after all, there would be no need for the advertising industry.

Between the crash of 1929 and 1933, the amount spent on advertising in America plummeted by two-thirds, from $3.4 billion to $1.3 billion.[80] With lower advertising budgets, manufacturers demanded that the money they spent on promotion go further. The result was a return to some of the hard-sell tactics of an earlier period, particularly in print advertising. Perhaps counterintuitively, one medium actually attracted advertising dollars, growing exponentially as the Depression deepened. "Real life in the 1930s was hard enough to bear," writes Stephen Fox. "When people clicked their radios on, they were seeking not reality but escape. Radio brought relief, with a message from our sponsor."[81]

The pressures of the Depression also inspired new theories and methods of advertising, as well as the identification of a new market, children.

As evidenced by Ruth's Equitable endorsement, his commercial work did not dry up during the 1930s. Indeed, if anything, radio's embrace of baseball and its stars made Ruth and his fellow celebrities even more marketable. This was particularly true of Ruth's appeal to children. For example, Ruth was an early endorser of General Mills' Wheaties, several years before it was branded the "Breakfast of Champions." He also endorsed Huskies, a bargain brand cereal introduced by General Mills' competitor, General Foods. Indeed, Ruth's cereal endorsements constitute a central strand in the Depression era's baseball and advertising narrative. Ultimately, his foray into breakfast food endorsements resulted in a long relationship with Quaker Oats, producers of Puffed Wheat and Rice as well as Muffet's Whole Wheat Biscuits.

Throughout his career, and even after, Ruth continued to prove that it paid to be personal, more often than not with the behind-the-scenes help of Christy Walsh. The unprecedented number of products he endorsed, including cookies for the Girl Scouts and milk for the Bureau of Milk Publicity of the State of New York, Esso and Sinclair gas and oil, Kew Bee and Mrs. Sherlock's bread, Battey's shoes for men, Simmons mattresses, and Studebaker automobiles, bore testament to his continuing popularity and selling power. So, too, did the number of products bearing his name. There were Babe Ruth undergarments and union suits for boys and men and Babe Ruth sweatshirts. There were Babe Ruth watches and Babe Ruth balls, bats, gloves, and caps. And the list goes on.

In 1948, Babe Ruth died at the age of fifty-three. His legacy as a product endorser, however, lives on. Based on Ruth's continuing place in the early twenty-first-century American zeitgeist and in early twenty-first-century advertising, it still pays to be personal, especially for sponsors looking for an endorsement from a celebrity athlete whose image is controllable and whose foibles—in Ruth's case, his seemingly insatiable appetite for booze, food, and women—are already well known.

Spreading the Endorsement Wealth

Cobb and Ruth were by no means the only baseball stars in the testimonial advertising game getting personal with consumers. Lou Gehrig also held his own in the testimonial arena. Just as he shared the diamond with his very personal teammate, the Yankee first baseman endorsed many of the same products as Ruth. Like Ruth, Gehrig pitched Old Gold cigarettes. In a frequently reproduced national ad, Ruth and Gehrig actually conduct an Old Gold "blindfold test" instead of taking one, tasking manager Miller Huggins to choose his favorite of four brands. Naturally, Huggins's choice is Old Gold, "for its zippy flavor and mellow smoothness."[82] Gehrig famously also pitched for Wheaties. And as Ruth's did, Gehrig's Wheaties endorsements played an important role in Depression-era advertising. Gehrig also gave the commercial thumbs up to Camel cigarettes, Aqua Velva, Williams shaving cream, and a host of other products. And his legacy as an endorser, like that of Cobb and Ruth, continues on.[83] In 2001 French communications company Alcatel stirred up significant controversy by using altered footage of Gehrig giving his farewell speech—which was, in fact, delivered in front of a large crowd—to an empty Yankee Stadium. Part of a larger campaign entitled "Speeches," which also included an even more controversial altered clip of Dr. Martin Luther King Jr.'s "I Have a Dream" speech, the Alcatel spot did not engender praise from American consumers or critics. As Gary Ruskin, director of a consumer watchdog group, told *Sports Illustrated*, "Alcatel is cheapening this moment by turning it into a commercial property that's no different from the Taco Bell Chihuahua."[84] Although Alcatel protested that the campaign was meant as a tribute, it seems more likely that the company was operating under the assumption that no publicity is bad publicity. More than a decade later, the company, which primarily sells cell phones and smart watches to the U.S. market, is hardly a blip on the memory channel. If the brand has any recognition, it is for the bad taste of its advertising in appropriating the images of Gehrig, King, and other iconic, deceased celebrities.

During his twenty-year career, Jimmie Foxx was also a star endorser. Foxx gave his imprimatur to Camels, Old Gold, Wheaties, and Ward's Tip Top Bread. New York Giants' star Mel Ott also got into the testimonial game, giving his seal of approval to Nestlé Milk Chocolate and Gillette Blue Blades, among other products. And while Dizzy Dean preferred Grape-Nuts for his morning repast, Hank Greenberg, Frankie Frisch, and "Schoolboy" Rowe pronounced their preference for Huskies. The 1931 World Champion St. Louis Cardinals preferred Camels to all other cigarettes, as did the 1933 Champion New York Giants. And the list goes on.

When the Business Model Changes

As early as 1929, an editorial campaign to limit testimonials, initiated by *Printers' Ink*, asked readers, "Do you believe that the use of purchased testimonials is good for advertising in general?" The resounding response was "no."[85] Babe Ruth's continuing testimonials—and those of Gehrig, Foxx, and Greenberg—belied this. Still, it no longer paid to be personal during the Great Depression in the same way it had in the teens and twenties. As the business model changed for both baseball and advertising, so, too, did the nature of celebrity endorsements.

Despite all the bad economic news, growing consumer consciousness, and falling advertising volume, there was one bright spot on Madison Avenue's horizon—the overwhelming success of commercial radio. And it should come as no surprise that baseball and its stars were key players in the new game too. Although baseball was slow to embrace and exploit commercial sponsorship, the possibilities of the new medium became quickly apparent. In the coming decades, baseball on the radio would prove that it still paid to be personal, just in new and different ways.

CHAPTER THREE

Breakfast of Champions

Tales of Depression-Era Baseball and Advertising

From the outset, professional baseball and the business of advertising developed along remarkably similar tracks. So it should not come as a surprise that both industries initially responded to the new reality of the Great Depression in remarkably similar ways—denial, followed by panic—or that both ultimately adjusted to harsh economic realities by embracing innovation. Driven by desperation as much or more than by the desire to embrace the spirit of the new, Major League Baseball reluctantly accepted commercial radio as a way to market its product, while advertising expanded its markets, selling products to new categories of baseball fans with other new techniques.

Advertising, a business founded on the principle of encouraging escalating consumption, took an immediate hit when the economy faltered. Looking back at the 1930s from the end of the decade, *Printers' Ink* knowingly observed, "The catastrophic collapse of the whole flimsy post-war inflation structure, with its worldwide reverberations, removed all semblance of balance between production and consumption. The national income plunged from $78,000,000,000 in 1929 to $45,000,000,000 in 1933. Millions lost what buying power they ever had as unemployment spread like a pestilence; millions more suffered reduced income. The machinery of production gagged on its own product."[1] Even as the machinery gagged and buyers for surplus goods, especially nonessential goods, could not be found, the pace of advertising's response was glacial. "Advertising practitioners, as resident cheerleaders for the economy," writes Stephen Fox, "kept up appearances longer than most Americans." When they did respond, they followed the lead of other industries, cutting salaries and laying off staff, all while being pressured by clients to cut prices, rather than adjusting practices. By 1932 it was abundantly clear that changes needed to be made, but the scope of necessary alterations in tactics was still foggy. "Hard times meant a hard sell," Fox observes.[2] Agencies returned to the aggressive, carnivalesque tactics of an earlier era, an era when ads featured fantastic claims, scantily clad women, and fearmongering, all in the service of continued consumer spending, with limited, if any, success.[3] Notes Fox, "Advertising's continued celebration of a materialist cornucopia appeared obscene in a nation headed toward breadline and relief roles. Nothing worked anymore."[4]

For professional baseball, it was also business as usual until 1931, when Major League attendance fell by 15 percent, a harbinger of what was to come. Just one season later, in 1932, total attendance plummeted below seven million for the first time in more than a decade.[5] In response, baseball, like the advertising industry, slashed costs. Team rosters were reduced from twenty-five to twenty-three players, and clubs increasingly relied upon player-managers to direct the game on the field. Fewer coaches and front-office personnel were employed. Salaries, too, were reduced dramatically. "The new policy spared few," notes Jules Tygiel. "Commissioner Landis voluntarily accepted a reduction in pay from $65,000 to $40,000. Babe Ruth, despite again 'having a better year than the President,' saw his salary drop $28,000 below his $80,000 peak. The cuts trickled down throughout the Major Leagues as owners reduced their payrolls by an estimated $800,000."[6]

The Medium Is the Message

It is not as if radio was entirely new in the early 1930s. By the time the New York Stock Market crashed on Black Tuesday, October 29, 1929, broadcast radio had already become a cultural and commercial institution. When the 1930 U.S. Census for the first time asked, "Does this household have a radio?" twelve million respondents—a full 40 percent of the population surveyed—answered "yes."[7] Nor was baseball a stranger to the broadcast medium. Baseball had been flirting with radio since 1920, when, according to media historian James R. Walker, the *Detroit News* station (later w w j) offered a detailed description of the World Series via wireless.[8] Advertising, too, made its mark on radio during the twenties, though there was considerable resistance to commercialization of the broadcast medium. Much early programming was not commercial at all. Rather, it was produced by fledgling stations as a public service. There were those, including then commerce secretary Herbert Hoover, who would have preferred that it remain that way.[9] Even *Printers' Ink* called for restrictions on radio advertising, agreeing with the findings of the Department of Commerce that "direct advertising would not be effective by radio, and that the public itself would probably resent the intrusion of advertising in musical and literary programming." Direct advertising—commercials inserted into programs, pitching products directly to consumers—was strongly discouraged in the early years.[10] But indirect advertising—the commercial underwriting of programming—though initially restricted, soon became common practice. So were born evening broadcasts featuring bands like the Clicquot Club Eskimos, sponsored by Clicquot Club Ginger Ale, the a & p Gypsies, sponsored by the a & p grocery chain, and the Lucky Strike Dance Orchestra, sponsored by the American Tobacco Company. Still, by 1926, a few advertisers began to cautiously dip their toes into the pool of direct radio advertising.[11] By 1929 radio was well on its way to becoming a central advertising medium.[12]

For much of its first decade, baseball on the radio was unsponsored. Even as other programming embraced advertising, both indirect and direct, baseball broadcasts were produced on a noncommercial or "sustaining" basis, positioned as a public service.[13] This is not to suggest that broadcasting baseball on the radio did not have its commercial purposes. In 1925, for example, radio manufacturer Atwater Kent advertised his company's product as "Your seat at the World's Series [*sic*]," telling consumers, "You can be at the center of a miracle; you can be in two places at once. All you need is a radio." Radio had the ability to transport listeners from Los Angeles, where this ad ran, all the way to Pittsburgh and Washington DC, where they could "become part of that great throbbing interested crowd," participating in the excitement via "play by play, vividly, realistically, immediately"—or at least by means of dramatic re-creation—simply by listening to local station KNX at home or at one of the public locations where Atwater Kent placed demonstration radios for the enjoyment of potential consumers.[14] Atwater Kent may have produced radios, but according to this ad, its real product was magic.

Atwater Kent and other radio manufacturers were not alone in using baseball on the radio to boost sales. Radio retailers such as the Broadway Department Store, also in Los Angeles, invited customers to "have what dozens of fans are fighting for—a reserved seat at every game of the World Series," while having lunch "in solid comfort" at their Roof Garden Café, "a cool delightful place."[15] Third-party print ads for baseball on the radio, like this one, became increasingly common during the 1920s, especially at World Series time, when there was widespread interest in the game.

Retailers and radio manufacturers like the Broadway Department Store and Atwater Kent seemed to have understood what the majority of Major League owners did not, that baseball and radio made an excellent commercial match. Nevertheless, a majority of East Coast owners were reluctant to embrace radio, fearing that broadcasts would hurt attendance. After all, why would consumers pay for a product they could get for free? In America's largest media market, New York City, owners of the three Major League clubs, the Yankees, Giants, and Brooklyn Dodgers, resisted regular-season radio broadcasts, with a few exceptions like home openers, until the 1939 season. Though not as obstinately resistant as New York's clubs, the Philadelphia Athletics and Phillies, the Boston Red Sox and Braves, and the Washington Senators were also slow to embrace the broadcast medium.[16]

Bucking the trend was Chicago, where the Cubs led the radio vanguard. Chewing-gum magnate and team owner William K. Wrigley Jr. was the earliest of early adopters. Wrigley, Walker notes, "immediately recognized the value of the felicitous spring-to-fall marriage of youthful radio and the baseball establishment.

The radio game offered owners a two-hour daily commercial for their teams. Weekday daylight games could reach women, children, and some men, while weekend contests could add most of the male population to baseball's radio audience."[17] That Wrigley was the first owner to embrace the promotional possibilities of radio should come as no surprise. His gum empire was built on a foundation of savvy advertising. Wrigley, who began his career in sales in 1891 hawking soap, including free baking soda into the deal as a premium to merchants who carried his products, understood the power of promotion. When consumer demand for his baking soda outstripped demand for his soap, he adapted and became a full-time baking soda salesman, offering a new premium to his customers that was far more popular than his baking soda—chewing gum. In short order, he was out of the baking soda business, becoming a gum manufacturer in 1892. But his real success came as a result of a counterintuitive move during the financial panic of 1907, when, according to his official company hagiography, he "did the unthinkable, mortgaging everything he owned to launch a massive advertising campaign, a move that skyrocketed the company into national prominence and set the stage for the company's future groundbreaking advertising strategies."[18]

Among Wrigley's closest advisers in the advertising game was Albert D. Lasker. Lasker was also the largest minority owner of the Cubs in 1916.[19] In 1925 Lasker sold his shares to Wrigley, making the chewing-gum king the team's majority owner. Lasker, author of the eponymous Lasker Plan, which led to the establishment of the office of baseball commissioner in the wake of the 1919 Black Sox scandal, was first and foremost president of Chicago's largest advertising agency, Lord and Thomas. Considered to be one of the fathers of modern advertising, Lasker was never one to let a good sponsorship opportunity go by. His parting advice to his friend and former partner in the baseball business was to rename Cubs' Park (originally Weeghman Park) Wrigley Field, claiming that it would do his "chewing gum business a lot of good" by increasing name recognition.[20] As such, Wrigley was also a pioneer in another aspect of baseball advertising and sponsorship, that of corporate naming rights. Reaching out to a consumer base beyond the "friendly confines" of Wrigley Field, the Cubs became the first team to consistently broadcast regular-season home games on WMAQ and some, also, on WGN, the same year Wrigley became the team's principal owner. As Wrigley had surmised, the regular radio coverage of Cubs games helped rather than hindered attendance. In fact, the Cubs set a National League attendance record in 1928.[21] Moreover, the constant repetition of the ballpark's name on the radio served as a potent source of free advertising for Wrigley's primary business, also doing his chewing gum business a lot of good.

To say that MLB's embrace of radio was inconsistent, differing widely from team to team and from region to region, would be an understatement. Like the Cubs, the White Sox began regular broadcasts in 1925. They were joined by the Detroit Tigers in 1926 and St. Louis's teams, the Cardinals and the Browns, as well as the Cleveland Indians in 1927. By 1929, with the addition of Cincinnati, all the western franchises were on the air.[22] Over the next decade, the eastern teams gradually relented. But it took another decade for all the eastern owners to admit that baseball on the radio might just be good for business.

Until the mid-1930s, the majority of baseball broadcasts remained unsponsored. It was not that Major League owners did not comprehend the commercial possibilities of baseball. Western team executives, following Wrigley's lead, realized early on that radio served as excellent advertising for their product, expanding their respective fan bases, and hence, attendance, significantly. Moreover, since live baseball was a daytime affair, radio broadcasts reached a new demographic, women. Quoting from an article in the November 1929 issue of *Baseball Magazine*, Walker observes that broadcast baseball "was not driving current fans away; it was enlarging the pool of fans by converting women to the game. Radio coverage and not 'Ladies; Day,' drew 'women as steady customers at the turnstiles.'"[23] Though it took the better part of a decade to learn, baseball's owners had begun to understand what radio advertisers already knew, that women made up the largest segment of the daytime listening audience, and women were the primary decision makers when it came to household spending. They also tended to control household entertainment budgets.

Pitching the World Series

Regular-season baseball in the 1920s and '30s was a fundamentally local product. The same cannot be said of the World Series. "World Series broadcasts," writes Walker, "were the most forcefully protected from the stain of overcommercialization. The combination of a monolithic commissioner, radio-wary owners, a Major League–level monopoly, and an American culture increasingly suspicious of advertising kept the crown jewel of all sports broadcasts unsponsored until 1934."[24] But Depression-era economics wore on Commissioner Kenesaw Mountain Landis's resolve to keep the World Series "pure." As the Depression deepened, and Major League Baseball, like the majority of American businesses, faced financial issues, Landis finally relented and sold the radio rights to the World Series to the Ford Dealers of America, Inc. for $100,000. By this point, Ford was already engaged in a heated competition with General Motors' Buick division to become the largest sponsor of broadcast sports. Since Buick dominated sponsorship of heavyweight boxing matches—by far the second most popular sport in America in the 1930s after baseball—Ford's sponsorship of the Series was almost a necessity, constituting a major feather in the automaker's advertising cap. That the hometown Detroit Tigers were vying for the 1934 American League pennant solidified Ford's resolve to win the Series rights. Based on the popularity of his company's sponsored, weekly, pennant-race updates hosted by Tigers' player-manager Mickey Cochrane, and urged on by his son, Edsel, Henry Ford was convinced that Landis's high price was worth it.[25]

In order to help cement the connection between its product, its dealers, and professional sports' premiere event, Ford engaged in heavy cross-promotion, advertising in major newspapers around the country. A national ad that ran in cities from Boston to Los Angeles as well as in smaller cities and towns like Sandusky, Ohio, and Beckley, West Virginia, relied on Cochrane's endorsement to clarify the connection between the cars and the broadcasts. Under a large headline reading "Control of Power," smaller display copy announces, "Big league pitchers know that power is not enough. The important thing is to control that power—particularly in tight situations where you've got to bear down and win." A photograph of the broadly smiling Cochrane in a catcher's crouch sits directly beneath the headline and above the actual endorsement, "Mickey Cochrane, manager of the Detroit Tigers says: 'I've caught a lot of great pitchers and they've all had two things . . . power and control. That's what has put us up there this year. All top-notchers have it—in baseball and in other lines of sport.'" [26] In this ad, the transfer of meaning from the endorser to the consumer via the product is quite explicit. Who better than Cochrane, the 1934 American League Most Valuable Player, to understand the importance of power—as in the power of pitchers and the power of his bat—and control—both of the ball and the team—to imbue the automobile with those qualities? More importantly, the ad completes its work by reminding consumers to listen to "Exclusive Ford play-by-play description of the World Series. Every day of the Series, over both Columbia and National Broadcasting Systems." In this way, the ad also links Cochrane's superior expertise regarding power and control to the power of the radio and control of the World Series' broadcasts to sell Ford cars.

Various local Ford dealerships piggybacked on the company's World Series sponsorship, engaging in cross-promotion through the print media in order to bring baseball fans into their dealerships. Five Atlanta dealers, for example, placed ads in the *Constitution* telling the city's fans, "Ford dealers of Atlanta have arranged for the colorful play-by-play descriptions of the World's Series to come to you at their showrooms. Loud speakers have been installed and arrangements have provided for your comfort." [27] In this way, the dealerships reverted to the same sales techniques as earlier radio manufacturers and retailers like Atwater Kent and the Broadway Department Store, inviting customers into their places of business where they might at the same time hear the Ford-sponsored broadcast and see the power and control of a new

Ford with their own eyes. And maybe they would also consider the purchase of a new car.

Sadly for Edsel Ford, his Tigers lost the seven-game 1934 World Series to the Cardinals. Both teams, however, benefited from the Ford sponsorship deal. Each of the Cardinals received a World Series share of $5,941.19, while every Tiger received a share of $4,313.00. Notes an article in the *Chicago Tribune*, the player pool was increased $51,000 by radio receipts, more than half of the proceeds of the commissioner's sale of the rights. In fact, the second- and third-place winners in each league profited as well, as did the commissioner's office.[28] Subsequently, Ford made the same deal with Landis to sponsor the Series in 1935 and 1936. While the 1935 Series, a Tigers victory over the Cubs, appears to have been a good investment for Ford, the automobile company was not as happy with the results in 1936, an all–New York affair between the Giants and Yankees. According to Irving Vaughan, writing in the *Chicago Tribune*, "One series is said to have cost Ford approximately $275,000 in addition to the original $100,000. So when a survey of the 1936 series, also played in New York, indicated a drop in listener interest from 1934 when the Cubs played Detroit, Ford asked for a release from his 1937 agreement." But because another sponsor could not be found to underwrite the broadcast, Ford remained on the hook for the $100,000, which was paid as a contractual obligation.[29] Even without Ford's sponsorship, fans could still hear the games on NBC and CBS as sustaining broadcasts, and the players still received their sponsor-funded, generous World Series shares.

This is not to say that the 1937 World Series was advertising-free. America's newspapers were filled with splashy print ads placed by radio retailers encouraging baseball fans not to miss a minute of the action. Davega City Radio, with thirty stores in the New York Metropolitan area, urged Giants and Yankees fans to listen to the World Series on the Emerson 6 Tube Air Queen, with its "Self Contained Arial," "Splendid Tone Quality," and "Good Looking Compact Cabinet," "made to sell for $19.95" for only $8.88.[30] Appearing on the first day of the Series, this ad pitches the relatively small radio as an impulse buy, something affordable that a consumer might purchase in the morning, take home, plug in, and be listening to by 1:30 in the afternoon. Unlike the Broadway Department Store or Atwater Kent, Davega was not offering fans the collective experience of listening to the Series with other fans while demonstrating the superiority of their radios. Rather, Davega's merchandise was positioned for individual consumption in the privacy of the home, presaging the way in which television would influence fan viewing practices two decades later.

But what about World Series fans without the ready cash? How might they listen to the World Series on a Davega radio if they couldn't come up with $8.88? The country was, after all, still mired in the Great Depression, despite an improving economy. But they had no need to despair. For them, the Air Queen, sporting a "Three Color Airplane Dial," and modern Art Deco styling, was also available on installment for just fifty cents a week, "no money down," with a "small charge for credit." Given that one of the causes of the Depression was the then unprecedented level of consumer debt, it might seem surprising to see Davega offering credit so easily.[31] But this is not the case. The practice of selling consumer goods on installment plans, a feature of everyday life during the 1920s, did decrease at the onset of the Depression. But the downturn in installment buying did not last for long. By 1933 retailers were once again offering credit as a way to stimulate sales.[32] Thus, Davega's offer of easy credit and low monthly payments for the privilege of listening to the World Series on the radio was indicative of this continuing trend.

The image of New Yorkers rushing to Davega to buy new radios on which to listen to the 1937 Subway Series in the privacy of their own homes, or, as baseball mythology would have it, blasted from every home on the block, so that a pedestrian might take a stroll and not miss a single pitch, may not be a terribly realistic one. Nevertheless, it is easy to see how an all–New York Series might have boosted sales of local radio retailers. But World Series–related radio print ads appeared in other parts of the country too. "The World Series Begins at Sterchi's," pronounced an ad for the Atlanta furniture store in the *Constitution*, for example. There, consumers might purchase the new 1938 Philco model 7xx. "No Squat. No Stoop, No Squint," trumpets the ad, next to an illustration of an elegant woman dressed in evening wear, effortlessly tuning in to her favorite sporting event.[33] The pictured radio is huge, a major piece of furniture, designed so that the fashionable female fan might easily find her station without awkward bending. The illustration, combined with the price of the radio, "only $89.95," suggests this is meant to be a luxury purchase. As such, the ad appears to target an entirely different consumer demographic than the Davega ad, which set its sights on working-class purchasers with its bargain price and promise of affordable installments. In contrast, the Sterchi's ad seems to target middle-class consumers, those who aspire to the gentility of the chic, presumably well-to-do woman depicted with the product. Listening to the World Series on a Philco 7xx radio purchased at Sterchi's might not elevate the social status of the consumer to that of the illustrated woman, but it would provide a material symbol of social mobility, telegraphing the message that mobility was possible, even during the Depression—all it would require was the purchase of a new radio from Sterchi's.

Both the Sterchi's and Davega ads share an important feature in addition to the similarity of their products and the World Series tie-ins. Both ads prominently display the price of the merchandise. By including the price, especially preceded by "only," the Sterchi's ad implies that it does more than offer luxury; it offers it at a lower price than other retailers. Prior to the Depression, advertising the prices of durable goods as these two ads do was unusual. But, as the *Advertising Age* publication *The Principles of Advertising and Marketing Communications at Work* explains, during the Depression, "the look and feel of creative executions changed . . . and the genteel and elegant ads gave way to hard sell efforts with more graphics, less copy, and more low price appeals that some call the 'tabloid aesthetic.'"[34] When prices were included in pre-Depression-era advertising, as they were in ads for department stores, dry goods emporiums, and grocery stores, they were always small and unobtrusive. But the Sterchi's ad, like the Davega ad, relies upon characteristic of Depression-era tabloid aesthetics. It is large and loud. Its graphics, though they depict a quality item being used by a well-dressed, chic listener, are crude. It eschews copy in favor of large display type and illustrations. And it includes a low price appeal even as it attempts to appeal to status-conscious consumers.

Thank Goodness, We've Solved the Breakfast Problem at Last!

For a few weeks each October, World Series broadcasts helped to sell radios, baseball, and, from 1934 to 1936, Ford cars. Still, these broadcasts did little to market either baseball or consumer goods during the rest of the year. Finding other means to sell the game to consumers and to sell consumer goods with the game was essential. As Depression-era advertising budgets became increasingly slim, notes *Printers' Ink*, "the selective attitude became paramount. Advertisers began to realize the need of a better allocation of advertising in accordance with the potential market. Advertising was specifically directed to types of markets, and in the presence of complete knowledge of sales potentials and market characteristics."[35] Out of necessity, advertisers also identified a new demographic, complete with the knowledge that it was readymade for baseball and baseball-related pitches, both on the radio and in print. Women may have controlled the family purse strings, but increasingly, many of their purchases were controlled by another force, their children. Children represented a new demographic ready and waiting to be exploited. Cigarette manufacturers already knew this. The American Tobacco Company most certainly marketed its product indirectly to children by packaging baseball trade card premiums with tobacco products as early as the 1890s. Nevertheless, few if any advertisers targeted children directly prior to the Great Depression. According to *Printers' Ink*, "The 45,000,000 boys and girls between infancy and eighteen years of age caught the eye of many an advertiser who was searching for new ways of building volume. Because children were maturing earlier than they used to and took a wider interest in the world about them, many advertisers of products whose consumption was shared by the rest of the family set out after the youngsters' favor."[36]

Of the companies that pioneered advertising to children, making ample use of baseball, radio, and baseball on the radio, in addition to a great volume of print and point-of-purchase advertising, General Mills, the maker of Wheaties, led the charge. At the same time General Mills moved to position itself as commercial radio's largest baseball sponsor, the company worked steadfastly to extend its consumer base to include children. Certainly, other advertisers also pitched to children, and other advertisers sold them cereal, but none did so as thoroughly or as effectively as General Mills did with Wheaties. Its standardized, highly consistent advertising campaign was launched just as America's descent into economic chaos began, though the seeds of its success were sown in the years leading up to the crisis

A decade before it became the "Breakfast of Champions," Wheaties cereal was introduced to the market as a modern, healthful morning meal for adults by the Minnesota milling conglomerate then known as the Washburn Crosby Company.[37] According to cereal historians Scott Bruce and Bill Crawford, "General Mills hagiographers maintain that their whole-wheat flake was developed by a Minneapolis health nut named Mennen Minniberg, but it is much more likely that the cereal was the product of deliberate corporate planning."[38] Whether it originated in the kitchen of a sanitarium or a laboratory, Wheaties seems to have been conceived of with marketing in mind. Its naming, the subject of a corporate myth probably founded in reality, illustrates this notion. According to General Mills historian James Gray, "A contest held among employees, their wives, and husbands, was won by Jane Bausman, wife of R. F. Bausman, the company's New York authority on the export market. She was the first person to say "Wheaties," knowing that nothing endears a man, an institution, or a thing to the American heart quite so surely as does a diminutive nickname."[39]

The same year as Wheaties cereal was introduced, General Mills also got into the radio business, buying a moribund Minneapolis station, renewing its license, strengthening its signal, and renaming it wcco, for the company's initials. Gray observes, "Meanwhile the history of Wheaties had paralleled the history of radio itself. The virtues of both were presently to become known to gratified millions, but for the moment the public of each was still small, too small to provide a profitable market for a ready-to-eat cereal."[40] Nevertheless, on Christmas Eve 1926, a quartet went on the air on wcco, singing new words to the melody of "She's a Jazz Baby":

> Have you tried Wheaties?
> They're whole wheat with all of the bran.
> Won't you try Wheaties?
> For wheat is the best food of man.[41]

So was born the advertising jingle.

While the jingle—as well as a sponsored evening radio program featuring the Wheaties Quartet, later renamed the Gold Medal Fast Freight for another General Mills product—increased sales, it did nothing to expand the product's target demographic. To broaden its consumer base in the face of worsening economic conditions, the company looked to a younger audience, introducing its first scripted afternoon adventure program aimed at children, *Skippy*, in 1931.[42] Based on an extremely popular comic strip of the same name drawn by Percy Crosby (no relation to Washburn Crosby), *Skippy* succeeded in appealing to its audience and thereby promoting the brand and increasing sales, but it lasted little more than a year. In all likelihood, the Wheaties-sponsored Series would have had a far longer run but for bad timing. In the episode that aired on March 1, 1932, the title character, Skippy, a loveable scamp described by Bruce and Crawford as "the Bart Simpson of his day," and his friends were kidnapped.[43] On March 2, a real kidnapping dominated the news, that of the "Lindberg Baby." After that, *Skippy*'s days were numbered. Still, the experience of marketing Wheaties on the radio with the help of a character popularized in the funny pages taught General Mills several important lessons: radio sponsorship worked, characters drawn from the funny pages had a widespread appeal, children were a market ripe for exploitation, and, even at the height of the Great

Depression, mothers could be counted upon to buy their children what they really wanted, especially if what they wanted was "good for them."[44]

Even as *Skippy* and another massively popular broadcast series, *Radio Orphan Annie*, looked to the funny pages as a source for material, advertising was slow to recognize the potential of newspaper comics as an advertising medium in their own right until the mid-1930s. Advertising on the funny pages was the brainchild of a few progressive agencies that embraced a new, scientific technique in an attempt to improve their bottom lines as their clients' advertising budgets shrank. This was especially true of Young and Rubicam (Y & R), which hired George Gallup, a little-known professor of advertising and journalism at Northwestern University, to conduct surveys. "His newspaper studies," writes Fox, "extended to fourteen newspapers and some forty thousand interviews with readers, found that people most noticed the picture page (85 percent), the most popular comic strip (70 percent), and editorial cartoons (40–50 percent). Even the lead story on the first page and the lead editorial fared less well."[45] Although Y & R commissioned the polls and profited directly from Gallup's work, the first Gallup polls had a wide-ranging impact on the advertising industry as a whole. Roland Marchand observes, "Gallup's findings did more than provide 'scientific proof' of a low level of public taste; they also seemed to demonstrate that the 'tabloid mind' was neither a class phenomenon nor confined to the urban masses. Bankers and professors read the comics as eagerly as waiters and truck drivers."[46] So, too, did children.

And so advertisers began to place pitches in the funny pages, often emulating the strips. According to Marchand, "Enthusiasts for the comic section as an advertising medium quickly discovered that in the comic-strip format, the best techniques learned from other sources could be combined. From the movies came the ideas of continuity of action, quick-cutting from scene to scene, and focusing attention through the occasional close-up. From the confessional magazines came the power of personal testimony and the intimate drama. From the tabloids came the emphasis on brev-

5. "Babe Ruth—The Home-Run King and the Free 'How-to-Hit-a-Home-Run' Moviebook He Gives to Boys and Girls" was one of General Mills' most visible examples of advertising on newspaper funny pages, emulating the comic strip form and targeting children and their parents alike. Courtesy of General Mills.

ity and pictorial imagery. And from radio came the persuasiveness of a conversational style and the seductiveness of eavesdropping." Comic strip advertising also drew upon celebrity endorsements as potent advertising tools. Marchand continues, "The most powerful testimonial of all was the one embedded in an ostensibly private conversation that the advertiser arranged for the consumer to overhear."[47]

General Mills, making ample use of comic-strip advertising, was one of the first companies to harness the popularity of baseball, connecting the game to their product. To do so, the cereal maker utilized the conversational product endorsement to sell Wheaties to the *Skippy* demographic. And who better to spread the word about Wheaties in the comics section but ace product endorser Babe Ruth? In July 1933, a half-page strip titled "Babe Ruth—The Home-Run King and the Free 'How-to-Hit-a-Home-

Run' Moviebook He Gives to Boys and Girls" began its national run. The "ad as comic strip" follows the adventures of little Jerry and his unnamed brother, two suitably adorable cartoon tykes, as they catch a Ruth home-run ball and bring it back to their hero in the locker room. Like flies on the locker-room wall, readers "overhear" their private conversation as if it were actually happening, or as if it was part of a scripted radio series. Seated on Ruth's knee, little Jerry tells the Babe, "I wish I could play ball like you." Ruth responds, "Well, maybe you can someday, Jerry, if you eat lots of Wheaties for breakfast every morning like baseball players do . . . 'cause there's nothing like them to give energy and pep." To help them emulate his swing, the slugger bestows upon them his General Mills–branded Moviebook—a flipbook—on the condition that they eat their Wheaties. Of course, the boys promise that they will tell Mom to buy some immediately. The next morning at breakfast, Jerry brags to his brother, "Mm! I could eat a carload of Wheaties right now!" leading their beneficent, smiling mother to exclaim, "Well . . . thank goodness we've solved the breakfast problem at last." Later, as the boys are hitting away, dad admires their new husky frames, leading mom to give Ruth and his gift all the credit, saying, "Thanks to Babe Ruth's Moviebook that started them eating Wheaties."[48]

Certainly, the larger-than-life Babe Ruth, especially the cartoon Babe Ruth, was the perfect figure to appeal to a significant portion of those forty-five million children, just as he had appealed to their fathers in the previous decade with his adult-centered endorsements. By eating their Wheaties, little Jerry and his brother would be able share in the fabled source of Ruth's energy and pep. But energy and pep were not enough. Eating Wheaties alone would not confer upon them the secret knowledge of Ruth's swing. This could only be acquired through their direct participation. Little Jerry and his brother may have held the secret to Ruth's swing, a secret accessible only through the Moviebook, but the young consumers reading the strip had to take another step to secure the information captured in the magic tome. The final panel of the advertising strip depicts the cartoon Ruth holding a giant coupon, advising his readers, "Here y'are, boys and girls—send this in and get my new Moviebook showing my complete home-run swing from beginning to end," explaining to all those potential Wheaties eaters how to complete the process of transferring meaning from him to themselves via breakfast.

Unlike using comic-strip characters to sell cereal to children in print and on radio, redeeming coupons for premiums was not a new advertising technique in the 1930s. Common in the early decades of the twentieth century, the practice served as a form of market research years before the advent of the Gallup polls. Advertisers were able to study the impact of their work by looking at the response to given ads as coupons were submitted by consumers, often in return for a sample of the advertised product.[49] Not only did this help advertisers judge the general appeal of their ads, but it also provided a window upon the ways in which different advertising techniques played in different markets. In order to sweeten the pot and to assure continued sales, advertisers also began to offer premiums in exchange for box tops and labels. Most often, the redemption scheme required the consumer to submit multiple proofs of purchase in exchange for the promised item. But this practice changed during the Depression. Premiums like the Babe Ruth Moviebook did not require a purchase on the part of the consumer, making sending away for it much less of an economic commitment.[50] Nevertheless, since possession of the Moviebook was only part of the formula for a Ruthian swing, a significant proportion of those who sent in the coupons were also likely to purchase Wheaties.

It is highly unlikely that little Jerry and his brother would have had the financial means to have purchased that box of Wheaties on their own. A wise child, Jerry presumably knows enough to ask his mother to buy them for him. Just in case the juvenile comics readers were not aware that asking Mom was necessary, the ad spells it out in small print in the instructions under the cartoon. Outlining the procedure, it says, "Ask your mother to get you Wheaties from the grocery store. Start eating them right away." But asking Mother to buy the product did not mean she would.

She, too, would have to be convinced. Thus, the ad needed to speak to her. While in the strip Ruth addresses little Jerry directly, the ad addresses mothers as well, creating a demand that only their purchase of Wheaties will satisfy. In order to offer a solution, the ad had to create or at least identify a problem. And identify one it did—the dreaded "breakfast problem."

Thanks to Babe Ruth, Wheaties was able to solve a persistent childrearing issue without the need for coaxing or threats. This was indicative of another trend in Depression-era advertising. This trend, the move toward appealing to new concepts of "parenting," more specifically, the notion that parents, mothers in particular, should turn nurturing into a career with the help of advice and guidance from experts was evident throughout the media. "As child guidance authorities discerned more and more difficult 'problems' in attaining the proper diet for children and in properly molding their behavior without destructive discipline," writes Marchand, "advertisers eagerly publicized those problems and offered their products as solutions."[51] The result was a common advertising trope, identified by Marchand as "The Parable of the Captivated Child":

> As an advertising tool, the parable of the Captivated Child gave special emphasis to certain aspects of the new child-guidance theories that the manuals and advice books had suggested with far less intensity. For obvious merchandising reasons, the ads advocated parental indulgence with far less qualification than the experts. Sensing that family democracy meant earlier and wider participation in the joys of consumerism, advertisers enthusiastically endorsed the idea of family conferences and shared decision-making. Advertising tableaux surpassed even the child-rearing manuals in placing total responsibility on the parents for every detail of the child's development, thus magnifying the potential for guilt. And they exaggerated the ease with which children might be manipulated.[52]

Fortunately for Jerry's mother, she does not have to go it alone, for she has the help of one whose expertise extends to captivating small boys in ways that perhaps no other expert does, the great Babe Ruth himself. Ruth may not have been a trained specialist in the new art of parenting, but he certainly held sway over younger consumers, and his cartoon interaction with Jerry and his brother reflects this. With Ruth's help, Jerry's mother does not have to admonish her sons to eat a meal they don't enjoy. Instead, she happily watches them ingest their cereal while they praise its excellence. They are nothing if not captivated. So evident are the positive results of Wheaties consumption that even their father can hardly believe the fantastic outcome.

Wheaties baseball comic strips, like all forms of successful advertising, had their imitators. General Foods, the parent company of C.W. Post cereals, advertised its Grape-Nuts, for example, in a strip titled "Dizzy Dean Cuts Loose with His Smoke Ball!" In it, the St. Louis Cardinals' pitcher, nattily clad in street clothes, helps an adorable tyke outsmart an evil carney who has bilked the child for all his money at "the old ball throwin' game." Not only does Dean win a coveted scout knife for the child by skillfully knocking bottles over with his fastball, but he instructs the youngster in the secrets of pitching so the child won't be cheated again. Unsurprisingly, the secret lies in the consumption of Grape-Nuts. The strip ends with the Captivated Child exclaiming, "Gee—Dizzy forgot to mention how swell Grape-Nuts tastes. Boy, it's sure elegant!"

General Foods' entry into the flaked-wheat advertising sweepstakes, Post-branded Huskies, was introduced in 1936. In direct competition with Wheaties advertising, Huskies' advertising also capitalized on the parable of the Captivated Child in the funny pages. An early comic-strip ad, placed at the bottom of a larger ad featuring endorsements by White Sox first baseman Zeke Bonura and a variety of Olympic stars, tells the story of how Charlie Grimm, "fighting manager of the Cubs" saved the day for a mother wrestling with the dreaded "breakfast problem." In contrast to the other captivating players, Grimm, passing by an open apartment window, hears a mother cajoling her thin children to eat a breakfast they don't like, and appeals to her rather than to her offspring.

Here, consumers overhear Grimm overhearing the family argument, doubling the "radio" fly-on-the-wall effect at work in the other two ads. Grimm, of course, wins mother and children alike over to Huskies. In the final panel, the youngsters show Grimm their muscles, as they profess to love Huskies so much they breakfast on them every day.[53]

Jack Armstrong, All-American Pitchman

To induce even more Depression-era children to eat Wheaties, General Mills introduced a new radio adventure series in 1933, *Jack Armstrong, the All-American Boy*. Through it, the company expanded the use of premiums like the Explorer Telescope, the Hike O Meter (a pedometer), and the Torpedo Flashlight. Although *Jack Armstrong* was not a baseball-centered program, it occasionally featured promotions by baseball stars. On one notable occasion during the early 1930s, Ruth made a guest appearance, promoting a recipe for cookies made with Wheaties. But while Ruth was a powerful hitter and an ace pitcher, he was not yet a powerful ace pitchman on the radio, which was, of course, live. During rehearsal, according to Bruce and Crawford, "Babe kept saying 'cooookies' instead of 'cookies.' On the air, Babe got through the entire pitch before delivering the last line, 'And so, boys and girls, don't forget to tell your mother to buy Wheaties, so she can make these cooookies.' There was silence for a moment, before listeners across the country heard Babe blurt out, 'I'm a son-of-a-bitch if I didn't say cooookies again.' No one complained—a testament to the power of the Babe."[54]

Not to be outdone, Post enlisted Lou Gehrig to endorse Huskies on the radio. In addition to placing giant point-of-purchase displays featuring the Yankee first baseman's image in grocery stores around the country, General Foods promoted Huskies through sponsorship of the extremely popular radio program *Believe It Or Not*, based on Robert Ripley's newspaper cartoon. Like General Mills, it, too, was the victim of the vagaries associated with hiring ballplayers to endorse cereal on live radio. According to *Broadcasting*:

Radio learned a lesson the other day about testimonial advertising. It grew out of the battle of breakfast foods and big-name athletes to endorse them. . . .

On the last Friday of last month, Lou Gehrig, stellar slugger of the New York Yankees, stepped before an NBC mike as the guest star on the Kellogg-sponsored *Believe It Or Not* program on behalf of Kellogg's *Huskies*. After a dramatic build-up of Gehrig's prowess as a home run hitter and the "iron-man of the diamond" who hadn't missed a game in years, his interviewer asked him about his favorite breakfast food.

And believe it or not, the Columbia University graduate replied: "*Wheaties*."

Silence shattered the ether. After an eternity, the interviewer finally collected his wits and inquired whether there wasn't some other breakfast food he liked. Gehrig then admitted a deep affection for *Huskies*.[55]

Given the circumstances, Gehrig, hardly a professional pitchman, could scarcely be blamed for his mistake—he also endorsed Wheaties. After all, *Broadcasting* got it wrong too. In the next issue, the radio trade magazine was forced to print a correction, noting, "GENERAL FOODS makes Huskies, General Mills makes Wheaties, Kellogg's makes Krispies, Krumbles, and other cereals. Lou Gehrig mixes them up for a reputed fee of $1,800 and *Broadcasting* erroneously blames Kellogg's for making General Foods' Huskies. They're all good and we're all wrong. Please pass the cream and sugar."[56]

Ultimately, General Foods used Gehrig's radio faux pas to its advantage. In the midst of the 1937 World Series, Gehrig once again appeared on *Believe It or Not*. This time, announcer Ford Bond made a joke of Gehrig's error, and the player played along. But Gehrig's slipup, as well as *Broadcasting*'s erratum, proved an important point. Other cereals may have entered the "battle of breakfast foods" and celebrity baseball-playing endorsers, but Wheaties was the clear winner. As Jim Fish, a former General Mills advertising executive, observes, "The product is no different from anybody else's. . . . It's just a product of unique and consistent advertising."[57]

6. A 1931 Lou Gehrig print endorsement ad for Post's entry into the flaked-wheat cereal sweepstakes. Gehrig also promoted Huskies on *Ripley's Believe It or Not* radio show, once misidentifying the sponsor as Wheaties. Courtesy of Post Consumer Brands, LLC.

Breakfast of Champions

A large part of Wheaties' unique and consistent advertising involved reaching a broad demographic with an inclusive campaign. Once General Mills had successfully marketed Wheaties to children and their adoring mothers, the company sought a means to attract grown men to the product. Gray explains, "There seemed to be no valid reason why men, too, should not be enrolled among lovers of a substantial breakfast. But if the traditional love of ham and eggs was to be challenged on the behalf of Wheaties, then a special appeal must be made to the masculine imagination." Following the strongly expressed opinion of its advertising chief, Samuel Chester Gale, General Mills began to sponsor local radio baseball broadcasts.[58]

This decision had wider implications. General Mills most certainly reached the desired male demographic on weekends, especially on Sundays during the 1930s, when doubleheaders were the norm. On weekdays, however, baseball was an afternoon affair. Night games, having been pioneered by both the Negro Leagues and Minor Leagues, came to the Major Leagues in 1935 as an attempt to boost the box office by making professional baseball available to the employed, the majority of whom were men. But night baseball remained a novelty until the end of the decade. Of course, with unemployment rates hovering between 15 and 25 percent during the midthirties, weekday afternoon baseball broadcasts also attracted a significant male audience.[59] But Depression-era advertising was not aimed at the unemployed. So by aggressively pursuing baseball sponsorship in its quest to make men into Wheaties eaters, General Mills also solidified its cereal's brand recognition with its key demographics, children and their purse-string-holding mothers.

General Mills was not the only company to sponsor local baseball broadcasts, nor was it the first. The John R. Thompson Company of Chicago, owner of a string of lunchrooms, began sponsoring games on its home city's WGN in 1929.[60] In 1933 WGN sold sponsorship of its White Sox and Cubs home game broadcasts to Walgreen Drugstores, while WBBM sold Cubs sponsorship to the Prima Brewing

Company, as did WJKS, the Gary, Indiana, station that carried the White Sox.[61] And there were others. For the most part, early commercial sponsors of baseball games were local businesses. Some national advertisers did sponsor broadcasts, Orange Crush, for example.[62] But none did so with the concentrated effort of General Mills. "As a national advertiser, General Mills needed to make the baseball connection beyond the eastern-midwestern range of Major League Baseball, and it found many ways to do so," notes Walker. "It sponsored Minor League Baseball as aggressively as big league ball. Just as the Minor Leagues exploited night baseball first, many of them also welcomed sponsored broadcasts of their games and a new revenue flow before the Major League superiors capitalized on the opportunity."[63]

An essential part of Wheaties' baseball-centric strategy was the development of its slogan, which, like its origin story, is part of company lore. Notes Gray, "A neat and unforgettable verbalization was needed to link the sport and Wheaties inseparably so that, in the minds of devotees, a home run should somehow be an eloquent endorsement of a General Mills product." Coming up with just such a "verbalization" was the job of Knox Reeves, the advertising executive who handled the Wheaties radio account. Reeves, according to Gray, "knew that an advertising slogan, though it unlocks no mystery as real poetry may be expected to do, still shares with the true art the attribute of epitomizing drama in a phrase resonant with meaning." Gray continues:

It came to him, according to legend, one day when a representative of the ballpark arrived at his office to say that as a sponsor of the broadcasts, General Mills was entitled to a sign in full view of the grandstand. What was to be painted on it? the ballpark manager wanted to know. Without a moment's thought, but apparently under the prompting of an unconscious mind that had been brooding for a long time about the problem, Reeves wrote out the evocative declaration. Boys by the millions were to repeat it with awe for the next few years. Indeed, testimony to its aptness had been gathered in abundance before General Mills officials left the ballpark on the first day when the sign went up. (General Mills' advertising chief) Gale heard many a man, as well as many a boy, saying "Breakfast of Champions" over and over again as though it were some kind of incantation to the goddess of health.[64]

And so, in the outfield of Nicollet Park, home of the Minneapolis Millers, was born the Breakfast of Champions. And it was no coincidence that Millers game broadcasts were sponsored by General Mills.

Emphasizing the slogan, General Mills also redesigned the Wheaties box in 1934. The orange and blue front remained the same, though the slogan, displayed in blue type on a white band that stretched diagonally upward from left to right across a large blue circle, would be added shortly thereafter. The new back design was where the most important alterations were made. Supplanting Jack Armstrong, Lou Gehrig became the first athlete to grace a Wheaties box, his image closely resembling one that might be depicted on a baseball trade card. By the 1930s, baseball cards were no longer packaged with cigarettes. Instead, they served as inducements to buy chewing gum. Like Wheaties, gum was marketed directly, rather than obliquely, to children. And young consumers seemed to have treated Gehrig's image and the others that followed as if they were baseball cards. A survey of card sites in 2015 suggests that Wheaties eaters often cut the pictures off the backs of boxes, collecting them.[65] This not only increased Wheaties' sales numbers, it served as a powerful brand recognition tool, further cementing the slogan in the memory channels of young fans and cereal eaters.

In addition to sponsoring home games from both Major and Minor League ballparks, General Mills contracted with WOC-WHO of Davenport and Des Moines, Iowa, to sponsor 150 "play-by-play reports," re-creations of Major League games, beginning in 1933 on a "test schedule," and in 1934, on a daily basis. At the microphone, according to an announcement in Broadcasting was "Dutch Reagan, popular young sports announcer." Listeners to the Wheaties-sponsored re-creations could not possibly have known that this particular popular young sportscaster would go into pictures, then politics, dropping the nickname Dutch for his real name, Ronald. Even without the availability of such foresight, a reported sixty-five thousand listeners were moved to write General Mills in support of Reagan's broadcasts.[66] Reagan's General Mills–sponsored re-creations would continue through the 1937 season, when he won the coveted title of "Wheaties Sportscaster of the Year." For his efforts, General Mills sent him on an all-expenses-paid trip to Los Angeles for Cubs spring training. He never returned to the radio.[67]

As the 1930s wore on and sales of Wheaties increased, General Mills continued to aggressively pursue radio sponsorship of Major League broadcasts. To battle the continuing perception that baseball on the radio would hurt attendance at Major League ballparks, the company held a competition among its radio outlets and announcers in 1935. A fifty-six-inch silver trophy was to be awarded to the radio station responsible for the greatest increase in paid admissions in its home city. The announcer, too, would receive a trophy, a fourteen-inch replica of the winning station's prize. What metric General Mills used to determine the winner is unclear, but according to the contest announcement in *Broadcasting*, the maker of Wheaties sought the suggestions of the teams as to the method for determining the gate.[68] To the apparent benefit of the Athletics and Phillies, Philadelphia's WCAU was the victor, and William Dyer, who called both local teams' games, was the winning announcer.[69]

Better Late than Never

Even in the face of evidence that sponsored radio did not hurt attendance, New York's three teams continued their ban on home game broadcasts. A letter to the editor of *Broadcasting* from William H. Rankin, president of his eponymous advertising agency, urged the teams to reconsider. Repeating his agency's plea to New York City station WMCA, he wrote, "Even [Yankees owner] Jacob Ruppert, and the Giants, too, will look with favor upon broadcasting if every day you have your announcer say 'go to the ball game twice a week'—just as Amos 'n' Andy say, 'See your dentist twice a year and brush your teeth twice a day.'"[70] WMCA was apparently not responsive to Rankin's entreaty. Still, there were signs that the end was near for the New York radio blackout. On January 12, 1938, Harold Parrott, a columnist in the *Brooklyn Daily Eagle* announced what seemed to be inevitable:

> Radio's super-salesmen are poised to make a new frontal attack on the last sanctuaries of peace and quiet in the major leagues if Larry the Red MacPhail is awarded the job as Head Keeper of the Dodgers, it was learned today.
>
> They want to broadcast Brooklyn's gyrations during home games at Ebbets Field for General Mills, Inc., who was not a Civil War officer, but should be shot, anyway, if he had anything to do with writing those infantile rhymes about Wheaties.
>
> Yes, Ebbets Field is the new spot they covet, and they know that MacPhail is a broadcast bug and was during his tenure in Cincinnati. They plan to flatter him by dubbing the Ebbets Field hookup the Red Network. If the Dodgers play to form, they might do better calling it the silly circuit.[71]

Just eight days later, Tommy Holmes, another *Eagle* sports columnist announced the hiring, commenting, "Possibly the most important angle is that the red-headed Mr. MacPhail seems destined to be the first real boss the Brooklyn ball club has had since that wet and chilly April Day in 1925 when Charles H. Ebbets was laid to rest in Greenwood Cemetery."[72]

Brooklyn, the *Eagle*'s columnists reported, was the first of the three New York City teams to relent, putting an end to the five-year regional ban the teams had put in place in 1934. Using considerably less colorful language to announce the end of New York's baseball broadcast blackout, the *New York Times* merely noted that "definite arrangements for the broadcasting of all Yankee and Giant home games this year, with the exception of Sunday contests, were completed last night at a conference of local baseball officials." The *Times* also included the language of the press release, which specifically noted the sponsors. Not surprisingly, radio's super-salesmen were at the head of the list. Joining General Mills in shared sponsorship of Dodgers, Yankees, and Giants broadcasts was Socony-Vacuum Oil, and, in Brooklyn, Procter & Gamble.[73]

At the start of the 1939 season, *Broadcasting* reported, "The three-way responsibility of the radio announcer in broadcasting a baseball game is to produce the best results for station, sponsor, and ball team, and the most efficient methods of producing those results were the subjects of the General Mills announcers conference held at the Hotel Commodore, New York, April 15–16." As the primary sponsor for the New York broadcasts, in addition to others, General Mills and Knox Reeves, now head of his own eponymous agency, hired and trained announcers. Notable among the play-by-play men new to New York was Walter Lanier "Red" Barber, who had previously called games for McPhail's former team, the Cincinnati Reds. Barber signed with General Mills and Knox Reeves for the hefty sum of $8,000 a year for his role as the voice of the Brooklyn Dodgers.[74]

At the training conference, agency and cereal company executives as well as Barber himself, instructed the new announcers on the art and business of the baseball broadcast. The most important lesson they learned was to "handle the play-by-play descriptions in a way that will build attendance at the ball parks, listeners for the stations, and sales for the sponsors." The new employees were also instructed on how to properly read commercials, making sure that "every announcer's watchword should be 'not how much, but how well.'" They were also schooled on the all-important craft of promoting commercial tie-ins with sponsors and retailers.[75] Judging by the conference description, it is clear that General Mills and Knox Reeves controlled the show. Baseball on the radio might very well have increased attendance in these markets, all the while providing entertainment to listeners at home, but its real purpose was to sell Wheaties, gasoline, and soap. By any measure, the company's marketing strategy was a success. General Mills' advertising campaign tying its breakfast cereal to baseball both directly and indirectly helped sell approximately 4,500,000 cases of Wheaties a year during the 1930s, about three times the volume the company initially projected.[76]

Wheaties Synergy

With the Yankees, Giants, and Dodgers in the baseball sponsorship fold, General Mills would seem to have had all its demographic bases covered. Comic-strip ads featuring appealing players captivated children and solved the breakfast problem for their mothers. *Jack Armstrong, the All-American Boy* extended the spell, reminding fans to eat their Wheaties and to collect box tops to exchange for premiums. The new box design gave children, and perhaps some adults, pictures of their "Champions" to admire and maybe even collect, and baseball on the radio brought the message home to the men, while reinforcing it among women and children. By 1939 General Mills was also placing ingenious print advertising in newspapers that combined all these elements.

One such ad ran on the funny pages nationally during baseball season. Titled "'Home Run' Hank Greenberg Reveals Batting Secrets—as Presented by Jack Armstrong, All-American Boy," it features the fictional adventurer-turned-radio-announcer learning, and thereby revealing to his "audience," the secret of Greenberg's swing. In the upper right-hand corner of the comic-strip ad, next to the title, the fictional Jack Armstrong sits in front of a microphone, his head encircled as if by a halo. So pure, so angelic, so white does he appear that he actually radiates light—or perhaps radio waves. The body of the strip depicts a postgame interview. Greenberg, having just hit a home run, demonstrates to the All-American announcer Armstrong and, by extension, newspaper readers, precisely how he chokes up on his bat. What follows is a series of panels made to look like newsreel footage, with sprocket holes lining the top and bottom of each drawing, in which Greenberg lets Armstrong in on the real secret, which, of course, he already knows. "And Jack," Greenberg reminds the All-American Boy, "another thing to remember is that you've got to *feel good* to play heads up ball! That's why I train and eat right . . . and I like my Wheaties *often!*" In the final panel, the woman of the house gets her due, as a generic mother figure says, "My whole family likes Wheaties flakes. They're nourishing whole wheat, you know, and they taste grand."[77] The primary message of this ad is fairly obvious. Skill is necessary—certainly some of Greenberg's power comes from his perfect swing—but of course, there would be no power without Wheaties.

The use of the sprocket holes as a visual trope in this ad is essential to its meaning. Newsreels, which were presented along with feature films, short subjects, and cartoons, were screened in as many as 90 percent of American movie theaters at the time and provided audiences with contemporary news. For the most part, the news was soft. Newsreels tended to be sensationalist, appealing to the "tabloid mind." They focused on human-interest stories, fashions, fads, celebrity news, and of course, sports highlights. By using newsreel iconography, the ad telegraphs to readers that it is more than a pitch on a funnies page. It is a truthful representation. This ad, however, does more than illustrate the mechanics of Greenberg's swing and remind consumers that he derives his power as much from eating Wheaties as from choking up on his bat. Closely associating Jack Armstrong, however fictional, with Greenberg, the ad transfers the meaning of "All-American Boy"—one so pure, he sports a light-radiating halo—to Greenberg via the comic strip.

Certainly, as the earlier funnies-page ad featuring Ruth and his Moviebook demonstrates, in the 1930s depicting baseball stars as wholesome was hardly unusual. In a sense, all those who labored in the fields of the national pastime were "All-American Boys" made flesh, living exemplars of the Jack Armstrong ideal. But Greenberg was different. The sporting press frequently referred to Greenberg, unlike Ruth, Gehrig, or the other big stars of his day, in terms of his religious affiliation. During the 1938 season, when Greenberg challenged Ruth's single-season home-run record, for example, the *Hartford Courant* described Greenberg as "the lanky Jewish player from the Bronx."[78] Suggesting that the Tigers play some West Coast exhibition games before the 1939 season, *Los Angeles Times* sports columnist Bob Ray noted, "Greenberg especially would attract many Jewish fans

from around the Beverly-Fairfax neighborhood."[79] And specu-
lating on a potential trade that would have landed Greenberg in
the Bronx, the *Christian Science Monitor* called him "the Jewish
slugger." In contrast, the church-owned independent newspaper made no mention of the religious connections of the other
players involved in trade rumors, Babe Herman, Birdie Teb-
betts, and Rudy York.[80]

Although it was used by the *Monitor* solely as an identifier, the
label singled Greenberg out among his fellow players, especially to
fans. The Wheaties ad, in contrast, makes no mention of Greenberg's religion. Nevertheless, it was common knowledge among
those who might respond to his Wheaties endorsement either positively or negatively that Greenberg was Jewish. His generic representation in the Wheaties ad came at a time when antisemitic
sentiment ran high, and not just in Europe. Coming out of Detroit,
home of Greenberg's Tigers, the rabidly antisemitic radio priest
Father Charles E. Coughlin broadcast a weekly program that was
carried by as many as sixty stations across the country in 1938.[81]
His program attracted up to thirty million listeners nationally.[82]
Coughlin's polarizing opinions received a great deal of coverage
in the print media, a surprising proportion of which was positive.
Coughlin's rants inspired their fair share of editorials and letters
to newspaper editors in small towns and cities, especially in the
Midwest, supportive of his indictment of Jews as fomenters of
international communism.[83]

Detroit's own Henry Ford, the same Ford whose company sponsored the World Series from 1934 to 1937, was also the publisher
of the *Dearborn Independent*, the anti-Jewish rag that blamed the
world's problems on the "International Jew." During the 1920s,
Ford was personally responsible for publishing an English edition of the inflammatory forgery *The Protocols of the Elders of
Zion*, written under the auspices of Czar Nicholas II, claiming
an international Jewish conspiracy controlled world events.[84] The
vast majority of Americans did not buy wholeheartedly into this
antisemitic rhetoric. Still, it certainly informed the zeitgeist. That
radio advertising icon Jack Armstrong, All-American Boy, though

fictional, would embrace Greenberg, even the cartoon Greenberg, in a Wheaties ad, sent a powerful message at a time when the definition of "All-American" did not always include people of Jewish descent. While the intentional goal of this ad was to induce consumers to eat Wheaties as part of a synergistic marketing strategy, it indirectly promoted inclusion at the same time it promoted cereal.

A Swell Ball Game and a Swell Shave

On August 17, 1939, just two short months before the scheduled start of the fall classic, the *Chicago Tribune* reported that World Series history "was made yesterday when the Mutual Broadcasting System and the Gillette Safety Razor company were awarded exclusive broadcasting rights for baseball's biggest show." So important was this news to both the Mutual System and Gillette, that it was announced via national broadcast from the network's Chicago station, WGN.[85] Granting exclusive broadcast rights to a single network was controversial; in past seasons multiple networks had carried the Series simultaneously. CBS and NBC were far from happy with the arrangement, refusing Mutual the right to broadcast the games over some of their local affiliates. In response, the respective executive vice presidents of NBC and CBS, Niles Trammell and Edward Klauber, wrote letters to Commissioner Landis protesting the decision, arguing that the Series was an "outstanding sporting event with a national following." Landis did not respond. But in an odd twist, *Broadcasting* reported, "From sources close to Judge Landis it was learned that he refused Mr. Trammell's suggestion because he felt the Series to be of no greater interest than the Kentucky Derby, Rose Bowl game, and numerous boxing events that have been carried exclusively on a single network."[86] Landis's assessment as to the World Series' comparative lack of importance as a national event was extremely ironic, given that until 1934, the commissioner held that broadcasting the Series was a public service, and that the championship games had to be broadcast with particular care.[87]

The Yankees swept the 1939 World Series, defeating the Reds in four games. But the real winner was Gillette. This was not Gillette's first foray into either sports or radio. Gillette was an early adopter in the sports endorsement game, hiring Honus Wagner, Hughie Jennings, Johnny Evers, Ed Walsh, and other star players to pitch its safety razors in a series of print ads as early as 1910. In 1929 the men's grooming company sponsored a Friday-night music program on NBC, featuring the Gillette Blades Orchestras and the Gay Young Blades, a vocal group. The broadcast also included a five-minute sports wrap-up announced by longtime World Series announcer Graham McNamee.

After a few short years, Depression-era economics, accompanied by a minor scandal involving poor quality control, forced the company to pull out of radio sponsorship in the early 1930s.[88] Following years of moribund sales, during which the company's market share dropped to 18 percent, Gillette changed leadership, naming Joseph P. Sprang Jr. president in 1938. Sprang invested heavily in advertising, raising the budget by 50 percent to $1.5 million. Of the new advertising dollars, Sprang devoted almost 20 percent to secure exclusive radio rights to the 1939 Series. In addition to paying the requisite $100,000 to the commissioner's office, Gillette devoted an even larger sum to advertise its sponsorship prior to the games. Gillette retailers also ran a "World Series Special" promotion to induce consumers to buy their product during the Series.[89] Announcer Red Barber pushed the promotion to his listeners, promising "a swell ball game, and if you pick up a Tech razor tonight with a Gillette Blue Blade, it will bring you a swell shave tomorrow and every morning."[90] Newspaper ads also promoted the special, reminding baseball fans that just forty-nine cents would bring them the same new razor and five blades, "featured on the World Series broadcast."[91]

Although the Series lasted but four games, effectively cutting the airtime, and thus the advertising time, nearly in half, Gillette's gamble was fantastically successful. According to Gordon McKibben's corporate history, "Retailers couldn't keep up with demand. When the final count was in, about 2.5 million World Series Specials had been sold—more than double the company's expectations. Sprang's faith in sports radio as a means of persuading American males to buy Gillette products had been vindicated."[92] So successful was the marriage of Gillette and the World Series that the manufacturer retained the radio rights until 1964 as well as picking up the television rights in 1945.[93] The company also added other premiere sporting events to its advertising portfolio.

The World of Tomorrow

On August 26, 1939, those interested enough to see one of the many promised wonders of the World of Tomorrow ventured to the RCA pavilion at the future-themed New York World's Fair. There they, along with a handful of others in various venues, were treated to the first Major League game to be broadcast on television. Although this event is widely viewed as having changed the baseball world as we know it, it had few short-term implications. Following a promising beginning, sidelined by world events, television as a commercial broadcast medium would not begin in earnest until after the conclusion of World War II. Moreover, commercial television did not burst forth fully formed like Athena out of the head of Zeus in 1946. It took some time to develop. For more than a decade after the 1939 experimental program, radio would remain the way in which most fans consumed their baseball, Major and Minor League alike, and with it their baseball-related advertising.

But not all high-level professional baseball found its way onto the airwaves. In a country in which General Mills might be considered bold for asserting that Hank Greenberg was, like the fictional Jack Armstrong, "All-American," players of color received no play. Missing from baseball's commercial narrative were Josh Gibson, Satchel Paige, and Oscar Charleston, among a host of others. In fact, African American and Afro-Latino players, long barred from competing in the mainstream, heavily advertised game would continue to be conspicuously absent from baseball on the radio and endorsement advertising in print until 1947, when the Brooklyn Dodgers desegregated, and commercial baseball television broadcasts actually made the World of Tomorrow a reality. Until their ultimate demise in the 1960s, Negro League and barnstorming black baseball, two mainstays of an industry that developed in response to the privations of Jim Crow, had their own relationship to advertising, the vast majority of it limited to print and outdoor signage. In fact, the story of advertising and black baseball primarily, but not exclusively, in the black press provided a counternarrative to the tale of the long-term marriage of the two mainstream, intimately related industries.

CHAPTER FOUR

Pitching in Black and White

Baseball, Advertising, and the Color Line

O n May 13, 1947, an editorial by "America's ace sports writer," Jimmy Cannon, appeared in the *New York Times*. With the bold, startling headline, "Lynch Mobs Don't Always Wear Hoods," it begins:

> You don't always lynch a man by hanging from a tree. There is a great lynch mob among us and they go unhooded and work without the rope. They have no leader but their own hatred of humanity. They are quietly degraded, who plot against the helpless with skill and a coward's stealth and without fear of reprisal. Their weapon is as painful as the lash, the hot tar, the noose or the shot gun. They string up a man with the whisper of a lie and they persecute him with ridicule. They require no burning cross as a signal of assembly and need no sheet to identify themselves to each other. They are the night riders who operate 24 hours a day.[1]

Cannon's lynch mob, the quietly degraded whispering persecutors, was, in fact, a group of ballplayers. Prior to facing the Brooklyn Dodgers in early May that season, several members of the St. Louis Cardinals ballclub proposed a strike. Their reason was the breach of Major League Baseball's sixty-year-old color line by Jackie Robinson, whom Cannon famously referred to as "the loneliest man I have ever seen in sports," in this very editorial.

That a sportswriter for a New York newspaper should take such a firm stand in support of Robinson, reviling what he called "the venomous conspiracy" against the player, seems only right. After all, Robinson played for a New York team, and Cannon wrote for an editorially liberal newspaper. But Cannon did not write for the *New York Times*. Nor was Cannon's work syndicated in the *Washington Post*, the *Chicago Tribune*, the *Tucson Daily Citizen*, or a host of smaller papers in which this piece appeared. Nor was this an op-ed, an opinion piece written for the *Times* by someone other than a member of the editorial staff. In fact, Cannon was an immensely popular sports writer for the *New York Post*, where this column had appeared three days earlier.

So how did a column composed for a rival newspaper end up in the *New York Times* and the other papers that did not generally carry Cannon's work? The answer lies in a few small lines of type at the bottom of the column, reading, "Presented as a public service by International Latex Corporation, Playtex Park, Dover, Maryland. Paid Advertisement. . . . Buy U.S. Savings Bonds." It is an ad—one of a long series of opinion pieces paid for by the makers of Playtex Living Bras and Girdles. In acquiring Cannon's column and purchasing the advertising space in which to reprint it, International Latex engaged in a form of promotion pioneered by its founder, A. N. Spanel. The company, founded in 1932, was profitable throughout the Great Depression. But once resources like rubber were diverted to the war effort, the business of manufacturing latex garments became complicated. To keep International Latex in the public eye, Spanel purchased ad space in as many as four hundred newspapers at a time, using it as a platform to disseminate either his own original political and social commentaries or to reprint like-minded pieces such as Cannon's. He continued to do so after the war.

According to his *New York Times* obituary, "Mr. Spanel's expression of his opinions won him both devoted friends and fierce foes. A $6 million libel suit against Westbrook Pegler, the syndicated columnist who attacked Mr. Spanel for what he called 'pro-Red,' New Dealish views, ended with Mr. Pegler's retracting in 1949 his charges that Mr. Spanel's editorial advertisements were 'Communist inspired.'"[2] Given the divisive racial politics of the late 1940s, International Latex's vocal support of Robinson was a bold move. While Playtex certainly could not credit all its success as the preeminent producer of girdles after World War II to its paid advertising in support of baseball's desegregation, its progressive politics did not hurt the company's bottom line, and may even have helped in some markets.

As is well documented, the St. Louis Cardinals did not strike. The desegregated Dodgers went on to win the National League pennant. Robinson was crowned Rookie of the Year—the first in Major League history—inspiring volumes of coverage in the mainstream press and traditional black newspapers alike. His ascent to the Major Leagues also led to his ascent in advertising. Robinson was paid to endorse cigarettes, haberdasheries, and without a hint of irony, white bread. Scores of businesses lined up to connect their names to Robinson's in congratulatory advertising and by invoking his name in ads. And not a few companies promoted their products with Robinson-licensed premiums. But just as the full desegregation of Major League Baseball took more than a decade, so, too, did the desegregation of mainstream American advertising.

Advertising and Black Baseball before the Negro Leagues

By the time Jackie Robinson took the field in a Brooklyn Dodgers uniform, New York City was home to a sizable, economically and socially diverse African American community. So, too, were Kansas City, Chicago, Detroit, Pittsburgh, Philadelphia, Baltimore, Washington DC, and a number of other large American cities. But even before the preeminent black newspaper of its day, Robert Abbott's *Chicago Defender*, urged African Americans laboring on the Mississippi Delta and other parts of the rural South to come North to work and live, spurring the first wave of the Great Migration in the early twentieth century, black baseball was played in the Northeast, and games were advertised in the mainstream press.[3]

As early as 1888, ads for games by "colored" nines appeared in the *New York Times* and other dailies. "Baseball. Polo Grounds To-Day. Colored Championship match. Cuban Giants Vs. Gorhams. Game 4 p.m. Admission, 25 cents," reads one such example.[4] At face value, there is nothing remarkable about this advertisement. It appears to be a straightforward game announcement. In this particular case, however, placement is everything. Printed nearly at the bottom of a column bearing the header "Amusements," this ad is sandwiched between an advertisement for Koster & Bial's Concert Hall, featuring "La Cuenca, Lady Bull Fighter," and another for the "Eden Musee Art Gallery, The Coolest place in New York," where the curious might see "The Whole World in Wax." Even without the column's more prominent ads—announcing "Imre Kiralfy's Latest, greatest, and supreme triumph, Nero; or, the fall of Rome," on display in Staten Island, or the "Biggest Show on Earth! America's Most Mighty Exhibition, Buffalo Bill's Wild West," as well as "an accurate account" of the battle of Gettysburg, including the "Death Scene of Lieut. Cushing"—it's easy to see that the ad for the "Colored championship match," the only game announcement in the column, might serve as an attempt to pitch a carnivalesque attraction rather than a conventional game.

Taken in the context of the other entertainments in this Amusements column, especially Buffalo Bill's Wild West Show, the advertised ball game appears to have been promoted as a curiosity rather than as an actual sporting event. Certainly, much nineteenth-century baseball, and even more nineteenth-century advertising, was carnivalesque, or at least had carnivalesque inflections. But the way in which the "Colored championship match" is advertised, combined with its placement in this column, seems to indicate that this particular event was more than just a ball game, it was a spectacle. Just as the ad for Buffalo Bill's Wild West Show, "America's Most Mighty Exhibition," offered those willing to part with the ticket price of twenty-five cents a peek into an exotic world, complete with a "night ablaze with splendid effect by electric light," so, too, might spectators who traveled to the Polo Grounds, prepared to spend their quarters, catch a glimpse of the exotic world of actual players of color, playing a real "championship" game.

Of course, the two amusements were fundamentally different from one another. While Buffalo Bill's Wild West Show was a carefully constructed version of the American frontier that never really existed, the game at the Polo Grounds was just that, a baseball game, and the contestants were baseball players. "The 'Cuban Giants,'" wrote black baseball's first chronicler, Sol White, "were heralded everywhere as marvels of the base ball [*sic*] world. They were not looked upon by the public as freaks, but they were classed as men of talent."[5] That White would find it necessary clarify that the Cuban Giants were not natural anomalies, coupled with the placement of this ad, seems to suggest that the amusement-seeking public might have thought otherwise, or at least that is what *New York Times* readers might have assumed. As if to counter this assumption, the *New York Sun* called attention to a piece in the *Sporting Life*, describing the Cuban Giants as "neither Giants nor Cubans, but thick-set and brawny colored men."[6]

In all probability, true baseball enthusiasts would have at the very least been aware of the Cuban Giants. But this ad is not aimed at true fans. It did not appear on the same page with the *Times'* baseball coverage, of which there was a significant amount.[7] Placed as it was in the Amusements column in close proximity to announcements for the Wild West Show and a re-creation of Nero exhibiting his questionable musical talents, featuring one thousand "Grand Terpsichorean Corps," as well as "Scenes of Splendor Exceeding Actual Belief"—a full fifty cents' worth—seems to suggest that at least for a portion of the *Times'* readership, the Cuban Giants were at best exotic curiosities, and at worst, freaks.

At a time when baseball trade cards had emerged as a major form of advertising, there was a dearth of representation when it came to the professional African American game. Although trade cards featuring black athletes were not unheard of, they were certainly extremely few and far between. But one, issued to advertise an appearance by the team, featured the 1897 Page Fence Giants, a black team organized by Bud Fowler and Grant "Home Run" Johnson—both of whom had played in organized baseball prior to the color line's establishment—and their partners, two white businessmen, to promote the Page Wire Fence Company of Adrian, Michigan, and Monarch Bicycles. According to Jerry Malloy, creative promotion was the name of the game for the Page Fence Company. He writes, "As a permanent demonstration of the capacity of its product to contain livestock, the company maintained a park in town stocked with various animals corralled by its woven wire fencing. This menagerie was transported by rail to nearby country and state fairs with Page Fence cages, thus displaying the strength and versatility of the company's line of goods."[8]

On the front of the Page Fence baseball card, a photograph depicts the team wearing their black uniforms with white letters. Also included in the group shot is the team's white manager, identified as A. S. Parsons. On the reverse side, an ad for Page Fences announces, "Play Ball! Play Ball! Whatever your hands find to do, do it with all your might." The card, in all likelihood, would have been distributed to curious spectators attracted by the sight of a luxurious private Pullman car disgorging the Page Fence Giants in full uniform to parade through town on their Monarch Bicycles. The language of the card, however, does not equate the ballplayers with parades or other forms of public merriment. Rather, it connects the team to the act of building fences.

As Sol White explains, the team's private railway carriage was the brainchild of Johnson and Fowler. It afforded the players the certainty of comfortable accommodations in Jim Crow America.[9] It also served to separate the team from the predominantly white spectators for whom they performed. In this sense, the private carriage marked "Page Fence" bore perhaps too close a resemblance to the Page Company's wire fencing that separated the company's traveling menagerie from their audience. Taken together, the trade card and the promotional nature of the team appear to suggest that colored ballplayers might best be kept at a safe distance from their white fans, preferably corralled in with a sturdy Page Fence, be it real or implied.

Sol White's *Official Guide*

With its slightly misleading title, Sol White's 1907 *Official Guide: The History of Colored Baseball* did more than tell the story of the Cuban Giants, the Gorhams, and the Page Fence Giants; it also served as a medium for advertisers wishing to reach baseball lovers of color, appealing to readers with a serving of race pride. In its ad, John W. Connor's Royal Café and Palm Gardens in Brooklyn, New York, headquarters for the Royal Giants ball club, owned

7. An 1897 Page Fence Giants trade card. Arriving in their private Pullman car in towns across the Midwest, team members would distribute their advertising cards to potential spectators. An ad for the team's sponsor, the Page Wire Fence Company of Adrian, Michigan, adorned the card's back.

and managed by John W. Connor, lets readers know that it is a black-owned establishment. Not so coincidentally, the smiling Mr. Connor is pictured on the facing page.[10] The message of black ownership is made even more explicit in an ad for "The Roadside" in Philadelphia. Occupying a full page, it consists of nothing more than a photograph of a man who is presumably the establishment's proprietor, a serious, bewhiskered gentleman of color. The adverting copy is similarly sparse, indicating only the establishment's address, 514 South 15th Street. There is no suggestion in the ad as to what type of business the Roadside might be. According to a listing in the 1938 *Negro Motorist Green Book*, the annual guide to accommodations, restaurants, gas stations, and other travel-related businesses that welcomed black consumers, a hotel called the New Roadside was located at the same address.[11] But there was no *Green Book* in 1907. Travelers were on their own. As such, baseball aficionados visiting Philadelphia must have been familiar with the business. The ad seems to suggest that the Roadside's reputation was strong enough to negate any need for description, essentially claiming, "All you need to know about the Roadside is that it is black owned."

At the same time these and other ads in White's *Guide* used race pride as a selling point, some reminded the pamphlet's target consumers that as members of "the race," they were relegated to the status of second-class citizens with limited economic possibilities, however inadvertently. An ad for the Chauffeur's Rest, a "first class" pool parlor and "Headquarters for North Philadelphia Sports," suggests that its patrons represent the upper crust of its city's sporting life.[12] The name says something else. It makes it clear that the establishment's high-class clientele were, in fact, tired chauffeurs. In the same regard, another ad for a race business—an African American–owned establishment that emphasized its race pride and contributions to the betterment of the community—which like the others uses a photograph of a dignified African American gentleman as shorthand for black ownership, promotes Washington's Manufactory, a dry goods emporium. Right underneath Washington's North Philadelphia address, the ad touts "Washington's Custom Made Shirts and Waiters' Supplies."[13] That Washington's emphasized its fine tailoring suggests that the retailer aimed to attract a prosperous clientele. But by promoting Waiters' Supplies in the same phrase, the retailer also proclaimed that its target market was made up of consumers laboring in the service industries. In fact, those custom-tailored white shirts were not positioned for purchase by "white-collar" workers in a white world, but, rather, for those who waited on them. In this way, the ad, very much like the spot for the Chauffeur's Rest, reflects the reality of life for readers of White's *Guide*.

Although many of the businesses advertising in White's *Guide* used black proprietorship as a selling point and targeted African American consumers, not all the advertised establishments were black owned. Among the purchasers of ad space were Schlichter and Strong, booking agents for the Philadelphia Giants, "the premier attraction among colored teams," whose "presence is eagerly looked for in all sections of the country."[14] Given that H. Walter Schlichter actually published White's *Guide*, it stands to reason that he would also advertise in the pamphlet. Schlichter's partner in his booking and promotion enterprise was Nat Strong, a New York–based promoter who would come to control bookings in the majority of the region's semiprofessional ballparks where black nines often played. In order to play in New York, Philadelphia, and pretty much everywhere in between, teams had to go through Strong, Schlichter, and other white booking agents who took a percentage of the gate for their services. Though African American baseball positioned itself as a "race business," White's *Guide* unintentionally reminded readers that the professional game was still subject to white control on certain levels. This was underscored by the fact that Strong was part owner of Connor's own Royal Giants.[15]

The Black Press

Among the others featured in White's *Guide*, a full-page advertisement for the *Philadelphia Tribune* stands out. Billed as "Our Only Daily Colored Paper," the *Philadelphia Tribune* was, and continues to be, the oldest black daily newspaper in the United States. In his landmark 1899 publication *The Philadelphia Negro*, W.E.B. Du Bois observed, "The *Tribune* is the chief news sheet and is filled generally with social notes of all kinds, and news of movements among Negroes over the country. Its editorials are usually of little value, chiefly because it does not employ a responsible editor."[16] This is certainly not the message communicated by the ad, depicting G. Grant Williams, city editor, with an extremely serious expression on his face. Whether or not Williams—who joined the *Tribune* in 1903, later becoming the paper's managing editor—fit Du Bois's description of "responsible" is unclear. What is clear is that Williams understood advertising. A man of many hats, he was also proprietor of the G. Grant Williams Advertising Agency.[17] Perhaps this is why the *Tribune* staked its claim as "the best Medium [*sic*] for advertising when you want to reach the people," in small print at the bottom of the ad.[18] Who are the people it sought to reach? They were, no doubt, the very readers of White's work—knowledgeable, serious baseball fans of color.

The *Philadelphia Tribune* did, in fact, offer its advertisers excellent access to "the people." Between 1901 and 1916 the *Tribune's* circulation increased from 700 to 20,000.[19] But the *Tribune's* reach paled in comparison to the influence of Robert Abbott's weekly *Chicago Defender*. Founded in 1905, the *Defender's* readership grew exponentially—from just 300 at the outset to approximately 90,000 in 1917 and 270,000 in 1920—and these statistics included only copies purchased, not the actual circulation, which was impossible to quantify. The *Defender* was, in effect, a national newspaper. More than 60 percent of its readers lived outside Chicago, many of them in the South, where they depended upon Pullman porters coming down from the city for their copies, which they passed from hand to hand.[20]

Certainly, a number of factors were behind the Great Migration of African Americans from the rural South to cities in the Midwest, Mid-Atlantic, and Northeast that began in earnest in 1914—unskilled labor shortages resulting from international immigration quotas, coupled with new employment opportunities in the rapidly expanding war industries supplying the growing conflict in Europe, a massive failure of the cotton crop destroyed by an infestation of boll weevils, and, of course, devastating Jim Crow policies, among them.[21] Of the mass migration, Isabel Wilkerson writes, "Over the course of six decades, some six million black southerners left the land of their forefathers and fanned out across the country for an uncertain existence in nearly every other corner of America. The Great Migration would become a turning point in history. It would transform urban America and recast the social and political order of every city it touched. It was the first big step the nation's servant class ever took without asking."[22]

This mass movement, one of the largest, if not the largest, demographic relocations in the history of the United States, was encouraged by Abbot in the pages of the *Defender*. The paper regularly included articles, poems, cartoons, and editorials urging readers to leave the privations of the delta, giving them advice both on how to do so and on how to behave in their new urban homes.[23] Inevitably, the *Defender*'s readers were also exposed to the advertising that kept the newspaper afloat financially, appealing directly to the needs of the new city dwellers. So, too, did other weekly and biweekly newspapers owned and operated by African Americans, such as the *Broad Ax* and *Bee* also in Chicago, New York's *Amsterdam News* and *Age*, the *Pittsburgh Courier*, the *Indianapolis Freeman*, the Kansas City *Call*, and Baltimore's *Afro-American*. Their rapidly expanding readership was also involved in the development of businesses and social institutions that advertised in the pages of the papers, black baseball among them. So in a sense, organized black baseball, collectively though not entirely accurately known as Negro Leagues baseball, owed its existence to the black press, in no small part.

The Negro National League (NNL), born in 1920 at the Paseo YMCA in Kansas City, Missouri, as well as the other leagues that would follow, depended upon the black press for publicity. The most consistent, cost-effective, and reliable means of marketing black baseball, or anything else for that matter, may have been by word of mouth, disseminating information about games through informal network of neighborhood institutions like barber shops, beauty parlors, and social clubs, as well as by formally spreading the word on window placards and by sound trucks. But since black ball clubs depended upon gate receipts for revenue, this was not enough. Advertising in the black press was an absolute necessity.

Entrepreneur Ed Bolden's Hilldale Club, one of the charter members of the Eastern Colored League (ECL), organized three years after the original NNL, was one of the very few African American teams to control its own venue, Hilldale Park in Darby, Pennsylvania, a "satellite community" or suburb of Philadelphia that was home to a significant African American enclave. As much as a decade prior to establishment of the ECL, Bolden began to rely heavily upon the *Philadelphia Tribune* to publicize his then-independent team and its ballpark. Hilldale Park opened in 1914, drawing as many as three thousand spectators to its first game.[24] According to team ledgers, in 1921 and '22, just before the formal league was founded, the Hilldales routinely budgeted between six and nine dollars monthly during baseball season to promote games in the *Tribune*. Although this seems like a paltry sum to dedicate to newspaper advertising, it represented a significant investment for a team that consistently operated in the red during this period.[25] In order to ensure that Philadelphia residents would be able to attend games in the nearby mill town, many of the team's ads included specific directions to the park, which could be reached by trolley, the "No. 13 Car on Walnut Street."[26]

The relationship between the black press and the teams was reciprocal. Ball clubs depended upon advertising on the sports pages and promotion by the editorial staff to insure that there would be spectators in the seats, and the newspapers depended upon the teams to provide content. For the most part, the papers could not afford dedicated beat writers to cover games, even official league games, and so they relied upon the teams for game accounts. A sampling from the *Philadelphia Tribune* of May 16, 1925, bears this out. Directly below several Hilldale Club game ads, an announcement reads, "Feature your Own Ball Game—Send Snappy accounts to the *Tribune* as soon as the game is over.—We boost clean sports."[27] No matter how snappy, team-provided accounts were likely to be unreliable, at best. But the *Tribune*'s ad copy makes one thing clear, the games it promoted had to be "clean," free of the taint of gambling. By virtue of its proximity to the Hilldale ads, this notice serves a purpose beyond soliciting copy. Though indirectly, it implies that Hilldale's games were on the up-and-up. This connection was further reinforced by the advertising message on Hilldale Park's scoreboard—the only ad on the scoreboard—that urged fans in attendance to "Read the *Philadelphia Tribune*."[28]

Playing by the Numbers

The implication that the Hilldales and the other clubs represented in the *Tribune* were "clean" or gambling-free does not necessarily imply that team owners or the ECL, NNL, or other leagues had no connection whatsoever with games of chance. The reality of black baseball is that it was often, though not always, financed with proceeds from numbers and policy rackets. At first glance, the *Tribune's* insistence on cleanliness appears to be out of line with the gambling-related capitalization of the game, but the fact of the matter is that without financing from numbers and policy kings who often owned teams in whole or in part, black baseball would not have emerged as a going concern across urban African America. According to historian Juliet E. K. Walker, "What is especially significant in black business history is the extent to which the informal, often illegal business activities, including policy, provided venture capital for the establishment of many legitimate black enterprises. Some notable black entrepreneurs built legitimate businesses on profits made from enterprises considered less than reputable."[29]

Numbers and policy were different iterations of illegal lotteries introduced to the United States, most likely from the West Indies, in the late nineteenth century. In policy, the dominant game in Pittsburgh, players selected three-number sequences or "gigs." The winning numbers were drawn from a drum or "policy wheel." Drawings were public, so there was little or no opportunity for game fixing. Winning gigs in the numbers game, dominant in New York, were derived from various public sources such as the NYSE totals and the Federal Reserve Clearing House Report, published daily in newspapers. As with policy, the public nature of the results meant that the games were theoretically fair. Although these lotteries were technically illegal, in many communities, though certainly not all, they were "protected." Greasing the right political palms was, after all, part of the price of doing business not just for African American city dwellers at the time, but for all city dwellers. From the 1890s through the 1940s, numbers and policy games played an important financial and social role in most urban African American communities as well as in other ethnic, working-class enclaves, providing capital where traditional financial institutions would not.[30] Indeed, policy and numbers continued to be important economically through the 1960s and into the '70s, long after the demise of the Negro Leagues.[31]

With payoffs as high as six hundred to one, and bets as low as a penny, numbers and policy games, like the cereal and radio industries, bucked the trend during the Great Depression. Even before the 1929 crash that marked the beginning of the Depression in the popular imagination, economic conditions were steadily worsening in certain industries and in certain communities. Black-owned businesses, professional baseball teams and leagues among them, failed at an unusually high rate.[32] By the mid-1930s, approximately one-third of urban, African American household heads, male and female, were unemployed, in comparison with roughly 15 percent of Caucasian household heads.[33] Given the economic situation, the appeal of such a large payoff on such a small investment was as substantial as were potential winnings. Numbers and policy bankers were also major employers in their own communities. Among the entrepreneurs with hands in both industries was Pittsburgh Crawfords owner Gus Greenlee, who founded the second Negro National League at the Depression's height in 1933. New Yorkers Alex Pompez, owner of the Cuban Stars, and James Semler, owner of the Black Yankees, and Newark Eagles owner Abe Manley, also made their initial fortunes in the rackets, though not all of them remained in the gambling business. And there were more.

The industry also fed a number of constituent businesses that advertised alongside baseball coverage in the black press. Much as the patent-medicine industry targeted readers of baseball news in the nineteenth century, so, too, did publishers of dream books and lucky talismans aim their pitches at fans of black baseball. Publications like *Aunt Sally's Policy Player's Dream Book*, *Stella's Lucky Dream Book*, and *Number Hit Forecast and Guide* routinely asked black baseball fans, "Want to change your luck? Release your Lucky Number at a glance."[34] Not surprisingly, baseball and baseball images were often attached to potentially winning numbers in some of the advertised dream books.

The Second Wave

As the Depression lifted, in no small part due to an explosion in the war industries in the late 1930s, more and more African Americans were attracted to urban areas by the prospect of good job opportunities. The new migrants represented the first of what would become the Great Migration's second wave, extending from 1940 to 1970. Increased employment for the new migrants also meant increased disposable income, which also meant increased attendance at ball games and increased purchasing power. Organized black baseball, never that stable to begin with, faltered during the 1930s, though some resourceful owners, Greenlee among them, kept their enterprises afloat. In 1937 his new Negro National League was joined by a second league, the Negro American League. Relatively speaking, both leagues prospered during the war years, though individual teams and smaller leagues continued to start up and fail at a pretty regular rate. This new prosperity contributed to a rise in the number of game ads and other baseball-related advertising in the black press.

As would be expected, most baseball-related advertising pitched games or consumer goods. But some spoke to a higher purpose. Addressing defense workers in the "Afro Sports" section of the *Baltimore Afro-American* in advance of the local labor board election of September 25, 1941, an ad placed by the Steel Workers Organizing Committee asked baseball fans, "What is SWOC's Batting Average?" As if to emphasize its point, the large advertisement, nearly a full page, includes an illustration of a beefy ballplayer, clearly a slugger, of indeterminate race, swinging his powerful bat. It reads, "This is baseball season and everybody thinks in terms of batting averages. If you know a man's batting average you can tell he's a big-leaguer. If you know a team's batting average, you can tell whether that team is going places. So it's a fair question to ask the SWOC: What is your batting average?"[35] It continues by giving a series of reasons to vote for the union, each ending with the tag line, "Not a bad batting average is it?" in bold print.

Although it would take several decades for the Major League Baseball Players Association to sign its first collective bargaining agreement with the league (a full thirty-one years after the color line was finally breached in 1947), organized labor seems to have understood the centrality and universality of baseball language to promote its cause.[36] At the time, Bethlehem Steel was the largest single employer of African American labor. Specifically, the swoc used the game to promote its push to unionize Bethlehem Steel's Sparrow's Point plant, where as many as one-third of the workers were African American. As early as 1936, when the union initiated its efforts in Baltimore, the swoc focused on ground-level community organizing. Not only did it look toward both black and white ethnic neighborhoods where steel workers lived, it also built a strong relationship with the ethnic press and the *Afro-American*. According to social historian Andor Skotnes, "In segregated Baltimore, the Black steelworkers could be won to the union only if opposition to racism were a first principle of the organizing drive."[37] After an extremely contentious battle to organize Sparrow's Point, where conditions were particularly bad, swoc forced an election. Perhaps in order to fight charges that unionization was anti-American, the swoc chose that most American of images, the ballplayer in midstride. The fact that the illustrated player bears a strong resemblance to Lou Gehrig, no longer the Iron Horse, but nevertheless an icon of American resilience and grace under pressure, is likely no coincidence.

For this reason alone, this ad differs substantially from the majority of baseball-related advertising in the *Afro-American* and the other black newspapers in a very pointed way. Similar to the image of the ballplayer, whose roughly drawn features may indicate that he is Caucasian, the language of the ad is also not targeted at a specifically African American demographic. The swoc ad claims that if you know a player's batting average, you can tell if he's a big leaguer. Quite apart from the spotty statistical reporting for which the black press was known, thereby complicating the ability of readers to actually know the batting averages of their favorite players, there is one thing that readers of the *Afro-American* knew for sure in 1941; star players for the Baltimore Elite Giants of the Negro National League were not big leaguers, nor could they be, no matter how talented they were.

Rare for an ad in the black press in 1941, the swoc advertisement eschewed the rhetoric of race to reach readers of color with the same ad used to appeal to white steel workers. At first glance, the language of the ad seems insensitive at best. Given MLB's long-term segregation, attempting to appeal to black union members with standardized language appears to be a misstep. But in its own way, it is quite the opposite. By refusing to pander to racial divisiveness to speak specifically to one segment of its demographic, it indirectly points toward an emerging sense of equality in the union, one that the union actively promoted by supporting civil rights groups. Indeed, the SWOC was more invested in visibly fighting Jim Crow than any other Baltimore-area CIO union during this period, sending white organizers into the African American community and African American organizers into white, ethnic enclaves as a strong, though ultimately purely symbolic, gesture.[38] That Sparrow's Point steelworkers, black and white alike, voted for the union overwhelmingly, to the tune of 68 percent of the vote, shows that the SWOC's cross-racial, baseball-themed promotional efforts were not wasted.[39]

It Pays to Be Personal?

Beginning in the early 1920s, celebrity product endorsement and testimonial advertising became a mainstay of mainstream advertising. Baseball players, representing strength, vitality, fortitude, American spirit, and eventually, wealth, were in high demand to pitch products ranging from patent medicines to cigarettes, breakfast cereals to insurance annuities, and everything in between. Black baseball certainly had its share of star power. The exploits of Cool Papa Bell, Oscar Charleston, and Josh Gibson were well chronicled in the sports pages of the black press. But for all its shining stars, product endorsements by Negro Leaguers were rare to virtually nonexistent. Only Satchel Paige was a master of promotion. Not only was he an ace on the mound, but he was a pitchman extraordinaire, especially when it came to his own image. Paige understood the power of his name to sell tickets, so he commodified it, sometimes appearing for several teams in a day, pitching one or two innings in return for a considerable fee, given the times and the circumstances. Baseball historian Donald Spivey observes, "Paige sold his baseball skills to the highest bidder. He understood that baseball was a business and that his growing superstar status had cash value."[40] But prior to desegregation, the only product Paige pitched was himself. While he might guarantee a good gate, he was not considered a good bet to sell cigarettes, razor blades, or breakfast cereal, not even to African American consumers.

As popular as the exceptionally talented ballplayers of the Negro Leagues were among their fans, they could not hold a candle to the iconic black athlete of the late 1930s and 1940s, boxer Joe Louis, in attracting both attention and advertising dollars. Louis endorsed everything from hair pomade to local haberdasheries across America. In that regard, he stands out as one of the only African American athletes to successfully double as a product endorser of note during this period. Even before his knockout of Max Schmeling at Yankee Stadium on June 22, 1938, during their second fight made him a champion to Americans regardless of race, Louis was featured prominently in advertising in the black press. So popular was he that he inspired the naming of Brown Bomber Baking Company of New York City, by their own account, "The World's Largest Negro Baking Company." A characteristic Brown Bomber ad features an illustration of a strong black pugilist—ostensibly Louis—pummeling a white boxer. Brown Bomber Bakery pitched its product with the slogan "11 cents spent for Brown Bomber gives you a double value . . . a loaf of tempting delicious bread plus part payment of some Negro's salary."[41]

This approach capitalized on the currency of the Double-Duty Dollar campaign that promoted buying from black-owned businesses in order to advance the race while shopping.[42] But Brown Bomber did have baseball connections. Another of the bakery's promotional tools was its sponsorship of a semiprofessional baseball team, the eponymous Brown Bombers. Taking a page from the Page Fence Company, the bakery used the ball club as a living marketing initiative, but to a different end. While the Page Fence Giants sold wire enclosures, the Brown Bombers sold race pride—and bread. But even Joe Louis the endorser was hampered by Jim Crow. His image seemed to be everywhere in the black press, pushing a vast variety of products, but his presence in mainstream newspapers and magazines was restricted to actual news and sports coverage. Louis's voice was also absent from product endorsements on the radio, though his fights attracted large listening audiences.

If Louis had no advertising presence in the mainstream media, it is hardly surprising that the rare Negro Leaguer did not breach the advertising color line, especially given the dearth of endorsement advertising. Therefore, it is perhaps unusual that one of the rare companies that employed a Negro Leaguer to pitch its product to black consumers prior to baseball's desegregation was a white-owned, seminational company. Bond bread, the major brand produced by the General Baking Company, a conglomeration of bakeries operating in eleven states in the eastern half of the country, was a regular advertiser in the pages of the black press, especially in New York, home of the original Bond Bakery. To advertise its "soft" bread, Bond generally relied upon photographs of happy homemakers, smiling babies, jolly grocers, chefs, and occasional military personnel. Until 1942 the bakery's approach to advertising was standardized—the same series of ads appeared in every area newspaper, mainstream and black alike. Homemakers in the ads were almost universally white, so, too, were smiling children and grocers.

Between 1942 and '43, however, Bond's advertising made a gradual shift from standardized to localized, appealing directly to readers of the Harlem-based *Amsterdam News* with photographs of African American homemakers, children, and grocers. The new ads featured testimonials by "real" people, providing not only photographic evidence of their enjoyment of Bond's products, but also supplying consumers with endorsers' addresses in order to prove the veracity of their claims. But not all the endorsers were housewives, babies, or grocers. Also singing the praises of Bond was Negro Leaguer Walter Wright of the perpetually cellar-dwelling New York Black Yankees. The endorsement ad, which also features a bathing beauty, a housewife, and a baby, just to cover all the bases, reads, "'A baseball player needs muscle,' says Walter Wright, famous 'Brick Top' [*sic*] of the Black Yankees. 'With rationing cutting down on the muscle-builders we used to get in meat, I'm mighty glad to get Bond's extra protein.' And 'Brick Top' is right. Every loaf of Bond gives *extra* protein that builds muscle—and helps to replace meat!"[43] Unlike the other testimonials in the localized campaign and even in this very ad, Wright's endorsement does not emphasize the product's taste, texture, or freshness, but rather, its nutritional value. Appealing to consumers, for the most part housewives, faced with the relative privations of wartime rationing, the ballplayer serves as an authority on the body's need for protein and Bond's ability to provide it.

Bond's choice of endorser, Wright, the Negro Leaguer, seems at first blush to be an unusual one, to say the least. Certainly, a baseball player, especially a famous one, by the very nature of his profession, could easily serve as an expert on nutrition. And Bricktop Wright, as he was commonly known, was, in fact famous—but not as a baseball player. A standout athlete at Lincoln University in Pennsylvania, he was known primarily for his skills at another sport, basketball. But there was more to his story than success on the field of play. In March 1940, Wright was convicted of assault for biting a white scorekeeper during a melee at the Penn Relays the previous year.[44] His situation became a cause célèbre. Later that month, a basketball doubleheader between teams fronted by two traditional black fraternities, members of the so-called Divine Nine, was held to benefit the extremely popular Wright.[45] Wright, according to local sentiment, was a victim of racial injustice, given the fact that he was sentenced to one to three years in prison, while a white Temple University student also convicted for his part in the melee was given only thirty days. The benefit, which raised funds to pay for Wright's appeal, was a major event on Harlem's social calendar, particularly given its connections to black Greek life.[46]

The benefit was a success, but the appeal was not. Nevertheless, after serving a little less than a year, Wright was released and went on to have a successful career in basketball, eventually joining the storied Harlem Rens. Like so many black athletes of his time,

Wright played more than one sport professionally. With its never very deep roster depleted by the war, the Black Yankees enlisted him to play right field and first base. Still, controversy followed the athlete. Just a week before the Bond ad appeared, Wright was in the news again, having angrily tossed his bat after being struck out in a game against the Newark Eagles, leading syndicated sports writer Al Moses to observe that "Wright was the sort of athlete who could never mask his feelings."[47]

So what made the volatile Wright the right endorser for Bond bread? Why did General Bakeries employ a Black Yankee rather than New York Cuban or a member of the extremely popular Newark Eagles, a team that in 1943 counted two name-brand players, Leon Day and the forty-two-year-old Mule Suttles, on their roster?[48] The answer to these questions is two-fold. Wright's volatility may have been a selling point, to be read not as temper but as passion. According to Moses, "Wright was thinking of blasting that ole 'balata' out of the ballpark and winning the game for the much-abused Black Yankees when the [bat throwing] incident occurred. The matter of being struck out at a time when he imagined that every fan in the yard was expecting great things of him was just too much for the explosive Wright."[49]

As Moses notes, Wright was passionate, not just about playing but about winning, about being the one to hit that walk-off homer. The passion for winning, therefore, was one of the meanings transferred from the celebrity to consumers by way of Bond bread. Every time readers of the *Amsterdam News* ate Bond bread, they also consumed Wright's passion, claiming it for their own. The indirect suggestion that by eating Bond bread, substituting its soya protein for that of meat, consumers were indirectly aiding the war effort was also amplified by Wright's passion for winning. If he could take winning so seriously, so could they. That Wright had been the victim of the systematically racist legal system and had survived to triumph as a professional athlete, even one who played for such a bad team, served to reinforce this notion. In a sense, purchasing Bond bread on Wright's suggestion was like participating in a different type of Double-Duty Dollar campaign.

Eating Bond, consumers participated in his winning spirit not just in the war effort but in the war for racial equality. It seems to have been unimportant to consumers that the bakery was white owned.

The Bond ad featuring Wright operates on yet another level. Including names and addresses of "real" New York residents, representatives of the bakery's target market of *Amsterdam News* readers, the Bond campaign was intensely local and intensely personal. While Leon Day and Mule Suttles were established Negro League stars, they were not local heroes. While Day and Suttles may have been race heroes, they were not local race heroes who had been victimized by the system and ultimately triumphed. They were not darlings of the local black elite, many of whom were alumni members of Divine Nine organizations, as Wright was. As such, the meanings of "one of our own" and "the best and the brightest," as well as one of the most athletically able, transferred through the product to community members. Moreover, because Wright himself was one of the social elite, the meaning of elevated status also passed from him to Bond purchasers. In this particular case, it may have paid to be both personal and local. Even those Harlem consumers who never interacted with the local bourgeoisie were exposed to the society pages of the *Amsterdam News* and no doubt knew Wright's name and his social status.

Now Pitching for the Dodgers

In its own way, Bricktop Wright's Bond endorsement may be seen as a bellwether of what was to come. Until World War II, national advertisers had largely ignored black consumers. Certainly, there were a few exceptions. Schenley distillery, for example, regularly advertised in the black press. But as the 1940s rolled around, more and more national advertisers began to realize that urban African America was a large and largely untapped market. Companies on the leading edge of selling to communities of color sought market research advice on how to appeal specifically to this new segment, many of them looking to David J. Sullivan, an authority on black consumers. In the March 1, 1943, issue of *Sales Management*, Sullivan published some important advice for companies intent on tapping the black market under the emphatic title, "Don't Do This—If You Want to Sell Your Products to Negroes!"[50] Sullivan's suggestions, though many, boiled down to a single piece of advice—don't trade in racial stereotypes if you want to sell to the race.

Seemingly from the moment Jackie Robinson stepped onto the field in Brooklyn, he also exploded onto the advertising pages of black-interest publications. Robinson was the perfect endorser for the new market, which expanded even more rapidly when African American servicemen returned home in the early postwar years. Strong, talented, handsome, college educated, and self-assured, Robinson was, in every sense, the opposite of the stereotypes Sullivan warned Madison Avenue to avoid. The first businesses to hop on the Robinson advertising bandwagon were not larger national advertisers, but rather small, locally owned businesses that catered specifically to the communities that read local black newspapers. New York City enterprises in Harlem and Bedford Stuyvesant regularly invoked Robinson in ways similar to those in which others had invoked Ruth twenty-five years earlier. Brooklyn's Silver Rail Bar and Grill, for example, placed ads in the *Amsterdam News* in August of Robinson's rookie year, announcing "A Jackie Robinson Gift Party." Billing itself as "The No. 1 Bar in Brooklyn," the Silver Rail's ad urged potential customers to "Watch Our Show Window for 'Jackie's Gift,'" beckoning prospective customers to have a look for themselves and, presumably, while they were at it, drop in for a beer and sandwich, even if they were not going to attend the party. Perhaps in order to prevent potentially disappointed patrons from expressing their disapproval in an unforeseen manner, the ad notes in suitably small type, parenthetically, "Jackie Will Not Appear in Person."[51]

Ads congratulating Robinson, thereby tying his name to specific businesses also appeared outside New York. Whenever the Dodgers came to a National League town for the first time during the 1947 season, supplemental congratulatory advertising pages sprung up like weeds in the black press. In the *Pittsburgh Courier*, which had by 1947 replaced the *Chicago Defender* as what was essentially the African American paper of record, an entire multipage spread was devoted to congratulatory advertising for St. Louis businesses the first time Brooklyn played the Cardinals.[52] Among a host of businesses offering their heartfelt felicitations to Robinson while simultaneously reminding consumers they were there for all their purchasing needs, a "Removal Sale" announcement for Zorensky Brothers stands out. That a business about to close its doors where "Everything Must Be Sold Regardless of Cost" promoted itself by congratulating Robinson is both odd and perhaps pathetic. More poignant still is the fact that Zorensky Brothers was one of the targets of the St. Louis branch of the Urban League's "I Buy Where I Can Clerk Campaign," protesting the department store's segregated policy when it came to its sales force though not its customer base, less than a decade earlier.[53]

In a perfect capitalist world, the moment Robinson stepped on the field in Brooklyn, forever desegregating Major League Baseball if not truly integrating it, he would have instantly become a star product endorser, not just in advertising targeting African American consumers, but in mainstream advertising as well. But this was not the case. In reality, the endorsement color line had rarely been breached prior to 1947. And with very limited exceptions, mainstream endorsement advertising would remain segregated during the early years of Robinson's Major League career.

Despite his conspicuous absence from mainstream national advertising, Robinson proved to be a valuable specialty endorser, pitching to African American consumers in the black media throughout the United States. Like Bricktop Wright before him, Robinson endorsed Bond bread. But while Wright's testimonial ran only in the New York area, Robinson's appeared in black-targeted publications across the eighteen states where Bond was by then sold. Wright's image worked to sell bread locally, where he was something of a celebrity. In fact, the personal and local essentially defined his appeal as an endorser—consumers trusted him, because he was one of them. Still, his fame was not such that he would have been valuable in a national campaign. Jackie Robinson, however, was a national race hero of titanic proportions, one who could pitch homogenized, enriched, white bread as easily in

Norfolk, Virginia, or Atlanta, Georgia, as in New York City. Bond as a brand was a natural fit for Robinson, and despite its almost national reach, his endorsement had a local appeal. The company's flagship Flatbush Avenue bakery was less than two city blocks from Ebbets Field. Old Dodgers fans fondly remember the aroma of baking bread greeting them as they exited the subway at the Prospect Park station on their way to the ballpark.[54]

Nostalgia aside, the meanings associated with Robinson—strength, power, resilience, wholesomeness—were desirable not only in an athlete but also in packaged bread. Indeed, these meanings transferred almost effortlessly from the ballplayer to the product. The fact that Bond was homogenized white bread may seem mildly amusing in a twenty-first-century context. This, however, was not the case in 1947. Most midcentury Americans ate store-bought white bread, often several slices at each meal.[55] In fact, consuming industrially produced white bread actually constituted a form of patriotism. According to Aaron Bobrow-Strain, "Part of the reason Americans stuck to gummy white bread lay in the way that wartime enrichment campaigns had cemented a sense that industrial white bread built strength for individual and national defense."[56] In this regard, Robinson's association with Bond worked in both directions. He imbued the brand with all the positive characteristics associated with being the first twentieth-century African American to play in the Major Leagues and, at the same time, the homogenized, enriched product transferred the meaning "American" and "patriot" onto Robinson, reinforcing his heroic status in the eyes of the target market.

So invested in connecting the player's image with its product was Bond that it issued a set of thirteen Jackie Robinson trade cards, available individually from grocers with the purchase of a loaf. While the endorsement was aimed at African American housewives and might lead them to buy Bond bread once, the promise of thirteen different Jackie Robinson baseball cards was all but guaranteed to encourage their children to demand repeat purchases. The cards may have actually increased the value of Robinson's endorsement by advertising Bond bread outside the target demographic. Robinson was, after all, a star player on a locally popular team. As such, the premium no doubt breached the advertising color line in Brooklyn, if not nationally, in all likelihood leading little boys who bled Dodger blue, regardless of race, to demand that their mothers also buy Bond.

But this breach was small and probably unintentional. Although Robinson's Bond endorsement ad ran in a variety of black newspapers and even on the back cover of *Ebony*, as did another Bond testimonial featuring Robinson along with his wife, Rachel, and his small son, Jackie Jr., it did not run in the *Brooklyn Eagle*, the local paper that followed the Dodgers' every exploit, including Robinson's, in excruciating detail. As it was in Bricktop Wright's day, national advertising remained segregated, if not strictly so. Robinson may have been the ideal athlete to extol the virtues of Bond homogenized white bread to black readers, but it took a white teammate to praise the wonders of Wonder Bread to white consumers. As if by careful planning and without a hint of irony, that teammate was Fred "Dixie" Walker. Walker, also known as "the people's 'cherce'" ("choice" in Brooklynese dialect), was, as his epithet suggests, extremely popular among Dodgers fans. But he was not popular with Robinson. A native Georgian who was apparently not terribly happy about playing alongside a teammate of color, Walker wrote a letter to Branch Rickey asking to be traded. It has often been suggested that Walker also attempted to organize his white teammates to resist Robinson's elevation to the big leagues. In his later years, Walker steadfastly denied having done so, stating that at the time, he simply preferred to play on an all-white team, and that even this had been a big mistake on his part.[57] But Walker stayed with the Dodgers throughout the 1947 season, offering his testimonial in favor of the Bond competitor in the white-bread market the same year Robinson pitched for Bond. Not surprisingly, Walker's Wonder Bread testimonial—*"Every Boy and Girl in America Is Entitled to a Bigger, Stronger Body!"* he opines in a dialogue balloon—looked a lot like Robinson's Bond ads, only whiter.[58]

While it is easy to see Robinson's relative absence from mainstream endorsement advertising as overtly racist, especially in the context of the contrasting bread ads, the reason behind the absence may be more subtle. A long-held practice, using African American endorsers to sell to African Americans is an example of market segmentation. "The basic rationale behind this strategy," write Richard W. Pollay, Jung S. Lee, and David Carter-Whitney, "is that a variety of marketing programs (unique combinations of products, advertising, packages, pricing, distribution, etc.), each designed to better match the psychology and interests of a separable segment, will ultimately generate more sales and profit than would a single undifferentiated marketing program, so-called mass marketing. In the 1940s and '50s, studies showed that black consumers preferred seeing black spokesmen and endorsers in advertising, just as white consumers preferred testimonials by other whites. And both groups preferred single-race or ethnicity advertising to ads featuring multi-ethnic endorsers."[59] Taken in this context, it makes sense that Walker's image would more effectively sell bread to white consumers while Jackie Robinson's appeal to consumers of color would be greater. The practice of segmented marketing to African American consumers was applauded and encouraged by community leaders as finally recognizing the power of the black dollar.[60] And while iconic athletes of color now effectively endorse products across market segments to mass audiences, market segmentation remains a potent advertising strategy in the twenty-first century, though perhaps less so than in the past.

Robinson's popularity among advertisers targeting an African American demographic led to more than one endorsement deal. Although he did not appear on a Wheaties box until five decades after his debut and twenty-five years after his death, Robinson enthused about the General Mills cereal in black newspapers and in *Ebony*. He also endorsed both Chesterfield and Old Gold cigarettes. This is especially notable, given that he was not a smoker. But no Ty Cobb was he. Unlike the Georgia Peach, whose name was frequently used to market tobacco products without his knowledge or permission and without compensation despite his vocal opposition to smoking, Robinson was paid to endorse cigarettes. And endorse them he did, though a copywriter was no doubt responsible for the words, "'Yes sir! Today!' says Jackie Robinson. 'For a treat instead of a treatment, I recommend Old Gold Cigarettes!'" as well as his tips regarding Chesterfield cigarettes' mildness.[61]

Robinson was the first twentieth-century, African American Major League player and major cigarette endorser, but he was not the only one. As professional baseball slowly desegregated and more and more players of color joined the big leagues, they also joined the endorsement game. Tobacco companies, more than any other advertisers, recognized the selling potential of other early postsegregation-era players. Robinson's Dodgers teammates Roy Campanella and Don Newcombe appeared in ads for American Tobacco's Lucky Strikes. They were joined by Henry Aaron and Ernie Banks for Philip Morris's Camels, as well as Willie Mays and Maury Wills for Taryton, another American Tobacco brand. And there were others. According to Pollay, Lee, and Carter-Whitney, "So common were [African American] sports stars as celebrity endorsers that they continued to be used even when the copy was inconsistent with athleticism." Indeed, "cigarette ads aimed at black readers of *Ebony* were significantly more likely to use athletes than those aimed at white readers of *Life*. For 1950–65, endorsements from athletes were about five times more common in *Ebony* than *Life*."[62] The vast majority of these athletes were baseball players of color.

There are a variety of reasons why Robinson, Campanella, and the others made such effective cigarette endorsers. After all, not only were they race heroes, they were American heroes, at least in the eyes of the target market segment. They were the true representatives of the American Dream for many African Americans, excelling on a playing field that had never been level. Though they were not yet embraced by mainstream advertising, they were legitimate stars on the big, mainstream stage. They were aspirational figures made flesh. For this reason, they could have effectively endorsed any number of products, and many of them did.

So what, specifically, made these pioneer ballplayers appropriate spokesmen for tobacco products? The answer lies in media and media markets. Although revisionist history suggests that consumers were unaware of the risks of smoking in the early postwar years, this was not the case. In the late 1940s and early '50s, a steady stream of articles appeared in medical journals, linking tobacco use with an increased risk of lung cancer. But most consumers did not read medical journals. They did, however, read *Reader's Digest*, one of the most popular general-interest magazines on the market at the time. The December 1952 issue included a condensed piece previously published in the *Christian Herald*, called "Cancer by the Carton." Written by Roy Norr, the shortened article briefly chronicled recent scientific literature regarding smoking and cancer, putting it into clear, understandable language.[63] Given the impact of *Reader's Digest*, it is safe to say that the article served to presage what would become an ongoing conversation, culminating in the 1964 Surgeon General's warning. Given Robinson's Old Gold "recommendation"—"For a treat instead of a treatment"—it is possible to suggest that a conversation about whether smoking might necessitate medical intervention was already becoming part of the zeitgeist three years before the *Reader's Digest* article was published. In such an atmosphere, it was important for cigarette manufacturers to attempt to counteract these growing concerns, and who better to do so than baseball players? Ballplayers were, after all, the very models of good health, stamina, strength, and virility. As such, they may have been able to counterbalance some of the emerging negative images associated with smoking.[64]

But why black ballplayers? White ballplayers also endorsed cigarettes during the 1950s, as Babe Ruth had in earlier decades. Chesterfield, for example, counted a whole stable of players among its spokesmen, Ted Williams, Stan Musial, and Joe DiMaggio among them. But at a time when the potential mainstream market for cigarettes showed signs that it might shrink, though in fact, this was not the case, the tobacco companies, like many other large, mainstream corporations, suddenly discovered a new market, ripe for exploitation. It is probably no coincidence that the tobacco industry recognized the potential profits to be made by advertising to the African American market segment at the same time as the desegregation of the Major Leagues. Advertisers had a product to sell, a newly identified, previously underserved market to which to sell it, and the perfect endorsers to pitch it. To smoke Old Gold or Chesterfield was not only to participate in the physical magnificence of Robinson, Aaron, and Mays, but also to consume a little bit of what made them race heroes and American heroes. By smoking their brands, metaphorically inhaling the same magical air as they did, consumers could be more like them, succeeding wildly where others like them had never done so.

Throughout the late 1940s and early 1950s, market segmentation practices and racism largely consigned African American big leaguers to an endorsement life behind a color line. But by the mid-1950s, long after they had proved themselves on the diamond, star baseball players of color began to enter the advertising mainstream. Taking a page from a long line of celebrity baseball men before him, giving credit to magical devices and nostrums for their excellent performance, New York Giant Monte Irvin endorsed the Niagara Massage Mechanical Cushion enthusiastically, if the ad is to be believed, giving it "credit for helping condition his ankle after last year's injury." The ad, which includes a picture of Irvin in midswing, is actually an advertorial (an ad masquerading as news), much like Ty Cobb's Nuxated Iron testimonials of old. Moreover, Irvin isn't the only celebrity in the ad. Also endorsing the device is Marie "My Friend Irma" Wilson, "famous star of stage, screen and television," as the ad would have it.[65] Market segmentation this was not. In fact, it seems highly unlikely that the vibrating cushion manufacturer would have had a large enough marketing department to engage in the practice. They seem to have metaphorically covered all their bases at once by employing both an African American slugger and a Caucasian, television sit-com actress and placing them in the same ad. Although this was hardly the work of a large, national advertiser or a major agency, it did appear in a large, mainstream publication of national repute, the *New York Times*.

So, too, did Willie Mays's endorsement of Rheingold beer. On October 1, 1954, just as Mays's Giants prepared to take a commanding three-game lead over the Cleveland Indians in the World

Series, Liebmann Brewing Company placed the testimonial ad in the *Hartford Courant* and other papers. Rheingold, though not a truly national beer, had a strong market presence in the New York metropolitan area, sections of the Mid-Atlantic, and, for a time, in Southern California. While Rheingold did not sponsor any of the local teams until the Mets were born, in 1962—Knickerbocker sponsored the Giants, Schaefer the Dodgers, and Ballantine the Yankees—the brewery wasn't shy about tying its product to baseball. In this regard, Liebmann was just like any number of national breweries. Certainly no product, with the possible exception of peanuts and Cracker Jack, was so closely connected to the sport in the public eye, thanks to decades of advertising and what might be described as a natural affinity with baseball. But Rheingold's producers were also fundamentally different from other breweries when it came to popular entertainment, race, sponsorship, and endorsement deals. Unlike other advertisers, Old Gold and Chesterfield, for example, that practiced what appears to be strict market segmentation, Rheingold placed ads in the black press featuring white and black ballplayers in the same ads. In 1951 and 1952, Gil McDougald of the New York Yankees and New York Giant Monte Irvin told readers of the *New York Amsterdam News* that their beer was "Rheingold—the dry beer!" In an ad featuring two side-by-side photographs, a standardized layout that was used in most Rheingold ads of the time, Irvin and McDougald are depicted on the left, conversing on what appears to be a train, and on the right, enjoying some cold Rheingold in a social setting. In this case, a picture really is worth a thousand words. The captions are what one would expect from a joint endorsement—on the left: "Hope both our teams get the chance to face each other in the World Series again next year!" say two of baseball's best players. And on the right: "But even though we're strictly opponents on the field, we're on the same side when it comes to beer. Like most of the millions around this town, we're both Rheingold rooters. No question about the original Extra Dry beer—it's the best! That's why it's New York City's largest-selling beer."[66] The pictures look fairly ordinary too. But the one to the right is far from conventional. In it the two players are seated side by side at a table in what appears to be the train's dining car. With their elbows almost touching, they dine and drink together. Behind them, other patrons are being served by a serious-looking waiter who is, contrary to both stereotype and the reality of the railroad industry in the early 1950s, white. That the two friends, whose connection is cemented by their good-natured competition and their choice of beer, represent opposing teams is not that unusual. In fact, it is an advertising convention. But in this case, although Irvin represents the desegregated Giants and McDougald, the still-segregated Yankees, they share a meal and a quaff in public. Whether intentional or not, this suggested to readers that off the field there was no color line, even if it persisted in the game, at least as far as Rheingold was concerned. In this regard, the meaning that transfers to the consumer from the endorser via the product is racial equality—a strong meaning to this ad's target market.

Although the Liebmann Brewing Company's best-known advertising campaign, the Miss Rheingold beauty contest, which ran between 1940 and 1964, neither employed endorsers from the world of baseball nor crossed color lines—Miss Rheingold was always white—the brewery was still an innovator regarding race. In fact its commercial color-line crossing was not limited to print advertising. Rheingold began sponsoring radio broadcasts in 1933, signing deals with several radio stations as early as October 1, more than two months before the official repeal of Prohibition, and continued to be an advertising presence on radio and, later, television.[67] Liebmann, along with several wine producers, sponsored the first major television program hosted by an African American celebrity, Nat King Cole.[68] Of course, Cole was not a baseball personality, but Jackie Robinson was. In 1959, the year in which the last Major League team finally desegregated, the retired Dodger signaled his desire to venture into the world of broadcast journalism, but sponsors were not immediately forthcoming. In paired industries that had survived the Great Depression in part by putting players on the air to sell products, from cereal to motor oil, it was still considered a major risk to tie a large corporate brand to

"Our beer is Rheingold —the Dry beer!"

say MONTE IRVIN and GIL McDOUGALD

"Hope both our teams get the chance to face each other in the World Series again next year!" say two of baseball's best players, the Giants' Monte Irvin and the Yankees' Gil McDougald. "But even though we're strictly opponents on the field . . .

". . . we're on the same side when it comes to beer. Like most of the millions around this town, we're both Rheingold rooters. No question about the original Extra Dry beer—it's the *best!* That's why it's New York City's largest-selling beer!"

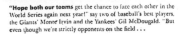

You can <u>always</u> rely on it —
It's beer as beer should taste!

8. Rheingold Beer ad featuring Giant Monte Irvin and Yankee Gil McDougald. The ad, notable for placing a black and white player side by side, ran in the black press.

a radio broadcast by an African American baseball player, even a
nationally prominent player. But Liebmann came through again.
Thanks to Rheingold sponsorship, Jackie Robinson's half-hour
weekly talk show premiered on WRCA New York.[69] It featured
guests from various walks of life, including New York City mayor
Robert Wagner and former First Lady and human rights activ-
ist Eleanor Roosevelt.[70] Called *The Jackie Robinson Show*, it was,
not surprisingly, cross-promoted in full-page print ads in *Ebony*
throughout its run.

Still Pitching behind the Color Line

The desegregation of Major League Baseball sounded the death
knell for the Negro Leagues and black baseball, in general. But that
death, like desegregation itself, was long and protracted. So, too,
was the death of advertising related to black baseball. As the official
souvenir program from the 1949 East-West Baseball Classic—the
Negro League All-Star Game—illustrates, black baseball at its best
was still popular enough to attract significant advertising dollars.
With ads on virtually every page, the program attracted national
advertisers like Coca-Cola, Pepsi, and Oscar Meyer. Among the
first national companies to advertise in the black press, these enterprises were a natural fit for East-West Classic program advertising.
More thoroughly represented than national advertisers, however,
were local, primarily black-owned Chicagoland area businesses,
as the game was played at Comiskey Park. As was the case back in
1907 in Sol White's *Guide*, the bulk of advertisers were saloons and
segregated hotels that served the game's fan base. Funeral homes
and pharmacies were also well represented.

East-West Game advertising also told a nuanced story. At least
one ad in the program, promoting the Payne School of Modeling
and Charm, offered instruction in "Fashion Modeling, Photographic
Modeling, Wardrobe Assembling, Body and Figure Control, Self
Assurance, Corrective Make-up and Hair Styling."[71] The ad was
clearly aimed at South Side women, women in search not of the
perfect loaf of homogenized white bread, but rather professional
careers in the fashion industry, an industry supported by Chicago-

area Johnson Publishing Company, publishers of *Ebony* and owners of Fashion Fair cosmetics. Different, too, was an ad for John
B. Knighten Jr. and Company, a South Side real estate company,
featuring an illustration of a nearly perfect nuclear family of color,
collectively dreaming, via thought balloon, of their slice of the
America pie, a home of their own. Outside the balloon, there is a
branch on which rests a nest, complete with chirping baby birds,
accompanied by copy reading, "Birds Have Nests! Do You Have a
Home?"[72] The only thing that distinguishes this ad from one which
might have appeared in a mainstream baseball program or newspaper is the family, whose faces are shaded with crude lines, indicating blackness. Its message is clear. It says, "You, too, African
American baseball fan, can participate in the American Dream
of Home Ownership." These ads, as well as a full-page advertisement for the Chicago School of Automotive Trades, endorsed by
boxer Joe Louis, spoke to a new, postwar, black empowerment in
what was still a largely segregated society, rather than representing the segregated status quo.

As the relatively large number of ads in the 1949 program suggests, African American baseball was still a going concern two
years after Robinson's Major League debut, but this was not the
case only a few years later. The Negro American League survived
until 1962, but only barely. Baseball-associated advertising in the
black press after 1949 was, for the most part, Major League–related.
At the same time, players of color began to build and maintained
a small presence as endorsers in mainstream media. There was,
however, one major exception. Black baseball ended, as it began,
with barnstorming teams owned by enterprising white promoters,
traveling to small towns, playing in front of predominately Caucasian crowds. The Indianapolis Clowns owned by Syd Pollack, once
a championship squad, became barnstorming baseball's equiva-
lent of the Harlem Globetrotters. The Clowns continued to advertise heavily in the black press as well as in small-town newspapers,
where they played into the 1970s, primarily in the still-segregated
South and the Upper Midwest, which had a long history of novelty barnstorming baseball. But the Clowns and their advertising

were anachronisms in a changing landscape, one that would, by the end of the century, see baseball's endorsement line, as with its color line, erode into oblivion, aided by the emergence and complete domination of that once experimental medium, television. After all, small-town Americans no longer depended upon carnivalesque live entertainment of the type provided by the Clowns for their baseball amusement. Their baseball heroes, white and black alike, were readily available with a click of a switch and the turn of a dial, right there in their homes in black and white and even in living color.

CHAPTER FIVE

Baseball, Hotdogs, Apple Pie, and Chevrolet . . . and Beer, Cigarettes, Cat Food, and Margarine

Tales of Television Advertising

O n July 1, 1941, a cataclysmic event shook the world, though it would take the better part a decade for its full impact to be felt. At 2:30 p.m., in New York City, many of those lucky enough to have access to television sets bore witness to the sight of something like a test pattern. But this was no ordinary test pattern. Instead of the usual abstract shapes, viewers saw a clock—a Bulova clock—splashed across a silhouette of the United States, ticking off a full minute. Finally, eager to watch the first-place Brooklyn Dodgers take on the historically bad, last-place Philadelphia Phillies, the audience heard the silken voice of an announcer. At once they all knew that "America runs on Bulova time." So was born commercial television with the first paid advertisement, and baseball attended the delivery.

This was not the professional game's television debut. Three years earlier, televised Major League Baseball premiered at the New York World's Fair and several other locations, conveniently including Macy's and other RCA retail outlets. Quick to realize the potential of televised baseball's power to boost the popularity of the experimental medium, the *New York Times* took notice, suggesting that "the greatest autumnal spur to television as an industry would be to telecast the world series [*sic*]." But, asked the *Times*, if somewhat rhetorically, "Who will pay for it?" The answer, of course, was "advertisers, known in radio parlance as 'sponsors.'"[1] This assertion no doubt resonated with the curious spectators who watched that first Major League broadcast on August 26, as it included three promotional spots. According to the *Times*:

Between the fifth and sixth inning [the announcer] spreads a table-cloth on his stand, reaches for a bowl, lifts up a package of cereal with the name of the box facing the camera, and then partakes of what he calls "a breakfast-sized sample," although he confesses it is rather late in the day. Mindful that he also is at the "mike" for an oil sponsor and for another who manufactures soap he displays a machine to spray bugs, and then two cakes of soap. There is said to be no violation of the FCC's regulations because the time is not sold for advertising purposes.[2]

Others also benefited from unpaid advertising during the telecast. The trade publication *Broadcasting* observed, "Advertisers whose messages are painted on the ball park's fence got extra value that day, as well, for their signs, especially the Gem razor ad in the right field, which showed up as well on the television receiver screens as in the park. It seems probable that when sponsored television arrives, sponsors of ball games will have to take over the billboards at the parks as well, or see other advertisers get as much benefit from telecast as they do."[3] Or as the *New York Times* put it, "Billboards do the trick!"[4] Whether Gem sold any more razors, Calvert any more blended whiskey, or whether any other company with Ebbets Field signage that happened to be captured by the camera sold any more of whatever they were selling is highly debatable. But once commercially televised baseball commenced in earnest, cameras would be judiciously placed in order to avoid including unpaid advertising during game broadcasts.[5] Television advertisers, in turn, would make certain to place billboards where they would have the most on-air impact.

A Brooklyn Dodgers game provided the content for another important experimental broadcast, this time the team's 1940 home opener, and unpaid commercials were part of the package. Procter and Gamble was the manufacturer, Compton Advertising was the agency, and Ivory Soap was the star of two one-minute promotions. *Broadcasting* described it in this way: "In one spot, Ken Towers, announcer, showed how the soap foams up by making suds in a glass; in the other, by wearing one red mitten and one white glove, he illustrated how Ivory keeps hands white."[6] This was but the beginning, an experiment in commercialism on a technically noncommercial, experimental medium. Following a protracted struggle between RCA and the Federal Communications Commission (FCC) over broadcast standards, the Bulova time-signal commercial made manifest that all this experimentation would eventually, if not immediately, come to an end. This was commercial television, and it was inevitable.[7] Not only would it change the face of American entertainment and American consumerism, and ultimately consumerism and entertainment on a global scale, it would also change the way in which Americans would consume baseball.

A New Advertising Medium for a New Era

Although the earth shook in 1941, commercial television's aftershocks were not really felt in full until 1947. After all, television ownership was hardly widespread in 1941. In fact, there were only an estimated two thousand sets available nationally in 1941, and the Dodgers-Phillies game was only broadcast locally in the New York City region. Televisions, though certainly attractive to a broad spectrum of consumers, were prohibitively expensive, well out of reach of the average American family.[8] Despite the extremely limited audience size, Bulova deemed its commercial successful enough to have been well worth the nine dollars the company paid—four dollars for time, five for "facilities and handling."[9] They would go on to sign a thirteen-week contract for daily time-signal commercials.[10] Adams Hats followed Bulova's lead, signing on as a Dodgers sponsor and doubling down on the company's Ebbets Field billboard. On July 4, the hatter, too, made history, bankrolling the first live, paid, television commercial.[11]

Commercial television's path forward was neither straight nor smooth. It hit a major road bump just five months after its introduction with the bombing of Pearl Harbor. When the United States entered World War II, the FCC strictly limited commercial broadcasting, issuing no new television licenses. With materials diverted to the war effort, no new sets were manufactured for the duration, either.[12] Some extant stations continued to broadcast during the war, but only for a few hours a week. And all programming was noncommercial, or sustaining.[13] This is not to say that there was no television advertising activity during the war, but it was unpaid, and therefore by definition experimental, as it was in 1939. New York City's DuMont network station WABD, for example, offered free advertising time to agencies eager to test the medium.[14] In 1944 Compton Advertising, a New York agency, signed on to produce experimental broadcasts as it had in 1939. Procter & Gamble and Socony Vacuum Oil were its clients. Programming consisted of puppet shows, *Truth or Consequences,* and not surprisingly, Brooklyn Dodgers baseball games, given the fact that both companies were Dodgers radio sponsors.[15]

Although the FCC put a temporary halt to truly commercial broadcasting during World War II, the agency did nothing to slow preparation for commercial television's return at war's end. The results of a survey conducted by *Broadcasting* of fifty-five large advertising agencies in major media markets, published nearly eighteen months before the final treaties were signed, indicated that the respondents were readying for the full-fledged return of commercial television.[16] The broadcasting industry urged the FCC to lift the ban as quickly as was expedient, pending the availability of materials and manpower after the war.[17] The FCC was listening. In 1946 commercial television resumed, using significantly better technology than in 1941. RCA engineer R. D. Kell, addressing a group of industry experts, enthused, "Now cameras are available which remove the limitations of programming, transmitters can be built for all the channels the Federal Communications Commission has allocated, ahead of us lie the facilities which will give us television networks, and we may have larger, brighter, pictures in the home. Nothing more is needed, except to do the work of producing in the factories, selling in the stores, and programming in the stations."[18] By October the FCC granted licenses to seventy-eight new stations in addition to the six that were already in operation.[19] In the summer of 1946, televised baseball, if not yet common, was becoming an increasingly regular feature of the broadcast schedule, with the Chicago Cubs telecasting home games during the second half of the season.[20]

If commercial sponsorship deals were any measure of success, the 1946 Cubs telecasts were extremely successful. By November the Cubs had already signed with Ford and Lorillard's Old Gold cigarettes to telecast home games during the 1947 season on WIND.[21] The Brooklyn Dodgers also found ready support, contracting with Ford and General Foods to sponsor their upcoming home games to be telecast on WCBS. The situation was not so financially rosy for New York Yankees telecaster WABD, the same station that had offered free experimental time to advertisers during the war. New Yorkers could certainly watch the Yankees if they had access to receivers. In fact, so could viewers in Philadelphia and Washington DC, where several Yankees games were televised, thanks to AT&T's coaxial cable. [22] The Yankees, however, were unable to secure regular sponsorship, so each game cost the station a reported $1,000 for rights, lines, and talent, as announcers were generally hired and paid directly by the advertisers or their agencies.[23] The New York Giants, too, broadcast their games on a sustaining basis.[24]

In 1947, for the first time, an expanding number of baseball fans could watch their favorite teams on television. Of eleven stations on the air, nine carried regular-season baseball games. Some carried Minor League games, and some telecast games of more than one team. Of sixteen Major League teams, ten broadcast home games.[25] On April 15, when Jackie Robinson made his Major League debut, breaking MLB's informal but long-standing and strictly enforced color line, he did so not only in living color at Ebbets Field, but also in black and white on New York City's WCBS Channel 2.[26] The television audience was by no means large. After all, there were only approximately sixty thousand receivers in the United States, forty-seven thousand of them in New York. Of those, however, approximately three thousand were located in bars, increasing the availability of the historic Dodgers telecast to a wider number of presumptive fans. Watching baseball was, after all, a communal activity. And the Dodgers' game was not the only game in town. It is safe to say that some baseball-loving viewers may have been watching a different game, as the Yankees were also at home in the Bronx and on station WABD Channel 5. It is impossible to say whether more fans saw Robinson's debut on television than in person—26,623 were actually in attendance at Ebbets Field.[27] It was, moreover, a Tuesday afternoon, not a time when bars were usually packed, not even in Brooklyn.

Despite the limited viewership, advertisers had a lot to gain by embracing baseball sponsorship, if not immediately, then in the very near future. To reach large audiences, commercial enterprises had to invest significant resources into placing ads in newspapers and magazines, as well as in abundant radio advertising. Television, however, had the potential to reach much larger audiences at once. In March 1947 *Printer's Ink* enthused, "Television is going to move very soon and very fast."[28] According to cultural historian Lawrence R. Samuel, "Television advertising was the stuff of dreams for companies like General Foods, offering potential unprecedented economies of scale and, ultimately, tremendous profits. Beyond its role as an advertising medium, television could and would act as a catalyst for selling the idea of consumption in general, a critical function in the first few years after the war."[29] Television advertising during baseball games proved to be sticky, claiming a solid place in viewers' memory channels. Brand recall levels were unusually high. Three out of four Dodgers viewers, for example, remembered that Ford sponsored their team's telecasts.[30] Potential advertisers were impressed by these recall numbers and looked for more opportunities to link the sport with their products.[31]

Although baseball and advertising connected with the new medium via sponsorship, it was not the only impact the advent of commercial television had on the twinned industries. Indeed, not all advertising related to baseball and television was actually on the new medium. As they had in the early days of radio, retailers used televised baseball as bait to lure potential customers into their outlets, even if they did not sell televisions. In Washington DC on April 14, 1947, in advance of the Senators' home opener against the Yankees, for example, the Potomac Electric Power Company

(Pepco) advertised a telecast opportunity, linking it to the company's product—electricity. Under display text proclaiming, "Television comes to Washington DC . . . and Pepco has a hand in it!" the ad proclaims, "You've talked about, read about, and felt pretty thrilled about Television. Now you're going to actually see it and hear it at no cost whatsoever!"

The special event that kicked off Pepco's "T-Week Broadcast Schedule," the totality of which was conveniently listed in the ad, was the game. To see their Senators open the season, all Washingtonians had to do was go to the main lobby of Pepco's building at 10th and E Streets, NW. They didn't even have to buy anything. In fact, they couldn't buy anything even if they had wanted to. "None of these Television Sets is for sale," emphasized the ad. Pepco's sole mission was to partner with "leaders in the industry" and to "take this opportunity to acquaint you with that newest miracle . . . TELEVISION." Of course, the small print, while not exactly contradicting the larger text, provided excited viewers a number to call in order to secure information about television dealers near them.[32]

This was not Pepco's first foray into advertising, nor was it Pepco's first advertisement using baseball. A large Pepco ad featuring the company's mascot, Reddy Kilowatt, already graced Griffith Stadium's left-field fence by the time the utility placed this ad. If Pepco, a public utility, was not selling televisions, then what did it have to gain by placing paid ads in the *Washington Post* and at Griffith Stadium? Why would a public utility, a virtual monopoly, need to advertise at all? Utilities like Pepco advertised for reasons of public relations. As early as 1922, when the PR industry was in its infancy, the editor of the trade publication *Public Service Management* made clear the need for such advertising, writing:

> Today nearly everybody reads, or has the opportunity to read, public utility advertising. More utility companies are advertising than ever before. Why? Because the companies want the public to know about their business and about its service. The utility has a service to sell. The merchant has a commodity to sell. The merchant advertises to create a demand for his commodity. The

demand for the utility's service does not need to be created—it exists already. What the utility advertises for is friends. By pointing out that it is a worthy friend the company improves its public relations, thereby improving its credit and enabling it to give more and better service.[33]

What better way for Pepco to engender the good will of its consumers than by promoting its excellent services with a televised ball game? And Pepco needed all the good will it could get. As the 1947 season opened, the utility was embroiled in a three-year lawsuit with the Public Utilities Commission that would be settled in May, leading to a sliding-scale rate increase.[34] The company was also locked in a dispute with several local communities that wanted their power lines buried rather than strung overhead.[35] While a televised ball game might not mollify angry consumers, it would go a long way toward branding Pepco as friendly to its customers.

Public relations aside, the real purpose of advertising was to sell commodities. If television was to realize its full potential as an advertising medium, more receivers would need to find their way into American homes. Just as radio retailers relied upon baseball to sell merchandise, so did television manufacturers and merchants, many of whom also sold the older, still more popular medium. The United States Television Manufacturing Company of New York City, for example, extolled the brilliance and size of its beautiful 1947 console model set in an ad in the *New York Times*. The ad's copy aims to tempt potential buyers with the promise of baseball on a big screen, touting the product's 340-square-inch projection screen, "almost 2 feet by 1½ feet, six times the average picture."[36] The magnificence of the picture, and of the product as a whole, is underscored by the artwork, which depicts the set's giant display complete with the image of a batter about to swing. In fact, the image of a batter in action quickly became a common visual trope in print advertising for television receivers, regardless of whether baseball was actually mentioned in the given ad's copy.

United States Television Company televisions were high-ticket items—very high. In September, an advertorial in the *Brooklyn*

Daily Eagle announced that the company was slashing the prices of some of its models from $3,000 to $480, thanks to "mass production and heavy sales."[37] While this certainly seemed like a bargain, even the reduced price was too high for most American consumers. In contrast RCA Victor offered a far more reasonably priced and considerably smaller tabletop model with a twenty-three-square-inch screen, one on which, according to advertising in the *Chicago Tribune*, fans could watch their Cubs for only $250. Even better, the ad suggested, the already affordable receiver was available on credit at Crown's for only "⅓ down, 15 Mos. to Pay." As in the illustration for the bigger, more luxurious set, a batter swings. As if this were not enough, the ad includes a crudely drawn baseball, superimposed with the words, "Batter Up!—see the BASEBALL GAMES from your easy chair with EYE WITNESS picture synchronizer." The ad also includes an equally crude drawing of an eye, for the benefit of consumers who had not yet gotten the point.[38]

With television receivers in less than 1 percent of American homes in 1947, it is hardly surprising that many Americans got their first taste of baseball on television in bars; so it stands to reason that television retail manufacturers would also advertise their wares to tavern owners.[39] With its giant screen projection sets and prices beyond the reach of even middle-income consumers, United States Television also advertised to bar, hotel, and club proprietors in the *New York Times*, emphasizing the promise of "big profits with the big picture." Baseball was the draw. Bar owners might potentially "give as many as 800 customers front-row seats at baseball" with the "Tavern Tele-Symphonic," the same receiver in the consumer model console advertised in the *Times*."[40] Obviously, the average urban tavern could not possibly hold that many customers. Nevertheless, the ad wasn't entirely wrong when it came to noting the potential profitability of installing a large-screen receiver. The promise of an establishment filled with drinking, paying customers watching the Dodgers or Yankees, especially on weekday afternoons, when business was characteristically slow, would have been more than enough to induce many a bar owner to invest in a United States Television model or other large receiver.

Once local drinking establishments invested in sets, they had to spread the word to potential patrons. Many bars, taverns, and restaurants advertised in local newspapers, using the availability of televised baseball to promote their places of business. In Hartford, Connecticut, the air-conditioned Villanova-Empire bar and restaurant invited drinkers and diners to catch a televised game while feasting on its delicious Italian cuisine. And the Villanova-Empire's television wasn't just any television—it was the "First U.S.T. Set in Hartford" with the "world's largest screen."[41] Indeed, it may very well have been the very United States Television model advertised to bar, hotel, and club owners in the *New York Times*. In contrast, the *New York Amsterdam News*, the city's major black newspaper, was filled with ads for taverns and restaurants making more modest claims. Most ads simply included the words "Television" and "Dodgers." Size did not matter. The very ability to watch Jackie Robinson and his team in action, the advertisers seem to suggest, was more than enough to appeal to their potential clientele.

It's an Old Goldie!

Commercial television in the last years of the 1940s remained a novelty. As the 1950s began, only 9 percent of American households owned receivers.[42] Although original television content—dramas, soap operas, quiz shows, and the like—increased significantly over the last years of the 1940s, baseball still provided the nascent industry with hours of commercially sponsored programming. At the outset, baseball advertising did not forge any new creative territory. Televised baseball tended to attract the same commercial sponsors as did baseball on the radio. Sponsorship was dominated by breweries, tobacco companies, and Ford. In turn these companies relied upon the same types of advertising that had served them well on the old medium, only this time with a visual component. Ford continued its on-air baseball presence with the Dodgers and Cubs, also acquiring rights to the Minor League Milwaukee Brewers telecasts for the 1948 season.[43] Ballantine sponsored Yankees broadcasts in 1948.[44] And in 1949 the Goebel Brewing Company contracted to broadcast thirty-five Detroit Tigers home games.[45]

Beer and automobiles notwithstanding, big tobacco was by far the biggest sponsor in televised baseball. In the late 1940s Lorillard and Liggett & Myers led the pack. Old Gold, a longtime Dodgers radio sponsor, replaced General Foods, sharing Brooklyn baseball sponsorship with Ford. The competition, Liggett & Myers' Chesterfield brand, sponsored the Giants and Cubs.[46]

With baseball, advertisers got a lot of bang for their buck, though certainly not as much as they would in years to come. According to Walker and Bellamy:

> NBC's sponsor of New York Giants games, Chesterfield, received six thirty-to-fifty-second filmed commercials that aired ten minutes before game time, at the end of the second, fourth, sixth, and eight innings, and after the game recap. In addition, there were "short" Chesterfield plugs at each half-inning. Chesterfield's signage at the ballpark was shown on camera, and the announcer was often shown "lighting up." Between games of a double header, the telecast switched to WNBQ's studio for a ten-minute program, "Chesterfield Baseball Quiz," in which fans attending the game competed for cartons of the sponsor's product.[47]

At the outset, Liggett & Myers also advertised the Chesterfield brand name with live crowd shots broadcast from the Polo Grounds. This practice, however, was short-lived. Notes Lawrence, "Crowd shots occasionally caught married men at the games accompanied by women other than their wives, eventually forcing advertisers to avoid televising scenes of fans over which they would superimpose their logo."[48] Although television ceased to be classified as "experimental" when it went commercial, advertising using live baseball as a backdrop was, in itself, an experiment, and sometimes it was an experiment that failed.

More than half a century before baseball's announcers declared the need for an "AT&T Call to the Bullpen"—the type of imbedded commercial message that infuriates twenty-first-century fans—Dodgers radio announcer Red Barber called home runs "Old Goldies." He did so not out of colorful tradition, but as a paid spot for the broadcast's sponsoring cigarette brand. What radio listeners at home could not see was a carton of cigarettes sliding down the mesh behind home plate, where PA announcer Tex Rickards, leaving his customary perch beside the dugout, would fetch the sponsor's product, bringing it to the eager players in the dugout every time a ball left the yard. Once Old Gold took over television sponsorship from General Foods, however, viewers could see both the home run and the promotion with their very own eyes.

Although the real source is obscure, someone, most probably either department store mogul John Wanamaker or Lever Brothers founder Lord Leverhulme, once said, "Half the money I spend on advertising is wasted. The trouble is, I don't know which half."[49] While it is unclear how much advertising money Lorillard and Liggett & Myers may have wasted sponsoring baseball on television, Old Goldies and all, the answer is most probably not much. In its June 1948 issue, *Television* magazine conducted a sponsor identification survey of 212 viewers, asking, "Would you please name three advertisers on television?" Cigarette companies associated with baseball telecasts received the top scores. Chesterfield's Giants games tied for first place on the list, while Old Gold's Dodgers telecasts were just a few places behind.[50] In April 1949, just as the season got underway, *Broadcasting* reported that cigarette sales had hit an all-time high, and were expected to improve even more in the coming year. Not surprisingly, Chesterfield stayed in the game, sponsoring the Giants and the Washington Senators both on radio and television during the 1949 season. And Old Gold once again sponsored the Cubs as well as the Chicago White Sox, though ceased to sponsor the Dodgers on TV.[51]

Although using sports to sell tobacco products seems counterintuitive to twenty-first-century consumers unaccustomed to widespread cigarette advertising on television and radio—the result of the 1970 Public Health Cigarette Smoking Act that banned the practice beginning on New Year's Day the following year—baseball and tobacco advertising had been linked since the late nineteenth century.[52] After all, cigarette manufacturers were the first advertisers to distribute mass-produced, baseball trade cards in order to brand their mostly indistinguishable products and encourage repeat sales. Early baseball trade cards most often used names and images of ballplayers without their permission. As such, this form of advertising was not technically endorsement, but in effect, it did not matter. The meanings smokers associated with players like Ty Cobb and Christy Mathewson were transferred to the consumers through the product via the advertising whether or not—most often not—Mathewson and Cobb were paid.

That was also the case with Chesterfield advertising, but its endorsers were compensated. Chesterfield's use of player endorsements preceded baseball's entry into postwar commercial television by several years, with testimonial print and point-of-purchase advertising featuring Mel Ott and Bill Dickey, managers of the Giants and Yankees, respectively, in 1946, for example. So it is no wonder that as Liggett & Myers firmly cemented the connection between Chesterfield and the Giants, Cubs, White Sox, and others via television broadcast sponsorship, the tobacco company extended its baseball-related campaign. It blanketed mass-circulation magazines and newspapers as well as the precious real estate next to the nation's cash registers with paid endorsement advertising featuring Ted Williams, Joe Di Maggio, Stan Musial, and a host of other marquee players and managers. Chesterfield endorsements by Jackie Robinson and Willie Mays also graced the back pages of *Ebony*. Most of the ads depicted the players in groups of two or more and bore the slogan, "The Baseball Man's Cigarette," in addition to the brand's original slogan, "Always Buy Chesterfield," which emphasized the *A*, *B*, and *C* with large type.

Predating the Marlboro Man, the archetypical American cowboy image that imparted the meaning of rugged masculinity to the Phillip Morris brand that had previously been marketed exclusively to women, by seven years, the 1948 slogan, "The Baseball Man's Cigarette" aimed at a similar result. Chesterfield did not share Marlboro's burden, in that it was marketed to men and women alike, most particularly with endorsements by Hollywood icons of both genders.[53] But by labeling the brand as the "Baseball Man's" smoke of choice, Chesterfield became not only a symbolic conveyer of masculinity, but of a very specific type. Baseball as played by Chesterfield's endorsers was a game not only of masculine power, but of grace, skill, and knowledge. While Williams, DiMaggio, and Musial typified every consumer's idea of star players and strong men, they were also possessors of a quality limited only to their kind. With every puff of a Chesterfield, smokers inhaled not only nicotine, tar, and satisfying flavor, but also some of the essence of Musial, Williams, and DiMaggio. Only Stan Musial could be Stan Musial, but any man could become a baseball man simply by smoking Chesterfields.

"How R'ya Fixed for Blades?"

At the conclusion of the 1947 baseball season, curious viewers within telecast range witnessed the first commercially televised World Series, a seven-game contest between the Dodgers and the Yankees. Though it was an all–New York affair, the Series drew the largest out-of-park audience in the championship's history. Of course, most fans enjoyed the games as they had for more than a decade, on the radio, with broadcasts within reach of a vast majority of America's homes. In fact, thirty million out of a little more than thirty-three million households were within radio earshot of the Series. Nevertheless, television audiences were impressive, given the limited scope of the new medium.[54] As J. R. Poppele, president of the Television Broadcasters Association, observed before the first pitch, "Now, with over 50,000 television receivers distributed in homes and public places throughout the metropolitan New York, New Jersey, southern Connecticut, the Albany-Troy-Schenectady area, Philadelphia, Baltimore, and Washington, it is quite likely that 600,000 to 700,000 will see the Yankee-Dodger games."[55] To say that Poppele underestimated the audience size is itself a huge understatement. According to a *Hooper-Billboard* survey of World Series viewers, approximately 3,962,336 people watched at least a part of the Series over the course of seven games—3,514,749 in bars and 447,587 on home receivers.[56]

From the standpoint of sheer numbers alone, the televised World Series was a success. The winners, along with the victorious Yankees and the bars and taverns that saw their patronage grow as much as

500 percent around game time, were the sponsors.[57] Advertisers were well aware of this, and they positioned themselves to associate their brands with baseball's premier showcase. A World Series radio sponsor since 1939, Gillette was deemed to have a "moral prior right" to sponsor the telecasts and so got first dibs. After a great deal of wrangling with MLB commissioner Happy Chandler, who rejected Liebmann Breweries' offer of $100,000 for Rheingold sponsorship because beer simply did not fit the World Series brand, Ford signed on along with Gillette.[58] For their advertising dollars, Ford's sponsor identification rate measured at 69.6 percent, while Gillette's stood at 61.6.[59] But that was not all. According to *Billboard*, "The commercial value Ford and Gillette got for the $65,000 they laid on the line for the Series telecast rights can hardly be estimated by the sponsorship identification figures alone. Both firms got countless thousands of lines of valuable publicity in newspapers and magazines as a result of bankrolling the blue ribbon ball games."[60]

All that publicity and the opportunity to cement the connection between baseball and safety razors was enough to induce Gillette to pay $175,000 to secure sole sponsorship of the 1948 Series.[61] Proof of the lure of televised baseball to advertisers, in 1950 Gillette paid the astronomically high amount of $7.37 million for combined radio and television rights for sponsorship of the World Series and the MLB All-Star Game for the next six years.[62] Six million of that, a flat million annually, went to television sponsorship alone.[63] For its money, the company received what would be considered a paltry amount of commercial air time by twenty-first-century standards. Still, the limited advertising minutes were vital from both a sales and branding viewpoint. During the 1952 Fall Classic, Gillette extended its "Look sharp, feel sharp, be sharp" campaign to include an advertising icon that helped define the company's brand image for more than a decade.

Beginning in 1952 Gillette's World Series commercials featured Sharpie the Parrot, a singing, animated bird. In his first appearance, Sharpie was accompanied by a parrot buddy, a mustachioed gentleman with an English accent of sorts, a room full of singing animal trophy heads, and a very animated bearskin rug. During the forty-five-second spot, the cartoon choir sang, "Listen, Mister! How are you fixed for blades? Do you have plenty? How are you fixed for blades?" with a rousing solo from the moose head hanging on the wall. Sharpie's own solo, a reprise of the chorus, was vocally rendered as "How r'ya fixed for blades?" delivered with an Irish brogue, perhaps in response to the gentleman's "King's English." Sharpie's message is reinforced by a winking elephant-head trophy.[64] The final twenty seconds of the spot feature the very recognizable voice of Series television announcer Mel Allen, connecting the commercial to the game. Gillette Sharpie television spots in later Series underscored the connection between the brand and the game more clearly than this early attempt. For example, between innings of Game Five of the 1956 World Series—a game not especially remembered for its singing parrot commercials—Sharpie is animated as a white line drawing, waving semaphore flags and powering a sailboat, superimposed on the field of play between innings. Nevertheless, Sharpie's connection to the game was tenuous at best, given Gillette's investment in branding the product with World Series sponsorship.

In addition to the Sharpie spots, the company aired a series of endorsement ads. One in particular, which premiered in 1956, seems at first glance to be little more than a conventional baseball product endorsement. In it Brooklyn Dodger Pee Wee Reese, who "has a way with Dodger Rookies and Sandlot youngsters," is "interviewed" about his work in youth baseball. Reese's wisdom is clear—he advises developing players to shave exclusively with Gillette razors, because "a boy has more respect when he's clean shaved." And lest any boy or man irritate his skin while aiming for his due respect, Reese informs viewers, Gillette produces a blade for every type of beard, each demonstrated by one of Reese's teammates. Reese himself, the team heavyweight in the respect department, demonstrates the razor for heavy beards, average player Don Zimmer demonstrates the blade for average beards, while the light blade is demonstrated by catcher Roy Campanella.[65]

This, in itself, seems unremarkable, except for the unmistakable fact that Campanella is clearly a player of color. Of course, Campanella was already a fixture in televised baseball in 1956, having appeared in four World Series by the time the commercial aired. But while African American players were clearly visible in the game, they had yet to become major players in the TV endorsement game. Shortly thereafter, Willie Mays joined Gillette's stable of baseball-playing endorsers, visibly increasing Gillette's African American star power. In this regard, the razor manufacturer's World Series sponsorship was groundbreaking, Sharpie the Parrot notwithstanding. More importantly for the company, Gillette's sports advertising, including its boxing-centered weekly *Cavalcade of Sports*, served the company well. By 1960 Gillette controlled approximately 60 percent of the men's grooming-product market.[66]

Like Chesterfield and many other TV and radio advertisers, Gillette also invested heavily in print. The company's synergistic advertising extended to a series of comic-strip ads first appearing in 1948. Connected specifically to the *Cavalcade of Sports* rather than the World Series, the ads featured profiles of athletes, baseball players among them. Most often reproduced in two colors, black and red, and very occasionally in four, the ads appeared on Sunday funny pages and in mass-circulation magazines like *Life*, *Look*, and the *Saturday Evening Post*. In the April 21, 1952, edition of *Life*, for example, a Gillette *Cavalcade* ad profiles Gus Zernial, the Philadelphia Athletics' power-hitting left fielder. With three illustrations of Zernial, one connecting with a ball, another writing in a pamphlet entitled "Major League Records," and the third, presumably off the field, dressed in a jacket and tie, the enthusiastic ad copy serves to acquaint consumers with Zernial's amazing exploits, punctuated with exclamation points galore.[67]

The Zernial *Cavalcade* ad shares an aesthetic with all the others in the series, of which there were many. Every ad is similar, both in terms of graphics and copy. In this regard, the print campaign was successful in supporting the brand image of the product as the razor of athletes and sports fans. The campaign, however, lacked completely in originality. In fact, the comic-strip-style art work, the layout, and the hand-lettered copy closely imitated the visual style of *Ripley's Believe It or Not!* cartoons. The resemblance to *Ripley's Believe It or Not!* might have been problematic had Gillette not already been so closely associated with baseball and other sports. That there was no confusion is testament to the success of Gillette's overall advertising strategy.

"I Love Mickey!"

When in 1947 *Printer's Ink* opined that the rapid spread of commercial television was all but inevitable, the advertising trade magazine was on to something.[68] According to Walker and Bellamy, "No media technology to date, including the Internet, has diffused as rapidly as television. From a near zero base in 1946, television was in over 87 percent of U.S. households by 1960. Not surprisingly, this unprecedented acceptance by the public triggered great concern in existing media industries (radio, motion pictures, and newspapers). It also troubled industries such as professional sports, which were just now coming to terms with radio, about which baseball ownership was still highly skeptical because of its possible impact of 'giving away' product."[69]

But while baseball had a fraught relationship with the new medium, advertising had no such concerns. As fans of *Mad Men* know, the late 1950s represented a period of unprecedented growth and creativity in the advertising industry. Some of the best and most enduring advertising of the period moved away from selling products by means of extolling their benefits and embraced the idea of selling images. Nevertheless conventional product endorsements remained a mainstay of the industry. And baseball provided a ready source of celebrities who were increasingly familiar to consumers accustomed to seeing them play on the small screen. The visual presence of players in consumers' homes day after day created a perceived personal relationship, and hence, a sense of trust, in ways in which earlier media simply could not. Even radio did not produce the same kind of perceived intimacy.

Not surprisingly, one of baseball's top endorsers during the late 1950s and into the '60s was the Yankees' golden boy, Mickey Mantle. In terms of endorsement potential, Mantle was the complete package. He was one of the premiere players of his era, winning three Most Valuable Player Awards, two batting titles, and in 1956, baseball's Triple Crown, when he led the American League not only in average but also in home runs and runs batted in. Certainly, there were other great players among Mantle's contemporaries, but their advertising presence did not measure up to Mantle's. He was, after all, also graced with both wholesome, All-American good looks and likability. Mantle endorsed a plethora of products both during and after his career. Like so many other players of the period, he endorsed cigarettes and beer, Camels and Ballantine, respectively. He endorsed sporting goods and menswear, and he endorsed tires, including, but not limited to, those produced by his own celebrity-branded Mickey Mantle Tire Company. And he endorsed breakfast foods, lots and lots of breakfast foods. Mantle lent his stamp of approval to Post Alpha-Bits, Florida Citrus Frozen Orange Juice, and Karo Syrup (for extra pep on pancakes). Perhaps most famously, Mantle, with his bat perched jauntily on his shoulder, whined into the camera, "I want my Maypo!" in imitation of cereal manufacturer Heubline's animated advertising icon Marky Maypo, the delightful tyke who whined the company's slogan in support of maple-flavored oatmeal from televisions across America beginning in 1956.[70]

Mantle's Maypo endorsement, along with promoting the brand, also demonstrated that the player had a sense of humor about his image. But this feature of his celebrity brand did not always transfer well in commercials. Although he retired in 1968, Mantle remained in the public eye via his commercial activity. In one television spot, Mantle was joined by fellow advertising ace Willie Mays, the first real African American endorsement superstar to truly cross the color line, accompanied by television stars Jamie Farr of *M*A*S*H* and Georgia Engle of *The Mary Tyler Moore Show* in what might best be described as the most bizarre athlete endorsement ad of the era, a commercial for Blue Bonnet margarine. In it, Farr and Engle appear as the characters who made them famous—Maxwell Klinger, the cross-dressing corporal, and Georgette Franklin, the ditzy partner of bombastic news anchor

Ted Baxter—praising the product. A single commercial featuring two oddly juxtaposed sitcom stars was perhaps a bit unusual. But the thirty-second spot becomes downright absurd as the camera turns to Mantle and Mays, dressed in identical red polo shirts and blue prairie bonnets, both trimmed with white lace, poised to tuck into two identical meals of steak, corn, and beer. Lifting the impressively sized ears of corn, they sing the product's jingle, "Everything's better with Blue Bonnet on it," in unison.[71]

According to Gay Sands Miller, writing in the *Wall Street Journal*, the Blue Bonnet ad, especially the segment with Mays and Mantle, targeted a new demographic for food products. In a cultural shift that found an increasing number of men both in the supermarket and the kitchen, the result of both the soaring divorce rate and the tendency of couples to share household chores as women took their rightful places in the workforce, grocery advertisers set their sights on male shoppers. Miller observes, "Inspiring male brand loyalty isn't easy. 'Men are less imaginative, less giving of themselves to a commercial,' says Bernard Owett, an executive of the J. Walter Thompson ad agency. Women, he continues, are easier to manipulate with 'fantasy and romance.'" In order to capture the new male market, advertisers tried a number of different strategies. Various manufacturers relied upon explicit names for their products, such as Hungry Man frozen dinners and Manhandlers soups. Conventional athlete endorsements also appealed to male consumers. Writes Miller, "Blue Bonnet margarine resorts to outright silliness, putting frilly women's bonnets on the heads of Mickey Mantle and Willie Mays. 'The oddness of men wearing bonnets makes the ads more memorable,' says David Graham, a Standard Brands Inc. marketing vice president."[72]

The image of Mantle and Mays, two exemplars of American masculinity, in bonnets is more than just odd. By 1980 there was nothing unusual about African American baseball players endorsing products alongside white players, or for Mantle to be connected with Mays, since both had been superstar outfielders for New York City teams and were constantly compared to one another, both by fans and the sports media. And, as the Maypo endorsement demonstrated, Mantle was no stranger to self-mockery. But the Blue Bonnet message goes well beyond silliness and self-deprecating humor, given the roles of Farr and Engle in the same ad. Farr, in character, is a cross-dresser. Though Farr's Corporal Klinger is aggressively straight, his comfort in women's clothing, originally donned as a strategy to secure a discharge from the army, is clear. Indeed, what makes Klinger funny is the very contrast between Farr's masculine hairiness and love of cigars, the Toledo Mud Hens, and the ladies, with his feminine wardrobe. Engle's Georgette is the very embodiment of femininity of a specific type. While decidedly not a sexpot, she is pretty, scatterbrained, and blonde. With her small high voice, she was infantilized both on *The Mary Tyler Moore* show and in the ad.

Following Farr and Engle in the spot, Mantle and Mays, men whose livelihoods once depended upon displays of masculine athleticism, are divested of their masculine qualities. The fact that they are depicted enjoying their margarine with big steaks, big steins of beer, and big ears of corn undercuts the ad's emasculating effect, however slightly. But the spot manages to rob Mays and Mantle of the very characteristic that made them great. On the surface, the ad seems to suggest that if the great Mays and Mantle are so excited about Blue Bonnet that they can sacrifice their masculinity to sing its praises while wearing prairie bonnets, then male consumers ought to be excited too. But the subtext is different. It implies that men's new domestic roles are, in fact, emasculating, reducing them to wearing bonnets and singing the praises of imitation butter, where they were once warriors like their former baseball idols.

"Who Knows More about Cats Than Puss 'n Boots?"

Blue Bonnet notwithstanding, Mickey Mantle was the shining example of All-American manhood, baseball edition, in the 1950s and '60s. As a product endorser, he transferred the meanings of strength, power, good looks, and devil-may-care attitude to consumers through the products he endorsed. As an idol of millions of children, he boldly sold untold boxes of breakfast cereal. He was, however, eclipsed as an endorser by his teammate Yogi Berra. It is not that Berra necessarily endorsed more products than Mantle, though he did, or that he was more visible. But as the postwar era advanced, Berra represented a new type of baseball celebrity, one whose brilliance lay in his imperfection. Advertisers harnessed that imperfection to create an entirely different type of idol, expressing an entirely different image of American masculinity.

In contrast to Mantle, whose well-documented battle with alcoholism ended with his death from liver cancer in 1995, and whose endorsement activities prior to his death were limited to paid public appearances on talk shows singing the praises of Voltaren, an arthritis drug, Yogi Berra enjoyed an unprecedented, unbroken streak in the public eye.[73] Known in the twenty-first-century first and foremost for his malaprops, his "Yogi-isms," some of which read like Zen koans, he was one of the greatest hitting catchers in the history of the game. When he could no longer catch, he moved to the outfield. As a result of his stellar play, he was the first to be named Most Valuable Player at two different positions. That Berra blossomed as a pitchman between the early 1950s and 1970s was no accident. Unlike many of the other players who dominated the baseball advertising game, the ethnically identifiable, physically awkward-looking Berra appealed to his fans specifically because he was ethnic and looked awkward.[74] Before Berra, Joe DiMaggio helped to reconstruct the Italian-American image with his perceived elegance and savoir faire during and after the war years. Berra, however, was cut from a different cloth.

Neither suave nor handsome like DiMaggio, the homely Berra, whose appearance belied his athleticism, resembled his fans. Playing on a team that included DiMaggio and Mantle, Berra stood in contrast to them as baseball's everyman. He was, in a sense, a living embodiment of the American Dream. If he could succeed as a professional athlete, or so it seemed, so could anyone. If Mantle, with his golden hair and winning smile, scored high on the likability scale, Berra broke it. In 1957 Berra, like Mantle before him, teamed with sportscaster Budd Palmer to pitch Frozen Florida Orange Juice. In an unusually long spot, clocking in at one minute, twenty-eight seconds, Berra hits a home run, and meets up with Palmer in the clubhouse. Wondering how Palmer magically knows the player wants a glass of orange juice, Berra learns that his "Body Wisdom" is telling him he needs to replenish his energy and vitamin C. Just in case consumers haven't gotten the message, the words "Body Wisdom" in large type are superimposed over Berra's now-wise lower body.

While most product endorsers tell consumers precisely what they need to buy, and perhaps why, Berra cedes the power of testimonial to Palmer. Berra doesn't necessarily know why he needs orange juice. But he is an athlete and his imperfect body is wise, even if he doesn't know it. Berra's Body Wisdom is, of course, underscored by his verbal wisdom. He does not recognize the import of the philosophical gems that come from his mouth, he just says them. In this regard, Berra is both ordinary, like his fans, and the possessor of mystical wisdom. Fortunately, they, too, can access it via a glass of reconstituted orange juice from Florida.

A testament to Berra's popularity and likability, in 1958 Hanna Barbera animation studios introduced a character named for the Yankee catcher, Yogi Bear. Although Yogi Bear was only tangentially related to Berra, most notably by the wise words that made the cartoon character "smarter than the average bear," the emergence of Yogi Bear helped reinforce Berra's lock on the memory channel, that elusive quality that keeps celebrity names in the public eye and the public memory, increasing their value as endorsers.[75] More importantly, while Berra's stellar ball playing coupled with his regular endorsement activity ensured that his name would be locked in the consumer consciousness of his fan base, the cartoon character introduced the Yankee catcher to a whole new audience— small children who were too young to appreciate baseball, but old enough to influence the buying patterns of their parents.

Berra, like his contemporaries, began his advertising career when the celebrity industry was not yet controlled by agents, lawyers, and public relations firms. Of course, there were exceptions. Babe Ruth, way ahead of his time in terms of managing his image, employed Christy Walsh as his own personal ghostwriter, publicity agent, and business manager. Walsh's ghostwriting syndicate also handled the journalistic needs of many of Ruth's contemporaries. But two years into Berra's playing career, the celebrity industry changed in ways even Walsh could not have foreseen. As the result of a serendipitous exchange between Berra, his wife, Carmen, and recently fired Yankees road secretary Frank Scott, involving a drawer full of gold watches given to Berra in lieu of payment for personal appearances and commercial work, Berra became the one of the first baseball players, one of the first professional athletes, to employ an agent. Scott saw a potential gold mine in product endorsements for his client, not to mention healthy commissions for himself. In fact, he also went on to represent Mantle, Mays, Roger Maris, and Jackie Robinson, among others. When Berra hired Scott to represent him, the business of professional baseball was fundamentally altered. The age of player agents and professional handlers, specialists in their fields rather than generalized accountants or business managers, had arrived. No longer did players have to create their own images. They hired others to do it for them.

Berra had an easier job when it came to image construction than some of his contemporaries, professional assistance notwithstanding. Unlike Mantle and Mays, whose turn as Blue Bonnet pitchmen, albeit after their playing careers were over, was definitely off-message, Berra's goofy-yet-wise everyman image lent itself to creative endorsement advertising. While baseball-related advertising and ballplayer endorsements continued to be a television mainstay, they remained, for the most part, conservative. Mickey Mantle pitching Alpha-Bits to children as a way to start their days was no doubt effective, and the concept behind it was tried and true. As advertising narrative, it continued in a tradition that stretched back to Lou Gehrig speaking the praises of Huskies on *Ripley's Believe It or Not!* radio broadcasts. Yet, at the same time, advertising was moving in a new direction. Madison Avenue was in the midst of what became known as a "creative revolution." Among the qualities that characterized new advertising trends were gentleness, humor, credibility, candor, and a willingness to treat consumers as equals. In this respect, the new direction ran counter to the traditional advertising wisdom that still dominated the mainstream.[76] And no baseball player more closely embodied the spirit of the creative revolution than Berra.

George Lois was a founding partner of Papert, Koenig, Lois, one of Madison Avenue's first boutique agencies. The hallmark of his work was offbeat humor. Among his early ads was a 1955 print promotion for American Airlines. It asked the question, "Thinking of going to Los Angeles?" The copy was simple and fairly generic, but it was the artwork that told the story. The ad featured an unnamed Brooklyn Dodger—Lois himself, unable to get any of the players to pose for the ad—hiding behind a headline reading "Fly American Airlines Aircoach." The Dodger player furtively peers to his left. Appearing two years before the team's departure, the ad addressed persistent rumors that Brooklyn's pride and joy were planning to follow Horace Greeley's well-worn admonition to go west and grow up with the country, using humor, honesty, and a willingness to approach what to many was an unapproachable topic, to sell the product.[77] Lois, who was responsible for Mantle's turn as whining Maypo pitchman in 1967, clearly understood Berra's appeal when he cast him in a Puss 'n Boots cat food commercial, the adman's first foray into celebrity advertising. Describing the spot, Lois writes:

> In 1962, Yankee catching great Yogi Berra, a pussycat of a man, starred in a beautifully photographed TV spot talking to a cat doing fantastic exercises on a trampoline, to show how fit he was. Then, shot from behind, the cat talked up a blue streak, bobbing and weaving, as the Yog listed patiently. *I work out every day. Gym, roadwork, you know.* When Yogi questions the source of the cat's energy, he gets a tome from the cat on Puss 'n Boots, winding up with *Yogi, I was once a five-pound weakling. Then I started eating Puss 'n Boots. Now look at me!*—followed by a Yogi punch line: *Who knows more about cats than Puss 'n Boots?!* The charming juxtaposition of the bearish Yogi Berra engaged in a dialogue with a pussycat was a visual tour de force as the cat's verbal wisdom convinced viewers that a real discussion was taking place.

9. Yogi Berra costarred with a cat who sounded remarkably like pitcher Whitey Ford in a 1962 spot for Puss 'n Boots cat food. Jeff Kaplan, Retro Brands USA, LLC.

Making this an all-baseball affair, the cat's thick Long Island accent was provided by Yankee-pitcher-turned-voice-over-artist Whitey Ford.[78]

Oddly, given the success of the finished commercial, Quaker Oats, Puss 'n Boots' former parent company, was not initially entranced with the concept of having a baseball player pitch its cat food. Despite the growing number of men engaged in grocery shopping, women purchased most of the country's cat food. To allay the manufacturers' fears, Lois conducted some market research. Of the 200 women he surveyed, 182 were familiar with Berra.[79] Berra transferred his likeability and his gentle sense of humor to Puss 'n Boots. At the same time, the ad helped cement Berra's image as everyman, willing to cede his expertise on things athletic to a cat in the same way he had ceded it to Budd Palmer in support of frozen orange juice earlier in his endorsement career.

Among other positive qualities that made him a perfect endorser for the creative revolution was Berra's perceived integrity. In 1955 Berra began a long relationship, really a love affair, with Yoo-hoo chocolate drink. His rationale for staking his claim with the New Jersey soft-drink company was influenced by a personal decision—he liked it. He was also the perfect endorser for the beverage. As the very slogan he made famous, "Mee-hee for You-hoo," indicated, the product was meant to be fun. Its success, like that of so many soft drinks and junk foods sold in the 1950s, '60s, and '70s, was predicated on the increase of disposable income among the youngest of Americans. The goofy but trustworthy Berra, a fan favorite with the young target market, familiar not only with Berra but with his cartoon namesake, made him the perfect pitchman. For Berra, pitching Yoo-hoo was a labor love. He knew the family that manufactured the product, and he did all he could to spread its gospel, enlisting teammates to join him in the venture. Because he believed in Yoo-hoo, he invested heavily in the company. According to Richard Sandomir, "In an era before athletes earned megabucks off the field, Yogi's Yoo-hoo endorsement was a big deal."[80] As Jim Bouton notes, "Yogi and Yoo-hoo just seemed to make sense."[81]

While the concept of truth in advertising had been around for decades and had been on the books as law since 1930, regulations were, at best, ignored.[82] All this changed in 1961, when the FTC cracked down on ads that made false claims. Even Mantle ran afoul of the FTC for endorsing a brand of milk he did not drink.[83] But Berra had no such problems. Although very early in his career, Berra, not a fisherman, endorsed Doodle Fish Oil, a product presumably intended to aid fishermen using lures known as doodles, by the time he endorsed Yoo-hoo, he adhered closely to the letter of the endorsement law. As such, it is hardly surprising that when Yoo-hoo fell into corporate hands in the mid-1970s, changing the formula to make it more cost-effective to produce, Berra sold his stock and severed the relationship. It is not that he did not approve of corporate ownership, it is just that Yoo-hoo no longer tasted good.[84] For Berra, there was no disconnect between perception and reality, as his experience with Yoo-hoo demonstrates.

In the world of celebrity endorsements, the match between athlete and product is critical.[85] Berra, however, could probably have endorsed anything, as evidenced by a pitch for Ozone hair spray in which he appeared with his wife, or his testimonial in favor of Jockey underwear. Over the course of his long career, he endorsed a long list of beers. Among his most notable beer commercials was his turn in Miller Lite's "Everything You Always Wanted in a Beer and Less" campaign. This landmark campaign effectively rebranded a low-calorie, low-alcohol beer originally produced with women in mind as the quaff of macho athletes by pitting mismatched pairs together in a barroom setting to argue whether the product tasted great or was less filling. The answer, of course, was both. In his version of the "Tastes Great, Less Filling" debate—one that in other TV spots also embroiled Mantle and Mays as well as sometime adversaries George Steinbrenner and Billy Martin, and star pitchman Bob Uecker, who shared many of Berra's everyman qualities—Berra essentially argues with himself, speaking in Yogiisms. Berra also parlayed his reputation for goofy but ultimately wise sayings into a Stroh's beer endorsement. In his Stroh's commercials, Berra enlightened his television viewers with two-minute movie reviews, also replete with his own unmistakable logic.

Testament to his appeal as an endorser, Berra continued to make television ads into the twenty-first century. He appeared in a Visa spot along with NBA superstar Yao Ming. He shared the spotlight with a computer-generated duck in a commercial for AFLAC disability insurance. And in the wake of the September 11, 2001, World Trade Center attack, he convinced tourists that New York City was still the place to visit as part of the "New York Miracle" campaign. "New York Miracle," which depicts iconic New Yorkers in incongruous, even miraculous situations—Berra conducts the New York Philharmonic in his spot—represented an attempt to tap into what advertisers wished to convey as the city's indomitable spirit. When choosing a spokesman, Batten, Barton, Durstein, and Osborne, the agency that handled the account, sought to select a celebrity whose meanings included integrity, grit, resilience, and humor, and who was anything but an elitist, as these were the qualities with which they wished to imbue their product. Since the product was New York City, it was all the more important that the right choice of celebrity be made. Commenting on the campaign, agency partner John Osborn observed that not only did Americans identify Yogi Berra with baseball and with homespun wisdom, but they also identified him with New York in the most positive way. "Quite simply put," observes Osborne, "People love Yogi."[86] Indeed, Berra remained a constant on the endorsement scene until just a few years before his death in 2015.

Baseball, Hot Dogs, Apple Pie, and Chevrolet

In a sense, Yogi Berra's everyman endorsements served as baseball's version of Volkswagen's groundbreaking "Think Small" print ad, one of the hallmark ads of the creative revolution. Of it, graphic design writer Joshua Johnson asks, "How did a funny-looking car that was named after a bug, known for being slow and manufactured in factories built by Nazis, ever become iconic to a generation of postwar Americans? Great design and fantastic marketing."[87] The 1959 black-and-white ad depicted a tiny image of the car in the upper left-hand quadrant of blank, white space. Below, under the caption, "Think Small," the copy, like the image, ran counter to conventional automobile advertising. Rather than singing the praises of speed and power, "Think Small" praised the product's practicality. The first car ad to take economy and gas mileage into account, it noted in prosaic language the vehicle's "aluminum air-cooled rear engine that would go 70 miles an hour all day without strain, sensible size for a family and a sensible price-tag, too." It ended with the tagline, "Beetles multiply; so do Volkswagens."[88]

Above all, what appealed to a new segment of the postwar, automobile-buying public, including the nascent counterculture, was the ad's honesty. Never before had an automobile ad called its product a "strange little car." Never before had an automobile ad used the word "sensible" repeatedly. Berra was, in his own way, very much like the ad's Volkswagen. In comparison to the era's baseball gods, he was small and fairly strange looking for an elite athlete. Yet like the Beetle, he could play all day and do it well. Above all, he seemed to be innately sensible, even when conversing with a talking cat that sounded just like Whitey Ford.

Of course, in order for advertising's creative revolution to exist, there had to be a mainstream culture against which it rebelled. According to Ron Briley, "The late 1960s and early 1970s were a time of upheaval and confusion in American society and the sport of baseball. Traditional values were under assault as 'pop' philosophers such as Harvard's Charles Reich proclaimed *The Greening of America* and the emergence of a counterculture based upon a new 'consciousness.' The post–World War II consensus of sustained economic growth, moderation, and anticommunism were openly challenged in the streets, university, and homes of America."[89] In baseball, the 1970s—a decade bracketed by Dock Ellis's LSD-fueled no-hitter and Mike Veeck's ill-conceived Disco Demolition promotion—witnessed continued team relocation, the aftereffects of expansion, the introduction of free agency, and the ascendancy of owners Charlie Finlay and George Steinbrenner, both of whom challenged the status quo, though in very different ways.

By the end of the 1970s, the U.S. auto industry would also be in a state of upheaval. In fact, it was in serious trouble, fueled by a series of energy crises and the refusal of the Big Three automakers—Ford, General Motors, and Chrysler—to explore new gas-efficient technologies. These factors, combined with the availability of new, fuel-efficient imports, Volkswagen not least among them, spelled potential disaster for this mainstay of the American industrial economy. In addition to the pressures of the Arab Oil embargo of 1973–74 and the availability of new imports, General Motor and Ford were faced with a crisis in consumer trust in the aftermath of the publication of Ralph Nader's *Unsafe at Any Speed* in 1966. Among the models cited by Nader were Chevrolet's Nova, Camaro, and V–8 trucks, all of which were subject to massive recalls. Other than the legendarily problematic Ford Pinto, perhaps the worst model of them all was the Chevy Corvair, which had a tendency to flip over and was implicated in a number of fatal crashes. Despite all the upheaval in their respective industries and in American life in general, professional baseball and U.S. automobile manufacturers held on to the traditional Americana image with all their might, if only by their fingernails. This stubborn, inherent conservatism was reflected in General Motors' "Baseball, hotdogs, apple pie, and Chevrolet" mid-decade advertising campaign.

"'Baseball, hot dogs, apple pie, and Chevrolet' was a jingle heard frequently throughout the country during 1975 and 1976," enthused Beverly Rae Kimes and Robert C. Ackerson in an *Automobile Quarterly* publication. "Chevrolet's campaign served to remind the car-conscious consumer that Chevrolet was really very close to the pulse of America's heart. Of course, as with any really successful advertisement, it was based on the truth."[90] Perhaps this was true in 1952, when newly nominated Secretary of Defense Charles "Engine Charlie" Wilson, General Motors president, told the Senate, "What is good for our country is good for General Motors, and vice versa," famously misquoted as "What's good for General Motors is good for America."[91] It was not, however, true in 1975. Still, Americana was in vogue in 1975, just a year ahead of the nation's bicentennial celebration. "Baseball, hotdogs, apple pie, and Chevrolet" represented an attempt to harness that temporary outbreak of national pride in the midst of social, cultural, and commercial turmoil by uniting the national pastime, the established signifier of Americanism, with the wholesome Americanism of a thoroughly American product. And the connection was made on that most American of media—television.

The first one-minute spot in a series of TV commercials features Ed Labunski, the jingle writer doubling as a country singer, sitting at a honky-tonk piano incongruously placed in the middle of a field.[92] He begins with a call-and-response, asking his audience, "America," "What's your favorite sport? . . . What's your favorite sandwich? . . . Pie? . . . And what's your favorite car, America?" The answers are as expected. His call-and-response is accompanied by a montage of images including the Statue of Liberty, Golden Gate Bridge, the Empire State Building, and a multiracial group of children sitting on a stoop, leading the enthusiastic Labunski to exclaim in his good ole boy accent, "You sure look like America to me." On cue, an "American" chorus breaks into the upbeat jingle, singing, "We love baseball, hotdogs, apple pie, and Chevrolet," repeatedly. Throughout, the montage continues, this time with the screen divided into four. Every image screams "America." Most of them depict "true Americans" frolicking in and around Chevrolet vehicles. The spot ends as Labunski reminds the folks at home that the commercial has been "brought to [them] by baseball, hotdogs, apple pie, and Chevrolet," though it seems unlikely that either the game or foodstuff were responsible for the ad.[93]

This commercial and others in the campaign, including one that featured a prologue declaring in no uncertain terms that while America has changed, the four things that America loves have stayed the same. In the later ad, the line "They go together in the good old USA" helps fuel the connection between the car and Americana. In an attempt to buck the cultural trend, the campaign seeks to define America in nostalgic terms that include America's game, not as played by free agents and mustachioed stars, but by blond children in fields. The ad, however, manages to nod to the counterculture, if ham-handedly. In both versions, Labunski sports long hair and a flannel shirt, a sure sign that the product embraces both the idea of "country" and the counterculture aesthetic. Moreover, the montage focuses on pictures of young people, including more than a few beautiful blond women in cutoff shorts. In this way, it tries to add youth and beauty to the list of extrinsic American qualities with which it attempts to brand Chevrolet.

Referring specifically to the words of the jingle, Kirsten Silva Gruesz notes that it serves as an attempt to define the very term *America*. She writes, "Foodways, cultural practices, and even consumer products are readily made to symbolize the nation's essence ('baseball, hot dogs, apple pie, and Chevrolet,' as a highly effective advertising campaign put it in the 1970s). Such metonyms gesture, in turn, at more abstract notions: Freedom, Liberty, Democracy."[94] The ad attempts to imbue the product with these American qualities. It seems to suggest that by driving a Chevrolet, consumers drive America—a potent message in the face of the rising popularity and rising sales of import vehicles. While the campaign was, in fact, effective from the point of view of its long-standing place in the American memory channel, it does not seem to have had a positive impact on Chevy sales. In 1962 Chevrolet controlled 30.8 percent of the U.S. market share in automobiles, a high-water mark for the decade, but by the end of the 1970s, it was down to 23.3 percent, a substantial drop for a company that had once sold nearly a third of all cars in America.[95]

While the campaign did not appreciably increase sales, its message retained its potency, so much so that it was revived in 2006. Suitably updated for the times, twenty-first-century American favorites included "free agents, rally monkeys, fantasy leagues, and Chevrolet," as well as "mascots, gourmet pretzels, retractable roofs, and Chevrolet," and "face painters, satellite radio, endorsement deals, and Chevrolet." The one-minute-long spot banks both on nostalgia for the past and enthusiasm for the twenty-first-century game. But the new Labunski, unlike the old, is willing to admit, "Apparently, baseball's changed over the years." But he'll never cede his position, qualifying his admission with "but not America's love of the game or our love for Chevy."[96] Baseball may no longer be America's most-watched televised spectator sport, though it is certainly healthy, and Chevrolet, though on the rebound, may control only 11 percent of the United States market share as of 2016.[97] But the mythmaking continues, whether on broadcast television, regional sports networks on cable, or in online viral videos. Chevrolet remains MLB's automotive sponsor.

Just Do It!

As the Chevrolet commercial rightly observes, baseball has changed over the years. But baseball-related television advertising has remained surprisingly stagnant as far as content is concerned. Certainly, the humor injected into baseball commercials during the creative revolution remains a feature of the advertising genre. Moreover, what is allowable in commercial speech has changed. But the basic message has remained the same. In a 1999 Nike commercial featuring Atlanta Braves pitchers Tom Glavine and Greg Maddux, for example, the players beef up and take round after round of batting practice with the hope of catching the attention of nighttime soap star Heather Locklear, because as the tagline preceding Nike's "Just Do It" slogan tells consumers, "Chicks dig the long ball." Regardless of its sexual innuendo, this spot relies upon many of the same meanings that made baseball a natural partner for advertising in the early days of television—hard work and perseverance combined with natural skill and talent. All of these can belong to Nike consumers. All they have to do is wear the right shoes, and "just do it."

But some change has occurred in baseball-related advertising, albeit at a slow pace. Cars, beer, sporting goods, and snack foods remain the mainstay of baseball-related television advertising—cigarette advertising having been banned from the airwaves in 1971—and celebrity endorsement deals have continued to proliferate. Added to these are pitches for new categories of products relying on the game for meaning, direct-to-consumer pharmaceutical advertising among them. The game, moreover, has produced a new class of celebrity endorsers who received no play in an earlier era, Afro-Latino players. New media outlets have also proliferated. With viral advertising videos, sponsors are no longer constrained to the thirty-second and one-minute formats associated with conventional television, leading to the creation of ads that are essentially minifilms. Nevertheless, all of these innovations owe a debt to the ticking clock, which, prior to the Dodgers game in 1941, told America that it ran on Bulova time.

CHAPTER SIX

"Let's Just Say It Works for Me"

*Major League Baseball, Viagra, and the Business of
Pharmaceutical Advertising*

S
ince their earliest days as profitable industries, advertising
and professional baseball have every so often partnered to
pitch products that do not necessarily fit. While the connection between the sport, its stars, and some consumer goods—
cigarettes, cigars, and other tobacco products, for example—have
been problematic, if not completely counterintuitive, none has
been so freighted as baseball's role in selling pharmaceuticals. Yet
from patent medicines and nostrums in the nineteenth century
to over-the-counter energy boosters in the age of performance-
enhancing drugs (PEDS), baseball and its players have actively
served as pushers for the pharmaceutical industry. So it should
have come as no surprise when Major League Baseball teamed up
with Pfizer pharmaceuticals to sell its new wonder drug, Viagra.
Nor should it have been shocking when one of the game's highest-
profile players, Rafael Palmeiro, signed on to pitch Pfizer's little
blue pills to baseball fans.

From 2002 until 2007, Viagra was an official and, as its ads would
have had us know, proud sponsor of Major League Baseball. For
five glorious seasons, MLB's ballparks featured prominent Viagra
advertising signage, most particularly behind home plate, providing a backdrop for televised action. As if that weren't enough to
remind armchair athletes that baseball was synonymous with Pfizer's product, Viagra branded "plays of the game" aired daily during
television and radio game broadcasts. MLB Advanced Media, the
league's new media promotional machine, publicized an online
sweepstakes tied to the 2003 All-Star Game. In 2005 MLB intro-

duced a new official award for Comeback Player of the Year (as opposed to the honor conferred by the *Sporting News* since 1965), bearing the name of Pfizer's magic pill and paid for by the pharmaceutical giant. And without a hint of irony, Viagra's Clutch Performances took its rightful place among the free fantasy baseball games featured on MLB.com.

So why was Pfizer so eager to link its blockbuster drug to Major League Baseball and its stars? What was it about professional baseball that made it such an excellent vehicle for Viagra promotion? To be fair, baseball wasn't the first sport to partner with Pfizer. A Viagra-sponsored NASCAR team was already circling America's tracks when the pharmaceutical giant made its mark on MLB. But given the demographics of baseball's television audience, MLB sponsorship seems to have been the logical next step. Although a much-publicized MLB multimarket study found that, in 2000, women preferred baseball to all other professional sports, according to a Gallup poll, the majority of baseball fans were, and continue to be, male.[1] And not only were they male, they were graying. The same poll indicated that during the height of Viagra's MLB sponsorship, between 2004 and 2005, baseball was most popular with men aged fifty and over.[2] So it made the utmost sense that Pfizer would eye MLB for a Viagra connection.[3] Despite the clear rationale, the deal raised eyebrows, as did thirty-eight-year-old Palmeiro's endorsement.

From Snake-Oil to Bitter Pills

Of course, Viagra was far from the first drug to advertise using baseball imagery, and Rafael Palmeiro was by no means the first baseball star to endorse a pharmaceutical product. After all, nineteenth-century advertisers sold American consumers a variety of patent nostrums with the help of testimonials from any number of celebrities. Celebrity patent-medicine endorsers were, for the most part, women, as were their target purchasers, but baseball stars were not unknown in the nostrum-pitching game. In the late nineteenth and early twentieth centuries, patent medicines like Dr. Barlow J. Smith's Caloric Vita Oil, endorsed by several entire team rosters, monopolized the advertising pages of many a newspaper and magazine. Patent medicines were categorically different from physician and pharmacist-administered cures. Drugs recommended and compounded by healthcare professionals—medicines considered "ethical" by the American Medical Association (AMA)—were listed in an official catalogue of standard drugs, the United States Pharmacopoeia (USP). Even USP-approved medications were not considered ethical unless they were administered according to preparation and dosing guidelines specified in the official catalogue. Ethical drugs were not advertised at all. In contrast, "unethical" drugs, patent compounds with secret ingredients that sometimes included ethical drugs like opium, morphine, and cocaine in unspecified, uncontrolled amounts, along with a lot of alcohol and colored water, most certainly were.[4]

With time and the enactment of the Pure Food and Drug Act of 1906, the unethical branch of the pharmaceutical industry came under serious scrutiny. The new law required that narcotics and alcohol had to be listed on the packaging, complete with specific dosing instructions. More importantly, the law made it illegal to deliberately make false or misleading claims on nostrum labels and in advertisements. Key to the regulation was the idea of intent. A patent-medicine manufacturer had to willfully make false claims—making them "accidentally" wasn't a problem. Much like twenty-first-century baseball players who continue to take performance-enhancing drugs despite the fact that they may very well test positive, the patent-medicine industry continued to sell dubious products in dubious ways, though on a much smaller scale than before the law's enactment. According to medical historian Julie Donohue, "It was difficult for the federal government to prove *intent* to defraud, and so the advertising provisions of the 1906 act had little effect on the behavior of the patent medicine industry."[5] Lax enforcement left the door open for the manufacturers of Nuxated Iron, Ty Cobb's patent performance-enhancing drug of choice, if his advertising testimonials were to be believed, and others like it to continue to appeal to American consumers. Nor did the new law prevent ads for impotence and venereal disease cures from dominating the pages of the *Sporting Life* and the *National Police Gazette*, both publications that counted a large proportion of predominately male baseball fans among their readerships.

But in 1938, under pressure from a newly energized consumerist movement, the Food, Drug, and Insecticide Administration, previously the Bureau of Chemistry (renamed the Food and Drug Administration in 1940), passed the Federal Food, Drug, and Cosmetic Act (FDCA), which required manufacturers to prove scientifically that drugs were both safe and efficacious. The government no longer had to demonstrate that medicine manufactures had specific, willful intent to defraud consumers; any potentially misleading claim, intentional or not, was forbidden.[6] Confusing matters somewhat, advertising was not regulated by the FDA or its predecessors. That was the job of the Federal Trade Commission (FTC), as specified in the Wheeler-Lea Amendment of 1938. Wheeler-Lea, according to the 1939 *Columbia Law Review*, represented "another attempt to curb the evils of false and misleading advertising."[7] Reinforcing restrictions imposed by the FDCA, the amendment made false advertising, specifically false advertising of food, drugs, medical devices, and cosmetics, a federal criminal offense.[8] Although ads for products like Blue-jay corn plasters and its ilk, which may have made slightly exaggerated claims but did no harm to consumers, persisted, the new law put an end to questionable large-scale, patent-medicine advertising in all but a few cases.[9] Of course small-print ads for liver purifiers, hemorrhoid cures, and the like continued to grace the back pages of sports publications and newspapers, but these virtually never included testimonials by athletes or other celebrities, instead relying upon a selection of dubiously credentialed "doctors."

Spelling Relief for the Pharmaceutical Industry

Between 1938 and the late 1970s, direct-to-consumer (DTC) prescription drug advertising of any kind was prohibited. It was legal to advertise over-the-counter (OTC) remedies, aspirin and the like, but ads for OTC drugs were subject to strict regulation. Making matters more complicated, there were no hard-and-fast rules as to which drugs were available over the counter or strictly by prescription. With very few exceptions, prior to the passage of the 1951 Durham Humphrey Amendment to the FDCA, it was left up to manufacturers to make the determination.[10] Once this amendment made it clear which drugs would be available without prescription and which wouldn't, OTC drug advertising moved to the fore, just in time to exploit the emerging new advertising medium, television. As had been true of patent-medicine advertising, subtlety was not a defining feature of OTC drug advertising. A landmark spot for Anacin, for example, featured the silhouetted head of a putative headache sufferer containing three boxes, the center one occupied by a pounding hammer. The takeaway was the simple but effective slogan, "fast, fast, fast relief." The Anacin ads, observed their creator Rosser Reeves of the Ted Bates agency, "were the most hated commercials in the history of advertising." They were, however, amazingly effective.[11] So, too, were ads for Rolaids antacid, also Reeves's work, which stressed the product's sponge-like absorbent properties, as illustrated by a screen full of animated amoebic blobs, theoretically soaking up "forty-seven times (their) weight in stomach acid." Both these ads used what Reeves called the "unique selling proposition" (USP), a single claim ostensibly unique to a given product, strong enough to cut through the advertising clutter.[12]

By 1983, when Los Angeles Dodgers manager Tommy Lasorda first pitched the product, the actual specifics of the claim had changed. In Lasorda's spot, the animated Rolaids amoebas were replaced by a round sponge echoing the antacid's shape, complete with its trademark R. In the commercial, a dramatization shows the sponge soaking up a noxious pinkish liquid, presumably stomach acid, from a petri dish, as a voice-over proclaims that a single tablet "consumes one hundred percent of the stomach acid required to give millions one hundred percent relief." The message is echoed by "100%," printed in large, black type at the bottom of the dish. Although "100%" seems like a bold claim, it is not. It is deliberately indeterminate; Rolaids absorbs exactly as much stomach acid as it needs to absorb, rather than a specific quantity. The move from specific to general no doubt reflected efforts by the FTC to enforce OTC advertising regulations. In order to be advertised at all, Rolaids' claim to soak up stomach acid had to be true. So quoting an unproven statistic might be interpreted as a fraudulent claim. Stomach acid quantities aside, the ad's USP remains the same—Rolaids work because they soak up stomach acid.

As the spot begins, Lasorda, known for his girth perhaps as much as his managing acumen, admits that he "doesn't always manage his stomach right." Following the sponge demonstration, Lasorda proclaims, "With that batting average, I spell relief R-O-L-A-I-D-S." In a close shot, Lasorda's actions echo his words—he inscribes the name of the remedy on a baseball as if signing an autograph. Here the baseball, both the source and symbol of Lasorda's power, is branded with the product name. In fact, Lasorda effectively transforms the ball into a Rolaids tablet by means of his inscription.[13] With the ad's emphasis on providing relief, Lasorda makes an ideal pitchman. After all, he has the authority to provide his team with the appropriate relief at the appropriate time. As such, Lasorda's superior knowledge regarding relief pitching effectively extends to other types of relief, most notably relief of his upset stomach. Just as a pitching change can save the day, so, too, can Rolaids.

The commercial link between baseball and pharmaceutical company Warner-Lambert's stomach remedy actually predates Lasorda's endorsement ads. From 1976 until 2014, Major League Baseball conferred the Rolaids Relief Man Award to the top relief pitchers in each league. Although this synergistic sponsorship deal did not conform to Reeves's USP principal—as it was extraneous to the advertising campaign's central message, adding to, rather than cutting through, the clutter—it served to cement connections between the drug, its slogan, and the idea of relief. Two commercials honoring 1983 Rolaids Relief Men Dan Quisenberry of the Kansas City Royals and Al Holland of the Philadelphia Phillies further reinforced the link, making even more explicit the connection between the product and relief pitching.

Ibuprofen, the commonly used nonsteroidal anti-inflammatory

drug also received the baseball treatment. It was approved for OTC sale in 1984, and with OTC approval, naturally, came advertising. First sold only under the brand name Advil, the original commercials stressed the drug's modernity, efficiency, and effectiveness, comparing it to aspirin and Tylenol. But in 1992, American Home Products (later Wyeth), Advil's manufacturer, went a step beyond emphasizing its product's strength and power by embodying it in the form of pitcher Nolan Ryan. Ryan sang Advil's praises in a thirty-second Super Bowl spot, the first of a series of Advil endorsement ads that ran throughout the 1990s and into the 2000s. The Super Bowl commercial, produced two seasons before Ryan's retirement, spotlights the pitcher in a no-frills gym, clad in a sweat-stained Texas Rangers T-shirt. In his thick South Texas accent, Ryan proclaims—almost complains—"If I want to keep playing baseball, I have to keep working. There is no off-season anymore, just a pile of iron, or a bike I ride forever." Once described by sports writer Ron Firmrite as "an uncommonly handsome young man with near-perfect features and a long, lean physique," who "would seem a natural for Western roles in Hollywood," Advil's Ryan is tired and visibly aging, with a receding hairline. He is no longer "no ordinary mortal . . . among the blessed, an exalted figure to be held in awe."[14] Rather, he is well past his prime, fighting to stay in the game, beset by aches and pains, ordinary, and mortal. But stay in the game he does—he takes Advil. "It's strong, it works, and I know it helps," he tells his audience with assurance and conviction. Ryan, who in his prime would hardly have been described as delicate, even extols Advil's gentleness on the stomach. Like the rest of us, the aged pitcher must take care. He concludes, "To last as long as I have, you've got to stick with what works."[15]

Certainly, the very fact that Nolan Ryan—who by 1992 had pitched seven no-hitters, the final one on May 1, 1991, just a few months before this ad aired—was already legendary is important here. Among the meanings he transfers to consumers by means of the product are strength, power, and the ability to throw "lightning, smoke, flames, heat, blue darters, dark ones, high hard ones, hummers, aspirin tablets," or Advil tablets, as the case may be.[16]

Even the most baseball-illiterate 1992 Super Bowl viewers would have recognized Ryan as "among the blessed." Yet he, too, is a tired, ordinary man fighting to keep his job. Like Advil's consumers, Ryan works hard. He feels pain. There is no magic to his longevity, just a magic pill that is strong, works, and helps. As such, the ad has a double message; it says, "Nolan Ryan is just like you. He works hard, he's aging, and he feels pain," at the same time that it says, "We, too, can be like Nolan Ryan. We, too, can be extraordinary, legendary, no ordinary mortals." In later Advil ads filmed after his retirement, Ryan seems less weary. But the message is consistent— Advil has the power to cure Ryan's pain; the consumer, too, may become powerful by taking Advil.

Had ibuprofen not been approved for OTC sale, Ryan's Advil spot would never have been made. Although initially there was no law limiting DTC prescription drug advertising, barring a few experiments, it simply was not done. Perhaps this is because in one case, the experiment went terribly wrong. In 1982 Eli Lilly aggressively marketed its arthritis medication Oraflex directly to consumers, issuing thousands of press kits, thereby assuring thousands of mentions in both print and electronic media. Demand was unprecedented. Despite knowledge that the drug had been implicated in a number of deaths during trials, Lilly's chairman and CEO decided to promote it anyway.[17] Ten weeks later, Oraflex was pulled from the market. As a direct result, the FDA placed a moratorium on DTC advertising. When the moratorium was lifted in 1985, it was replaced by strict regulations that prohibited the use of specific brand names in drug advertising.[18] Rather than abandon the idea of advertising altogether, the industry took two different tacks. In some cases, pharmaceutical manufacturers advertised certain drugs without mentioning their names. In others, they resorted to a type of stealth testimonial advertising, paying celebrities to publically laud branded drugs both on talk shows and during public appearances. Such was the case with Ciba-Geigy's antiarthritis drug Voltaren. To spread the word and to differentiate its product from any number of prescription anti-inflammatory medications, Ciba-Geigy hired Mickey Mantle. The fact that the oft-injured Mantle suffered from arthritis and had actually participated in clinical trials for the drug was unimportant. But the fact that viewers were not informed that Mantle was a paid endorser was. Mantle's Voltaren endorsement created something of a firestorm in the industry, and not just among regulators. Representatives of other drug companies expressed concern that the practice was unethical and would bring the wrath of the FDA down upon them.[19] As a result, Mantle's testimonials ended, but the practice did not.

There were, however, no restrictions on pharmaceutical marketing to the trade. In fact, from the 1950s on, drug companies spent millions of dollars both on advertising in medical journals and on promoting their wares directly to physicians. The numbers were startling. According to Donohue, "In 1958 the industry estimated that it had turned out 3,790,809,000 pages of paid advertising in medical journals, sent out 741,213,700 pieces of direct mail, and made up to 20 million calls by detail men [drug company sales representatives] to physicians and pharmacists."[20] These practices continued on into the 1990s, unabated.

You Gotta Have Heart

On December 31, 1998, Brian K. Jefferson, MD, of Johns Hopkins, unleashed his fury on the editors of the *New England Journal of Medicine* in a letter that reads:

> It is no secret that product endorsements provide a lucrative supplement to the day jobs of celebrities and athletes. Sports great Michael Jordan is the perfect example of this, making $47 million last year in endorsements alone. Another sports hero, Cal Ripken Jr., made $6.5 million in product endorsements last year. As a resident of Baltimore, I see the baseball great's face on everything from roller-coaster rides to milk cartons. But imagine my surprise when I opened up not *Sports Illustrated* but the *Journal* and saw a picture of Cal Ripken Jr. in a Prinivil (Lisinopril) baseball cap instead of his usual black and orange Orioles cap.

The letter continues, "I take issue with the Prinivil advertisement, however, for this reason: Cal Ripken Jr. does not have hypertension. The concept of a celebrity's endorsing a product for a medical condition he does not have or for a drug whose benefits and side effects he will never experience is, in my opinion, unethical."[21]

In its response to Dr. Jefferson's letter, physician Louis M. Sherwood, a spokesman for the drug's manufacturer Merck, offered an explanation for his employer's choice of celebrity:

> Regarding the question of why we chose to feature this baseball star in an advertisement for Prinivil, the answer is simple: Cal Ripken Jr. is not an ordinary baseball star. As the holder of baseball's record for consecutive games played, Mr. Ripken embodies the same hard-at-work ethic that we associate with Prinivil. . . .
>
> The aim of the advertising campaign has never been to urge consumers to "be like Cal," and physicians' responses to the campaign are tested periodically. Their reactions have been highly positive, because it is understood that Mr. Ripken is espousing a work ethic that our company and physicians alike can support.[22]

The choice of Ripken to promote a medication used to treat diseases of the heart seems to be intuitive. After all, who better to sell heart medicine than a player who is "all heart"? Who better to sell heart medicine than a man whose own heart, both literal and figurative, allowed him to break Lou Gehrig's streak?[23] Ripken's surplus of heart in addition to his work ethic—the same quality that made Ryan such a natural match for Advil—marked the resilient shortstop-turned-third-baseman as the perfect endorser for Merck's hypertension drug. There was one small problem, as Dr. Jefferson indicated. As the original ad itself pointed out in the finest of fine print, so small as to be barely noticeable, "Cal Ripken Jr. is not hypertensive and is not taking Prinivil."

Good health intact, Ripken entered into his relationship with Merck with open eyes. Ripken's celebrity image had already been carefully crafted, and it was controlled by a sophisticated industry. Even before his historic streak of 2,632 consecutive games played began, Ripken employed a public relations firm to help increase his name recognition and build his brand. Aware of the process and the potential of advertising to impact his identity, Ripken and his agent, Ron Shapiro, were very careful about what products the player signed on to endorse. Faced with a choice between two products, milk and Jockey shorts, Ripken writes in his as-told-to memoir, *The Only Way I Know*:

> Ron felt that I could do one or the other campaign, but not both, and he pressed pretty hard with the idea that this would be a defining moment for me in the public eye. In hindsight, I guess it was. I tease Ron now about not being so certain which was the right choice, but the choice for me wasn't that tough, really. I couldn't see myself posing in my under shorts. I'm a milk person, both in substance and in how I want to be seen, and not a male model in effect.[24]

However, appearing in medical journals in a Prinivil cap and jersey did not seem to bother Ripken. In fact, the player and his representatives gave their approval before the ad ran.[25]

Although the meanings of "heart" and "hard work" may very well have transferred from Ripken through the product to prescribing physicians by means of the endorsement ad, those meanings did not transfer to the FDA. In March 1997, the agency's regulatory review officer in the Division of Drug Marketing, Advertising, and Communications informed Merck that the Ripken Prinivil ads were "false and/or misleading." Since the ads appeared to be outright endorsements and the disclaimer was not prominently displayed, Merck was in violation of the FDCA.[26] Merck's response was not to drop the ad, but to print the disclaimer in clear, bold, readily visible letters, and to change the language to be more specific: "Cal Ripken has never suffered from CHF [congestive heart failure]. Cal Ripken has never suffered from MI [myocardial infarction]. Cal Ripken does not use Prinivil." This, according to the FDA, was acceptable. The *New England Journal of Medicine* concurred, stating, "In general, our policy is to accept advertisements for drugs approved by the Food and Drug Administration as long as they are not in bad taste."[27] Though controversial, Ripken's relationship with Prinivil's manufacturers did nothing to tarnish his glowing "milk" image, most probably because the ads did not appear in the mass media, but only in specialized medical journals. And even if the ads had been given wider exposure, their impact on Ripken's image would likely have been minimal. After all, they contained nothing off-message. If anything, their "Hardest Working Man in Baseball" slogan would have only served to reinforce Ripken's carefully constructed celebrity brand.

Ask Your Doctor

Given the political climate in the early 1990s and the combined movement toward consumer self-determination and continuing corporate deregulation, it seemed inevitable that the FDA would loosen restrictions on DTC drug advertising. But pharmaceutical companies were still not home free. The aim of the loosened restrictions, which allowed drug companies to advertise their products by brand names, was, according to the FTC, to empower consumers to take part in their own care by encouraging them to be informed when interacting with their physicians.[28] But drug manufacturers were still prohibited from telling consumers that by taking a specific medication, they would be cured of the condition or disease it was designed to treat. Remaining regulations kept "Big Pharma," as the multibillion-dollar industry came to be known, out of the business of offering salvation to the infirm as its forebears in the patent-medicine business had. But there was a workaround—and so was born the bit of commercial language urging each potential prescription drug consumer to "Ask your doctor if _____ is right for you!"

Emerging from an alphabet soup of regulation, deregulation, support, and criticism came advertising for Viagra, a drug that was, and continues to be, good at what it does and good at marketing what it does directly to consumers. Viagra, too, had predecessors in the DTC drug endorsement game. Before Rafael Palmeiro's Viagra deal was even a gleam in his and Pfizer's eyes, Mike Piazza, the New York Mets star catcher, was pitching antihistamine to American audiences on television, in print, and online. Claritin, Piazza's drug of choice, was, in fact, the first prescription pharmaceutical to benefit from the FDA's relaxed regulations, advertising on television and print in 1997.

Not only was Claritin the first prescription drug to be aggressively advertised directly to consumers, it was the first to enter into a licensing agreement with Major League Baseball, becoming MLB's "official allergy medication" in 1999. The first Claritin MLB commercial played on all the American baseball clichés. In it an announcer proclaims, "From spring to fall, you can feel it in the air. From the sunshine leagues of Florida to the farmlands of the prairies, from the school yards of New York to the golden fields of California." A montage of images drawn from the American baseball mythos, the fresh-faced, smiling player getting off the bus, children playing in a prairie pickup game and in an urban playground, and a little female outfielder retrieving a ball in the waist-high fields of summer accompanied his voice-over.[29] While the images say, "It's baseball season," the announcer says, "It's allergy season." Of course, he's got a way to convert the latter to the former—a visit to the doctor to ask about Claritin. The connection between the drug and the game is obvious. As a Schering-Plough spokesperson told Sports Business Daily, "Baseball is played outdoors, on grass, during peak allergy season. We think many of the 45 million Americans who suffer from seasonal allergies are baseball fans."[30]

In 2001 Claritin extended its MLB sponsorship, branding in-stadium, All-Star Game ballots, distributing thirty million paper punch cards to ballparks and related businesses around the country. Claritin's All-Star Game presence also included the sponsored "Claritin All-Star Workout Day." Just as baseball was a good fit for Claritin, so, too, was Piazza, the perennial All-Star. No Cal Ripken Jr. was Piazza, and no Prinivil was Claritin. In Piazza's endorsement commercial, the announcer makes it immediately clear that the player is also a user, proclaiming that "Claritin goes to bat for Mike Piazza." A montage of Piazza engaged in all sorts of baseball-related activities is accompanied by upbeat music while the announcer assures consumers that Piazza does not worry about allergy symptoms. In virtually every shot, Piazza grins broadly, even mid-pushup. Indeed, if one message is conveyed during the course of the thirty-second spot, it is Piazza's pure, unadulterated happiness, presumably the result of being allergy-free.

Clearly, this spot makes sense. Piazza is portrayed as a down-to-earth superstar who is serious about his craft, but approaches his work with a smile on his face. The Piazza of the commercial always has a minute for his fans, whether to sign autographs during batting practice or to interact with a little girl who looks a great deal like the outfielder in the earlier spot. Naturally, the ad also implies that by taking Claritin, consumers have the potential to be worry-free and allergy-free like Piazza, and they, too, can share in those ephemeral qualities that make Piazza such a happy superstar. At the same time, the Claritin spot is effective in contributing to the public Piazza's identity, his brand. It reinforces his image as happy and fan friendly, a hard worker who is not above clowning for his people, playing air guitar on his bat to the tune of the guitar-driven music that plays behind the voice-over. Piazza's other forays into endorsement advertising, most notably a series of spots for the telephone service 10–10–220, in which he appeared with the TV alien Alf, also contributed to the construction of his brand. That his commercial appearances aided in cementing his reputation, especially among those who were not his avid fans, was borne out by continuing success as an endorser. In 2005 he was named one of *Sports Illustrated* magazine's "Fortunate 50," one of the fifty top-earning American athletes of the year, raking in a reported $4 million in endorsements in addition to his robust salary, despite a media brouhaha surrounding his sexuality.[31]

"Let's Just Say It Works for Me"

Claritin's MLB ties, which also included a cross-promotion benefitting the Boys and Girls Clubs of America, exploited the undeniable relationship between summer, outdoors, green fields, and baseball by touting the drug's power over hay fever. In this regard, Schering-Plough had a much easier path forward than did Pfizer with Viagra. Frank discussions of and allusions to seasonal allergies and pitches for drugs designed to treat them did not require any particular delicacy. This was clearly not the case with Viagra. Erectile dysfunction, the condition Viagra is intended to treat, is not hay fever. Nor was it easily discussed in public in 2002, especially not during commercial breaks on primetime sporting events. Moreover, it was not intuitively connected to baseball.

There is no question that FDA approval of sildenafil citrate, the chemical name of Pfizer's patented drug, was welcome by any number of men and their partners. The condition it was designed to alleviate was neither new nor uncommon. But finding a way to advertise it directly to consumers was not that easy. How on earth were the creatives at the Omicron Group's Cline Davis & Mann, the agency tasked with finding a way to advertise the drug, going to find a way to talk about the condition publicly? The first step was to give the condition an acceptable name. As millions of consumers now know, the answer was ED. In earlier, less enlightened times, ED was popularly known as male impotence, a loaded term to say the least. While impotence, used in a medical context, might denote a physical condition, its connotations included powerlessness, loss of manhood, even psychological castration. The clinical-sounding term ED served to negate these connotations.

In an act of rebranding, Pfizer and Cline Davis & Mann stole a page from advertising great Everett Grady's playbook. In 1928 Grady brought America a new ill and a new way to cure it—BO and Lifebuoy soap. The clinical term "body odor" was deemed unfit for polite company to be exposed to in advertising. BO, however, sounded clinical, like a condition that could be treated.[32] Team Viagra neither created an illness nor a cure, but it did build a new brand identity for impotence. Positioning the drug in this way presumably lessened the discomfort of potential consumers.

But simply calling impotence ED was not enough. In order to thoroughly rebrand what was an embarrassing, potentially emasculating condition, unmentionable in polite or overwhelmingly male company, Pfizer had to find just the right pitchman. Senator Robert Joseph "Bob" Dole was their initial choice. It was not an exaggeration to say that Dole was a household name in 1998.

After all, the former Senate majority leader was the Republican Party's presidential candidate in 1996, losing to Bill Clinton. At a time when the partisan rhetoric surrounding presidential politics was becoming increasingly contentious, Dole was universally respected by his peers and voters of both major parties. Not only that, but he was a bona fide American hero, earning both a Bronze Star and Purple Heart fighting Nazis during World War II. As if this weren't enough, he was married to a strong, powerful woman thirteen years his junior. Perfect though he seemed to be, his endorsement had a major drawback. His appeal as a spokesman was essentially limited to his own demographic, aging white men. This was Viagra's initial market. But Pfizer wanted more.

To expand its consumer base from one made up solely of men like Dole, the pharmaceutical company had to change the drug's image from that of an old man's panacea to something a younger man might voluntarily take, not only without shame but with aplomb. How better to reform the image of a condition associated with the powerlessness of aging and ill health than to connect it to a sport synonymous with youth, health, and vitality, like baseball? Not warlike and testosterone driven, like football, and not a showcase for showboating teenagers, like basketball, baseball's image was that of a sport enjoyed by sons, fathers, and even grandfathers together. In a very real sense, baseball served as a big tent under which all potential Viagra consumers might be gathered. The symbolism was perfect too. ED, the enemy, could be vanquished by a man wielding a very large bat.

And who better to appeal to Viagra's new target market than Rafael Palmeiro? Prior to his testimony before Congress during its 2005 hearings on doping in Major League Baseball, Palmeiro was known as a strong, powerful player who could field as well as he hit, an almost certain Hall of Famer. While not as famous as Ripken or Piazza, the tall, strikingly handsome Palmeiro was certainly familiar to the MLB fans Viagra sought to attract. Perhaps more importantly, the choice of Cuban-born Palmeiro as Viagra spokesman was designed to broaden the drug's appeal to a more ethnically diverse as well as younger target market than the very

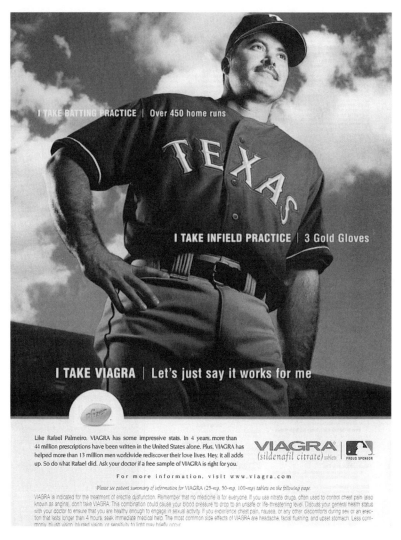

10. Rafael Palmeiro's Viagra endorsement ad targeted younger and more ethnically diverse consumers than the product's previous advertising. Courtesy of Pfizer, Inc.

white, septuagenarian Dole. So perfect was Palmeiro that it is surprising that he was not Pfizer's original choice for the job of official MLB Viagra spokesman. That honor went to Seattle Mariners designated hitter Edgar Martinez, who turned down the endorsement offer, ostensibly due to time limitations.[33] Though without

Palmeiro's fielding credentials, career designated-hitter Martinez shared important qualities with Palmeiro, qualities that also made him an excellent potential Viagra endorser. Martinez, like Palmeiro, was a well-known, well-respected Latino power hitter.

In 2003 MLB had no shortage of impressive Latino players with higher profiles than either Martinez or Palmeiro. Yet none of them had what Pfizer wanted—a quality Palmeiro himself summed up in a widely disseminated statement he made when his endorsement deal was announced. According to Palmeiro, "We need to change the perception of what macho is. You're more macho if you can step forward and send a positive message."[34] As the *Oxford English Dictionary* notes, *macho*, derived from the Spanish for "young man," is specifically defined as "a notably or ostentatiously masculine, tough, or vigorous man; one who is aggressively proud of his masculinity."[35] Admitting that one takes Viagra, suggested Palmeiro in a Pfizer press release, would not compromise this new sense of machismo. By stepping forward to send a positive message, Palmeiro also inferred that ostentation and aggression should perhaps be stricken from the macho formula.

Sending a positive message while at the same time redefining machismo as less ostentatious and aggressive seemed to be precisely Pfizer's goal. Nuyorican Martinez and Cuban-born Palmeiro were, and continue to be, light-skinned Latinos, appearing to be more European than African in origin. Indeed, for all intents and purposes, they are white. They both speak English with very slight accents, retaining just enough Spanish inflection to remind consumers of their heritage. Though they were both power hitters, neither was perceived as ostentatious or aggressive in their displays of that power. On the field they were both masculine, tough, and vigorous, but not ostentatiously, aggressively so. As potential Viagra pitchmen, they were both Latino, but not ostentatiously, aggressively so.

Pfizer's desire to link its ED drug to performance and endurance, toughness and vigor, and above all else, power, is hardly a surprise. But by its choice of endorser, the pharmaceutical maker signaled that it was looking for yet another quality, youth, or relative youth. In 2002 Palmeiro was still in his thirties. He may have been old in baseball-player years, but he was hardly geriatric like Senator Dole. ED is not a condition generally associated with healthy men in their thirties and forties, yet healthy men in their thirties and forties was precisely the market segment Pfizer sought to attract with Palmeiro's testimonial. As an anonymous advertising industry representative speaking to the *Boston Globe* observed, Palmeiro's selection as the face of Viagra represented "a repositioning of the product. We're not talking your daddy's Viagra. We're not talking postsurgical or dread disease sexual dysfunction or even Bob Dole." What Pfizer aimed for, he continued, was to market the drug to men seeking "that extra edge." Indeed, Pfizer stood to make an astronomical profit from exploiting what they defined as "male 'edge' insecurity."[36]

Certainly, if positioned correctly, Palmeiro's testimonial had the potential to reach these insecure consumers. But Palmeiro's endorsement could only be effective if the coveted edge seekers he was meant to attract actually believed that he was sincere. FTC regulations helped in that regard. Section 255.1c of the *FTC Guide Concerning the Use of Endorsements and Testimonials in Advertising* makes this explicit. It states, "Where the advertisement represents that the endorser uses the endorsed product, then the endorser must have been a bona fide user at the time the endorsement was given. Additionally, the advertiser may continue to run the advertisement only so long as he has good reason to believe that the endorser remains a bona fide user of the product."[37]

By Palmeiro's own account, his testimony was true. "I approached it as a regular endorsement," claimed Palmeiro in an interview with Jim Moore, columnist for the *Seattle Post-Intelligencer*. "I wasn't too focused on the product itself," he continued. Still, he managed to make it clear to Moore that while he used the drug, he did not need it.[38] Need it or not, Palmeiro's endorsement might have made him an easy target for less-than-complimentary clubhouse humor. But this was not the case. On the contrary, if he is to be believed, Palmeiro became the Texas Rangers' de facto Viagra pusher, claiming that all of his teammates were users and most were hitting him up for more.[39] Fortunately for Pfizer and Palmeiro, Viagra was not one of the performance-enhancing drugs on MLB's list of banned substances.[40]

To say that Palmeiro's endorsement ads were widely disseminated is an understatement. They appeared on television, in a variety of popular magazines, as well as on Pfizer's Viagra website and on all sorts of promotional items distributed to physicians by drug reps (the detail men of yore). Of several print ads, the most-often reproduced features Palmeiro in his Texas Ranger's uniform. Strategically superimposed over the body parts they refer to are three lines of bold type that read:

I TAKE BATTING PRACTICE/ Over 500 Home Runs

I TAKE INFIELD PRACTICE/ 3 Gold Gloves

I TAKE VIAGRA/ Let's Just Say It Works for Me

The first two lines of type overlay his right shoulder and his right hand—his glove hand—respectively. The third rests just above his athletic supporter. Each serves to underscore the connection between practice and performance. Power and skill do not come cheap, the copy suggests, and neither does virility.

Like virtually everything else in baseball, these claims are backed up by statistical evidence, vague though they may be. Without sparkling numbers, Palmeiro would have had little value as a product endorser. To both fans and the uninitiated, those who might have seen the ad in the *New York Times*, *People*, or even *Gentlemen's Quarterly*, the statistics serve to brand Palmeiro as someone with superior knowledge and skill, qualified to offer an opinion on the efficacy of a drug designed to confer power on the powerless. Broadly conceived, statistics like the ones in this ad make Palmeiro and all baseball players of above-average skill excellent spokesmen for pharmaceuticals, at least at first glance.

Arguably, no two industries rely so heavily on statistical evidence as to the effectiveness of their respective products as do professional baseball and medicine and, by extension, Big Pharma. Without statistical data, researchers might never have developed Viagra.

Without statistical data, Viagra would never have been approved by the FDA. And without statistical data, Palmeiro would never have been hired to endorse Viagra. This line of reason is borne out in the ad's smaller print, reading, "Like Rafael Palmeiro, Viagra has some impressive stats. In 4 years, more than 44 million prescriptions have been written in the United States alone." Indeed, the ad uses statistics to draw a direct comparison between Viagra's efficacy and Palmeiro's.

The ad's statistics may also function on a more abstract level. In his landmark work *Understanding Media: The Cultural Extensions of Man*, Marshall McLuhan examines, among other things, the magical properties of numbers. Citing observations by Bauhaus artist Laszlo Maholy-Nagy, McLuhan writes, "To Europeans, America seems to be the land of abstractions, where numbers have taken on an existence of their own in phrases like '57 Varieties,' 'the 5 and 10,' or '7-Up,' and 'behind the 8-ball.' It figures. Perhaps this is a kind of echo of an industrial culture that depends heavily on prices, charts, and figures. Take 36–24–36. Numbers cannot become more sensuously tactile than when mumbled as the magic formula for the female figure while the haptic hand sweeps the air."[41] Like the numbers in McLuhan's slogans and clichés, "500 Home Runs" and "3 Gold Gloves" take on an independent, tactile existence. They are more than just the magic formula that must be uttered to gain entrance into baseball's holy inner sanctum, the Hall of Fame; they are extensions of the players, themselves. McLuhan reasons that our numerical system, based as it is on the number of our fingers, ten, is essentially an extension of our hands, an extension of touch. Palmeiro's statistics, as the ad tells us by the position of the first two lines of bold type, are the result of batting practice and fielding practice, which are necessarily accomplished with a bat and glove, extensions of Palmeiro's hands, in McLuhan's terms. So, too, are the other numbers cited in the ad—"4 years" and "44 million." Like the magical incantation of yore, "36–24–36," these numbers may be associated with a haptic hand sweeping the air, though with a less socially acceptable gesture than the one that used to connote the ideal female form. And they, too, reflect an extension of the human body associated with tactile sensation, though, in this case, it is not the hand that is extended.

That Palmeiro's prowess with bat and glove were achieved only through long hours of practice is stated clearly in the ad. The results of the final statement, "I take Viagra," however, are considerably vaguer. By design, this final assertion is followed not by specific statistical evidence, but by a comment filled with innuendo. In a sort of "wink, wink, nod, nod" fashion, the comment "Let's just say it works for me" suggests that Palmeiro's Viagra-aided conquests may be far too many to enumerate. Let's just say it's more than a few.

Handsome and self-assured, standing tall and erect, with the knowing smile of one who possesses that elusive edge, Palmeiro towers behind the copy. Photographed from below, he looms against an almost impossibly blue sky, dappled with fair-weather clouds. The magic pill, the little blue diamond, symbolically connecting Palmeiro's workplace with the heavens above, sits on its side at a jaunty angle, pointing directly at the slugger's crotch, which, according to the laws of scientific perspective, serves as a vanishing point in the ad, the imaginary place on the horizon where all lines converge. This element of the layout, as essential to the ad's effectiveness as its copy, directs the consumer's attention both to Palmeiro's protective gear and upward to his testimonial.

As in all DTC pharmaceutical advertising, Palmeiro's Viagra endorsement also includes copy listing possible side effects, complete with its own numerical language. "For an erection lasting more than four hours," warns the ad, "seek medical help." Since priapism is a condition requiring medical attention rather than a source of macho pride, "four hours" probably does not constitute a magic number as described by McLuhan. Required by a law, which asserts that all DTC ads must include all the risk information associated with the advertised drug, the numerical side effect must be included in the ad.[42]

In addition to appearing in the print ad, Palmeiro also starred in a thirty-second television spot that aired repeatedly during the 2003 baseball season and playoffs, as well as during commercial breaks in primetime network programming. The spot contains much of the same imagery, information, and language as the print ad, but by virtue of its being video, it is considerably richer. It begins with a montage of Palmeiro in action, pawing the dirt with his spikes, swinging his big bat, and tagging a runner at first on a bang-bang play. Interspersed with these images are shots of photographers, aiming cameras with really long lenses at the slugger, as well as a short take of a rotating newspaper. In the background, pulsing music layered with crowd sounds and play-by-play calls build to a crescendo. The majority of shots in the sequence are canted up either to the right or left, and most have been taken either from below or at eye level. Over all, the message of the montage duplicates that of the print ad. The low-angle shots suggest power, while the canted shots duplicate the directional effect of the diamond shape of the pill pointing at the player's crotch. Moreover, the canted shots, especially those taken from below, give the overall impression of rising, particularly in the case of the angled lenses and the images of Palmeiro's bat, both in midswing and as it rests on his shoulder.

As the newspaper bearing the generic title *Sports Day*, and the generic headline, "Palmeiro Stars on the Diamond" comes to rest—at an angle, of course—Palmeiro in a voice-over tells his audience, "I've made a lot of news on the diamond, but if you want to find out about *this* diamond, you got to go talk to your doctor." His opening statement linking his press coverage to information about Pfizer's drug is clearly an unabashed attempt by copywriters to reinforce the notion that Viagra is somehow deeply linked to the national pastime via its shape. It is not, after all, too bold a leap to link power and performance with a bat to power and performance in the bedroom, to link that elusive edge in the public sphere to that elusive edge in the private. This is further underscored by the following shot, a sample pack of the drug resting on the grass next to a ball, accompanied by an announcer's voice-over asking male viewers if they "are ready to try Viagra for the first time," urging them to see their doctors to see if "a free sample is right for you."

Finally, Palmeiro, seated in the dugout with his bat on his shoulder, tells consumers, "My doctor says it's right for me. That's why I stay with it." The message here is that when Viagra is right for the implied *you*, as it is for Palmeiro, it is something to be used more than once. Just like Palmeiro, armed with his magic stick, ready at a moment's notice to spring into action, so, too, should the consumer be at the ready, armed with a refillable prescription for Viagra, prepared for whatever opportunity may arise to engage in his own feats of power. The spot ends with Palmeiro hitting a long home run. The ballpark stands are filled with fans eager to receive the ball and, with it, Palmeiro's wisdom. Of course, the signage below the seats features a Viagra ad, complete with the image of the diamond-shaped pill and the MLB logo. Just to the right is the bright-yellow foul pole, yet another phallic signifier, another visual reminder of the drug's purpose. Finally, the canted newspaper reappears. This time its headline reads, "Going, going, gone—to the doctor."[43]

Absent, however, is the list of side effects, including the dreaded four-hour erection. In place of the litany of warnings contemporary consumers have come to expect from DTC drug ads, Palmeiro advises his audience to go to Viagra.com for more information. This is where the commercial departs significantly from the print ad. While the print ad specifies that Viagra's purpose is to treat ED, providing scientific statistical information about the drug's efficacy in addition to stats proving Palmeiro's baseball prowess, balancing the information fairly with a statement of risks, the commercial does not. Nor does the spot, with all its canted shots, bats, lenses, and foul poles, specify what condition the product is intended to treat. It does not state, it only insinuates. Because it makes no claims, it is required only to direct consumers to their doctors and the company website for further information.[44]

Sometimes a Ball Is Just a Ball—Enter Levitra

At the outset, Viagra had the luxury of being the only FDA-approved ED drug on the market. But its virtual monopoly did not last long. In July 2003, just as Palmeiro began to refer to his Viagra-aided conquests with an implied wink and nod from the pages of American periodicals and from TV screens, Bayer and its parent company, GlaxoSmithKline, prepared to introduce its entry in the ED sweepstakes, Levitra. Perhaps inevitably, Levitra countered Viagra's

MLB licensing deal with one of its own. Following its competitor's lead, it became the official ED drug of the NFL.

While Palmeiro's Viagra ads may have been accused of lacking some subtlety, the football-themed Levitra ads were downright Rabelaisian. The first Levitra football spot was celebrity testimonial-free. Instead, it featured a young man, handsome and carefree, though not as carefree as he ought to have been, attempting to throw a football through a tire suspended from a tree, to no avail. After taking Levitra, however, he returns, and like Odysseus on his homecoming to Ithaca, throwing his spear accurately through an arch made by crossed arrows, his aim improves markedly. And just like Odysseus, he emerges a hero in the adoring eyes of his own Penelope, who watches him skillfully throw the football through the tire, straight and true. The spot seems to suggest that Levitra improves not only its consumers' chances of heroic performance, but also their aim.

Levitra was not to be outdone in the celebrity athlete endorsement arena, either. Countering Viagra's Palmeiro, Bayer hired Mike Ditka, former coach of the Chicago Bears. In fact, Ditka was on board as an endorser before the drug was even FDA approved.[45] Ditka first appeared in a forty-five-second spot that aired during the 2004 Super Bowl. In it Ditka and Levitra take aim not just at ED and the pesky tire, but also at baseball and, by extension, baseball's drug, Viagra. Like the Palmeiro ad, the Ditka spot makes no specific medical claims, but it does assert that football—a fast, powerful game, which is played no matter what the weather—is for real men, for warriors, while baseball, like Viagra, is for sissies, and could use a dose of Levitra. By making this comparison, the Ditka spot seems to refute Palmeiro's redefinition of machismo, returning to it all the ostentation and aggression associated with football. It implies that baseball may inspire fantasies of clutch performance, but football makes those fantasies reality. And the ball always goes through the tire, straight and true.

When It Doesn't Work for Big Pharma

The 2007 MLB season marked the end of an era, short though it may have been. In March, Pfizer ended its five-year relationship with MLB. Viagra would no longer be MLB's official ED drug. Where it had been a leader in the field, Pfizer followed the competition, as Levitra had ceased to be the NFL's ED drug of choice in 2006. The cause of death was the PhRMA Guiding Principles, a list of guidelines the pharmaceutical industry imposed upon itself to avoid government regulation. Pfizer was one of the signatories of the Pharmaceutical Research and Manufacturers of America (PhRMA) document in 2009, which stipulates, "In terms of content and placement, DTC [Direct-to-Consumer] television and print advertisements should be targeted to avoid audiences that are not age appropriate for the messages involved. In particular DTC television and print advertisement containing content that may be inappropriate for children should be placed in programs or publications that are reasonably expect to draw an audience of approximately 90 percent adults (18 years or older)."[46] It continues, "Companies should focus on whether the content—including text (visual or audio), images and themes—in the advertisement, taken as a whole, is sexually explicit in nature such that it is not suitable for children."[47] According to an industry expert, "With changes in pharma TV guidelines, Pfizer literally could not activate the [MLB] sponsorship in primetime advertising any more. So they are out of baseball and probably out of sports altogether."[48] Gone were the digital ballpark ads, specifically designed to show up clearly on television. Gone were clutch performances, at least from the MLB website.

But even after Pfizer ended its product's official relationship with the sport, Pfizer continued to advertise during baseball broadcasts, even though its commercials do not invoke the sport. In fact, Viagra was one of the first sponsors to sign on with the new MLB Network in 2009.[49] Signatory to the PhRMA guidelines or not, Pfizer continued to place Viagra commercials on afternoon and primetime broadcasts through the middle of the 2016 MLB season. So prevalent were spots for the little blue pill during the 2015 postseason, that St. Louis Cardinals pitcher Adam Wainwright turned to Twitter to protest: "@MLBONFOX @MLB I shouldn't have to turn the channel every single comm break because of erectile dysfunction ads. Millions of kids watching."[50]

Why did ED drug spots continue to air on baseball broadcasts during commercial breaks? A 2013 study released in the *Journal of Health Politics, Policy and Law* concluded that Big Pharma failed when it came to self-policing DTC advertising for ED drugs. According to Denis Arnold and Jim Oakley, the study's authors, Pfizer, BayerHealthcare, and Eli Lilly, manufacturer of Cialis, the third drug in the ED cure triumvirate, may have certified compliance with the guiding principles, but they did not abide by them. The study found that not only did Big Pharma put consumers at risk by failing to fully educate them as to the drugs' risks, they regularly exposed children to inappropriate content.[51] Three years later, the baseball audience continues to overlap with Viagra's target demographic. It seems that for the foreseeable future, viewers of regional sports networks as well as national and local baseball broadcasts will likely be told to ask their doctors if Viagra is right for them.

Nevertheless, as of 2016, MLB no longer counts pharmaceutical companies as official sponsors. And while ads for antihistamines and a host of other drugs, both OTC and prescription, continue to air during baseball games, they are virtually devoid of endorsements by baseball players. Like all advertisers employing celebrity testimonials to sell their products, the pharmaceutical industry runs the risk of selecting someone who seems perfect, but is not. As *Pharma Marketing News* observes, "Worse than falling out of the public limelight, however, is when a celebrity goes off the deep end at the height of his/her career while working for the drug industry."[52] In 2005, just five months after his finger-stabbing denial of steroid use under oath in front of Congress, Rafael Palmeiro was suspended from baseball for ten days, the result of a positive test for performance-enhancing drugs. Like so many of baseball's accused PED users, Palmeiro insisted that he took them by accident.[53] Palmeiro's suspension put an exclamation mark on his fall from grace, a victim of MLB's PED purge. Fortunately for Pfizer, the company had elected not to continue the use of celebrity endorsers for its ED drug, moving instead to portray ruggedly handsome "everyday men" in their ads.

Although baseball players seemed to be the perfect pharmaceutical endorsers, they were not. Were Palmeiro's Viagra endorsement the only issue, the practice might have continued, but there were other problems. In 1999 seven MLB headliners with visibly thinning hair, Sandy Alomar Jr., Gary Gaetti, Todd Greene, Stan Javier, Bret Saberhagen, John Smoltz, and Walt Weiss, joined in a publicity stunt to benefit their charities of choice. The fierce competitors took each other on to see which one could grow the most hair in a year in the Hats Off! Charity Challenge for Propecia, Merck's miracle baldness cure.[54] Walt Weiss was the winner.[55]

Although none of the players were paid for their Propecia endorsements, their involvement in the competition effectively functioned in the same way as paid testimonial endorsements. All the meanings associated with them as individuals and their game became available to consumers via the stunt, followed by use of the product. At face value, this semiendorsement does not seem to be problematic. But it was. Because Propecia works by changing the way in which the body utilizes testosterone, Propecia was sometimes used to mask PED use in drug tests. In fact, Propecia's active ingredient, finasteride, was banned for use in international competition by the World Anti-Doping Agency (WADA), as well as by the NCAA and a number of professional sports leagues in 2005. While the ban was eventually lifted at the urging of scores of balding athletes and, no doubt, its manufacturer, the association of the drug with PED use might have potentially been damaging to the reputations of players like Weiss and his Hats Off! cohort at the same time as baseball's PED scandal might have hurt the product's on-label sales.

Despite Big Pharma's recent rejection of baseball players as endorsers, it is hard to argue with the impact of Viagra's MLB sponsorship and Palmeiro's endorsement. From a branding viewpoint, Viagra's MLB campaign helped permanently change the image of impotence. Industry experts have given Pfizer kudos for making a drug meant to treat a shameful condition downright acceptable, and baseball helped. According to Kathleen L. Endres, "The direct-to-consumer campaign was more successful than anyone could have imagined. Within a year, the Viagra brand was as familiar as Coca-Cola; Viagra sales topped $1 billion, and Pfizer had become the second-largest drug company in the world."[56]

Of course, Rafael Palmeiro no longer assures potential Viagra consumers, "Let's just say it works for me." Although he is available for speaking engagements, Palmeiro is not in the public eye, either in baseball or in advertising. Nevertheless, Palmeiro's endorsement legacy, though not immediately apparent, remains extremely important. Palmeiro's tarnished reputation notwithstanding, he was one of the first Latino baseball players to be represented as digni-fied, emotionally sensitive, and strong at the same time, countering prevailing stereotypes. His redefinition of macho as characteriz-ing any man who is responsible and is willing to step forward and send a positive message, though perhaps not embraced by either American consumers or the *Oxford English Dictionary*, flew in the face of the way Latino baseball stars were conventionally por-trayed in advertising. In a sense, Palmeiro's Viagra endorsement ads, amusing though they may be more than a decade removed from their introduction, set a new standard for the representation of Latino players, one that was well ahead of its time.

CHAPTER SEVEN

Four Things We Love

Advertising, Identity, Big Papi, and the
Image of the Afro-Latino Ballplayer

As the 2015 Major League Baseball season was set to begin, MLB issued its annual press release listing the national origins of its players. Of the 868 players—750 on Opening Day rosters and 118 on disabled and restricted lists—198 were foreign-born Latinos.[1] Not included on the list were a significant number of U.S-born Latino players, Alex Rodriguez, Adrian Gonzalez, Matt Garza, and Dellin Betances, prominent among them. Nearly 30 percent of all MLB players, both foreign and U.S.-born, on 2015 Opening Day rosters identified themselves as ethnically Hispanic.[2] Considering their growing presence in the Major Leagues, it stands to reason that Latino baseball players have also become increasingly visible in testimonial and endorsement advertising. Indeed, the top MLB endorsement earners in 2015 were Latino. Robinson Cano, and Albert Pujols, both from the Dominican Republic, and Venezuelan Miguel Cabrera led the pack.[3]

This is borne out by a number of recent English-language commercials. For example, in 2017, before he tested positive for performance-enhancing drugs, Cano was featured in a Nike ad recalling the classic "Bo Knows" commercial. As he takes his swings, Bo Jackson watches, telling consumers, "Robbie Knows Boom!" In 2015 Cabrera's "Road to Greatness" was the subject of a Chrysler commercial. And Albert Pujols has assured his fans that he is "definitely comfortable in his own skin" with Dove for Men. But topping them all was the great Dominican player David Ortiz, fondly known as Big Papi for his outsized body, bat, and public persona—his brand. Even a season removed from the diamond, as he makes the transition from designated hitter to national baseball broadcaster, Ortiz is still active in the endorsement game, signing new deals, stamping new business initiatives with his imprimatur, making personal appearances, and even inscribing his name on a wine label—Arias Wines by David Ortiz.[4]

According to 2016 U.S. Census Data, 17.6 percent of the country's population self-identified as Hispanic or Latino.[5] Hispanic and Latino are not interchangeable terms, though they overlap significantly. The definitions are not necessarily clear. The U.S. Census defines Hispanics as people who come from Spanish-speaking nations, including Spain.[6] Demographically speaking, Latino encompasses those with roots in Latin America, including Brazil. Because it is regional and does not refer directly to the area's colonial past, Latino is the preferable label to many of those who identify as such.[7] With few exceptions, most MLB players with Spanish-speaking origins are Latino. So, too, are most recent Spanish-speaking immigrants.[8] In fact, the U.S. Census groups "Spanish/Hispanic/Latino" together as a single category with multiple subcategories.[9] Their data show that Latinos and Hispanics comprise the single largest minority group in the country.[10]

English-language proficiency among Latinos in the U.S. is on the rise. In 2014, 68.4 percent reported that they spoke only English at home or that they were effectively bilingual.[11] Nevertheless, in response to the growing population of Spanish speakers, Spanish-language media has grown at a rapid rate, outpacing that of its English-language counterparts.[12] Advertising outlays in the Spanish-language market have also grown, surpassing mainstream major-media spending. This is particularly true in the case of print advertising.[13] With an ever-expanding market and a ready source of celebrities, endorsement opportunities have also increased for MLB's Latino stars. According to agent Fernando Cuza:

> You have Univision and these other Latin networks that are going all over the place. And we don't have a lot of athletes that are Hispanics in other sports. Baseball and soccer are basically it. So the marketers realize that if they sign David Ortiz or Mariano Rivera

for a Pepsi or Coke commercial, they capture the local market. They are also able to capture their local market where they live in the Dominican Republic or Venezuela, Panama, or wherever they are from. On top of that, they are also able to tap into the bilingual market in the U.S. So they are really hitting three different demographics.[14]

But revenue from Spanish-language endorsements alone does not account entirely for the success of celebrity athletes like Ortiz, Pujols, Cabrera, or the other top earners. Stars of their caliber and charisma reach another demographic altogether—mainstream, English-speaking consumers.

Mike Fish of ESPN concurs, observing, "Not only are Latino stars from the Dominican Republic to Puerto Rico putting up monster stats and leading their teams to pennants, but sports marketing executives are also increasingly turning their way with lucrative endorsement deals. And with good reason: They're often the marquee players of big-city franchises. Perhaps more importantly, Hispanics have become the second-largest population group in the U.S.—ahead of African Americans but behind Caucasians—thanks to the influx of immigrants from Latin America."[15] As Cuza confirms, Latino players represent an emerging class of baseball product endorsers, often capable of pitching products in two languages.

The Chico Escuela Factor

The path to elite endorser status has not necessarily been easy for Latino players, despite their increased visibility and the growing purchasing power of the Latino consumer base. This is particularly true of players whose English is not perfect, many of whom have faced discrimination from the English-language sports media and the advertising industry. Prior to a 2016 policy change spearheaded by Carlos Beltran that assures Spanish-speaking players the right to have an interpreter present for all official media contact and baseball-related interviews, players with limited English were forced to muddle through on their own. Dedicated simultaneous translators were a luxury generally afforded only to Japanese players as negotiated in individual contracts, but not to Spanish speakers. Where Spanish-English translation was available, it was spotty at best, with many teams depending upon bilingual players, coaches, and other employees to fill in as interpreters. As a result, players lacking English fluency were often reduced to giving overly simple answers to questions from the media. Of his early days in the Major Leagues as a young player struggling with English, Beltran recalls, "I couldn't really say much other than, 'I feel good,' and 'I had a good game,' and 'I am happy I helped the team.' Just simple and short stuff, so I didn't do a lot of interviews. But at points, I felt I wanted to express myself a little bit more but I couldn't, and I didn't want to look bad with broken English, either."[16]

The long-standing practice of interviewing Spanish-speaking athletes lacking English fluency led to the construction and perpetuation of the stereotype of the bumbling Latino ballplayer. The exemplar of the stereotype was Chico Escuela, a fictional player. Embodied by comedian Garrett Morris, Chico Escuela appeared as a sports commentator on *Saturday Night Live*'s (SNL) "Weekend Update" segments in 1978 and 1979. The putative New York Met, hailing from the Dominican Republic, was originally introduced during a sketch about the Knights of Columbus, and quickly became a recurring character during the news segment. With his poor command of English, Chico Escuela responded to virtually every interview question in the same way—"Beisbol been berra berra good to me." According to Adrian Burgos Jr., "The character made comic fodder of Latinos in the midst of a new wave of Latino players breaking into the Major Leagues. His catchphrase and portrayal took the image of the bumbling Latino player who cannot speak understandable English to an audience beyond baseball circles."[17]

Symbolically, Chico Escuela came to represent all Latino players. It mattered not whether they were from the Dominican Republic, Puerto Rico, Venezuela, or Mexico. Though ethnically and culturally different, they were lumped into a single group, regardless of origin. In this regard, the public's response to the SNL character was not terribly different from organized baseball's response to the influx of players from Latin America, who the league, much like the U.S. Census, regarded as a single, culturally unified group. While this served to galvanize Latino players, essentially creating a group identity, it also racialized them. Burgos observes, "At different moments, league policies formulated to deal with 'Latin' player issues treated all those from the Spanish-speaking Americas as sharing a common identity. . . . With this in context it is clear that *Latino* as an ethnoracial category represents a process of racialization that affected many groups from the Spanish-speaking Americas."[18]

But Chico Escuela wasn't just Latino. As portrayed by Morris, an African American, Chico Escuela was also a person of color—an Afro-Latino, a Latin American of African ancestry. Although some Latino players, Rafael Palmeiro, for example, were European in appearance, many representatives of the new wave were Afro-Latino. Prior to MLB's desegregation, their predecessors, like all other black players, were consigned to play in the Negro Leagues or on black barnstorming teams. And like most other Negro Leaguers, they were almost never called upon to endorse products, not even in the black press or black-interest publications. Once the color line was breached, Afro-Latino players were odd men out in the endorsement game, even as their African American teammates were hired to pitch beer and cigarettes in *Ebony, Jet,* and black newspapers around the country. Unlike Jackie Robinson, whose celebrity elevated him to star endorser almost from the moment he joined the Dodgers, albeit in advertising addressed solely to black consumers, the same could not be said for Orestes "Minnie" Minoso, the first Afro-Latino Major Leaguer. In his home country, the Cuban-born Minoso was an endorsement mainstay, pitching products such as cigarettes, cigars, rum, and quite inexplicably, housing projects. He was such an advertising presence in Cuba that a writer for *Jet* in 1954 called him "Poster Boy of the Week," more visible on Havana billboards than President Fulgencio Batista, even during the election season.[19] But in the United States, Minoso, who had his first cup of coffee with the Cleveland Indians in 1949, did not endorse a major product until 1962.

Even then, his Marlboro cigarettes testimonial only appeared in black-interest publications. By that time, Robinson was an executive at Chock Full o'Nuts, having already been featured on his own weekly half-hour-long Rheingold beer–sponsored television talk show. Willie Mays was also fast becoming a star endorser in the mainstream media.[20] It was not until 1982 that Minoso, who desegregated the Chicago White Sox in 1951, appeared in mainstream English-language advertising, endorsing a local product—Old Style Beer.

Even as their numbers in Major League Baseball grew, Afro-Latino baseball players continued to be exemplified by Chico Escuela well beyond the character's shelf life. Morris, one of the original Not Ready for Primetime Players, left the cast of *Saturday Night Live* in 1980. Yet Chico Escuela lived on. The "Weekend Update" bits faded from memory, but his catchphrase remained part of the zeitgeist. Moreover, it continued to affect the mainstream perceptions of Latino ballplayers lacking English fluency for decades. Advertising played a role in perpetuating the Chico Escuela stereotype, disseminating it outside of the baseball sphere to a broader audience than even the wildly popular SNL skits.

Although prior to the 1990s endorsements by Latino players were rare, the few who appeared in mainstream English-language advertising did little to counter the image. Cuban-born pitcher Luis Tiant's Yankee Franks endorsement serves as a case in point. In a 1978 campaign that included a television spot and print advertising, Tiant, dressed in full uniform, poised to take a bite from the product, raises his finger in the air and tells his audience, "It's great to be with a wiener." That Tiant's Yankee Frank ad ran at the same time the fictional Escuela was providing regular sports updates to "Hane" ("Weekend Update" anchor, cast member Jane Curtin), only served to reinforce the connection between the character and the actual Afro-Latino ballplayer.

Sammy Sosa

Two decades later Sammy Sosa was something of a commercial darling during the 1998 home-run race. Sosa could be seen far and

11. Luis Tiant channeled Chico Escuela, the fictional, bumbling Afro-Latino ballplayer in Yankee Franks advertising.

wide, pitching for Pepsi, McDonalds, Nike, Armour Hot Dogs, MasterCard, and even the New York Stock Exchange. Even after Mark McGwire outhit him, Sosa's adverting presence remained high. Of all his commercials, one in particular stands out. It is a thirty-second spot for a 3-D baseball simulation game called *High Heat 2001*. The ad begins with Sosa about to take a swing against an animated backdrop. Just then his cell phone rings. He answers in Spanish. The Cubs slugger looks extremely befuddled as his manager says, "Hey, Sammy you're in the wrong game." Sosa, who seems to be playing in the virtual world rather than the real one, is confused by the naturalistic look of *High Heat*, leading him to exclaim, with an amazed look on his face, "High Heat. Iii-issssssoooooreeeeaallll." Several seconds later, his virtual manager, a live-action teenage boy, echoes his real manager's complaint. Again, Sosa, looking no less stunned, repeats the slogan in the same exaggerated accent.[21]

And as if acting the part were not enough, Sosa was known to echo Escuela's catchphrase in interviews, thereby doubling his association with the character. Burgos writes, "The resurrection of Chico Escuela in the midst of the home-run chase evokes the duality inherent in the clowning tradition in black baseball during the Jim Crow era."[22] He continues, "The performance of Chico Escuela by Latino players involved a similar type of duality. On one level, Sammy Sosa reclaimed Escuela's 'Latino' persona and gave it a Latino accent. . . . Invoking Chico Escuela meant performing a familiar Latino figure—the gracious immigrant exuberant about receiving an opportunity to improve his life. Hidden in the subtleties of Sosa's performance was his use of racial knowledge to possibly extract financial gain by endearing himself to fans and marketers."[23] African American ballplayers, the Indianapolis Clowns and their less successful ilk, had found a way to make a living "performing" stereotypes rooted in minstrelsy, thereby allowing them to ply their trade under the rule of Jim Crow even after Negro League baseball was no longer competitive or relevant. So, too, did Sosa made the image of the Latino ballplayer chasing the very American single-season, home-run record palatable to American consumers and to advertisers trying to appeal to them. Indeed, Sosa's performance of his own version of *Latinidad*—his sense of belonging to a wider pan-Latino community—as a latter day embodiment of Chico Escuela, may have contributed to his continued employment even after he was caught using a corked bat during a game in 2003.[24] After all, how could consumers really blame someone as simple as Sosa for not understanding the rules?

Although Sosa's Chico Escuela-esque turn may have been an act of subversion, a knowing play on the stereotype for personal gain, it may not have been perceived that way by everyone. In fact, it most certainly wasn't. During the 2002 MLB All-Star Home Run Derby broadcast, commentator Curt Schilling, then with the Arizona Diamondbacks, was inadvertently captured on tape mocking Sosa as the slugger gave an interview on the field. While Sosa responded to questions, Schilling laughed, assuring his fellow commentators, Mike Piazza, Joe Morgan, and Chris Berman, "He's gotta say it. Beisbol been berra, berra good to me," in an exaggerated accent.[25] If the oft-reviled Schilling, never known for his sensitivity and open-mindedness, had been the only one to mock Sosa, it would have simply been a case of Schilling behaving as expected. But he was not alone in mocking Sosa. More than one of his on-air colleagues laughed right along with him. This, too, was caught on tape; as the camera turns from Sosa to the broadcast desk, Piazza and Morgan can be seen laughing hysterically at the Arizona pitcher's Chico Escuela imitation, while Berman puts his finger to his lips in the universal gesture for "be quiet, they can hear you." So how did Piazza, one of MLB's golden boys, and Morgan, one of the game's elder statesmen, avoid scrutiny? Perhaps the answer lies in the pervasiveness of the Chico Escuela stereotype. Even in the twenty-first century, a little "good-natured" ethnocentric tittering is apparently understandable, as long as it doesn't go overboard. And this is only one example of Chico Escuela's staying power in baseball.

Enter Sandman . . . into Taco Bell

Despite the persistence of what might be characterized as the Chico Escuela factor, advertisers seemed ready to bank on a new generation of Latino stars who emerged alongside Sosa. The popularity of players like Pujols, Ortiz, Rivera, and, before his fall from grace, Alex Rodriguez, appeared to offer advertising the opportunity to leave Chico Escuela behind, acting as a corrective to the bumbling stereotype. According to ethnographer and media critic Arlene Davila, "The development of culturally specific marketing has been generally regarded as a viable means to correct the former stereotypical commercial portrayal of Latinos. We need only to contrast Latinos' earlier commercial representation as thieves, as in Frito Lay's controversial Frito Bandito character, or as stinky banditos, as in the Arrid deodorant ads in the 1960s and 1970s, with contemporary Hispanic-generated ads to note their pride-worthy images of beautiful, upscale, affluent, and successful Latinos."[26]

Of all the Latino baseball stars capable of putting Chico Escuela to rest among mainstream consumers by means of some well-placed endorsement advertising, perhaps none was better situated than the New York Yankees closer Mariano Rivera. The all-time postseason-saves leader, Panamanian-born Rivera played a pivotal role in winning five World Series Championships. But perhaps more importantly from a commercial viewpoint, he appeared to be the very anti–Chico Escuela, ever humble when victorious, ever gracious in defeat. Rivera told the *New York Times* in 2010 that he thought of himself as a "simple man." *Times* baseball columnist Harvey Araton described him as inscrutable.[27] Not once in his career was "the great Rivera"—as he had come to be called by national baseball commentators—tainted by even a whiff of scandal. Rivera was just the type of celebrity Davila called for—beautiful, upscale, affluent, and successful.

This was not lost on high-end Italian menswear manufacturer Canali. In 2010 the company signed an advertising deal with the closer, the first athlete ever to endorse the brand. He appeared in Canali print ads, television spots, and on the home page of the company's English-language website. Elisabetta Canali, the manufacturer's global communications director told Araton, "He reflects the positive attitude that we would like to deliver to our consumer. He is solid." Rivera's relationship with the brand actually predated his endorsement. That he was a customer first added to his credibility. "He just looked so good in the pinstripes," Canali observed.[28]

Rivera even went so far as to counter the Arrid stinky bandito spot referenced by Davila with his own Arrid commercial in 2011. It is a fairly typical antiperspirant ad, showing Rivera in an unmarked uniform, indicating that the advertiser did not license the Yankees logo from MLB, preparing to pitch. Rivera has but one line, "Why pay more to sweat less?" which he speaks as he holds the product up next to his smiling face. His accent, though discernable, is not exaggerated. His smile, though wide, is earnest. In the final frame, he is dressed in a suit, possibly designed and manufactured by Canali, his official outfitter, happily signing autographs for a suitably interracial, multiethnic group of children. Certainly in his Arrid spot, Rivera is not the picture of restrained elegance as he is the Canali ads. Still, he manages to project the desired image of someone who is always "cool under pressure"—the Arrid campaign's title.[29] More significantly, the shadow of Chico Escuela is absent from the picture.

The benefits of signing Rivera as an endorser were not lost on fast-food giant Taco Bell. As of 2010 Rivera had made more post-season appearances than any other relief pitcher. But not all his appearances were on the mound. That year, the New York Yankees were eliminated from the playoffs following an anemic performance against the Texas Rangers in the American League Championship Series. But Rivera pitched on, called upon by manager Joe Girardi, sometimes multiple times during a single game, thereby defying baseball's rules, to perform the seemingly impossible task of finishing off a Taco Bell xxl Chalupa.

Taco Bell became an official mlb sponsor in 2004. Banking on big events to spread brand awareness, the Yum! Brands subsidiary sponsored the Taco Bell All-Star Sunday as well as the Taco Bell All-Star Legends and Celebrity Soft Ball Game during mlb's All-Star Week. The fast-food giant also made major ad buys during mlb's regular season, especially on nationally broadcast fox and espn games, and until 2011, on *This Week in Baseball*.[30] In 2007, 2008, and 2012, mlb's official fast-food restaurant partnered with the league for a World's Series promotion called "Steal a Base, Steal a Taco." The rules were simple. If a runner for either participating team stole a base, the whole country would be entitled to a free taco. So popular was the promotion that Taco Bell upped the ante during the 2015 Series with "Steal a Base, Steal a Breakfast." "We think there is no better way for us to share in the excitement of the World Series than to celebrate and reward all our fellow fans with a Taco Bell breakfast," noted the company's chief brand management officer in an official company press release. "This year, in partnership with Major League Baseball, we are encouraging the whole country to root for a stolen base in the series—from either team—because the player who steals that first base will have thereby 'stolen' a free breakfast, our A.M. Crunchwrap breakfast sandwich, for all of America."[31] At first glance, this seems like any other promotion. Fast-food giants frequently offer free or discounted food tied to specific feats on the baseball diamond. But this one was a little different. Stolen bases are certainly a feature of exciting, well-played baseball. But stolen tacos are not. And "stolen" is different than free.

The concept of stealing vaguely Mexican food, even when done by officially sanctioned means, carries with it visible traces of one of the most stereotyped advertising icons of the past, also singled out by Davila—the Frito Bandito. From 1967 to 1971, the animated figure, a small "Mexican" bandit wearing crossed bandoliers and a giant sombrero, sporting the requisite drooping moustache, speaking with an accent that would make Chico Escuela proud, sang, "Ay-yi-yi-yi, I am the Frito Bandito/I love Fritos corn chips, I love them I do/I love Fritos corn chips, I'll get them from you," to the tune of the Mexican folk song "Cielito Lindo." So offensive was the campaign that the Senate, the House, local television stations, newspapers, and advertising trade publications, joined with Mexican American groups to successfully pressure Frito Lay, the manufacturer, to pull the ads.[32]

With the Frito Bandito in the background, the notion of taco theft may certainly be read as perpetuating an unfortunate stereotype. Then again, Taco Bell is no stranger to ethnic stereotyping. One need only recall Gidget, the Spanglish-speaking Chihuahua, who ran amok during the 1990s, telling consumers, "*Yo quiero* Taco Bell*,*" in many an ad, including one featuring something best described as Taco phone sex delivered by a very small talking dog, ending with the slogan, delivered in an exaggerated Mexican accent.

But Gidget the Chihuahua is nowhere to be seen in the Rivera Taco Bell ad. Indeed, there are no Mexicans, stereotypical or otherwise in the spot. As noted, Rivera is Panamanian. Joe Girardi is Italian American, and the defeated Chalupa eater, a generic Caucasian. There is not even any Mexican food in the ad. Nevertheless, most Americans would define Taco Bell's fare, if not as Mexican, then as an iteration of Mexican food—Tex-Mex or Cal-Mex—and therefore Latin American. But Taco Bell, most particularly the XXL Chalupa in question, may be read in another way. In this ad, Taco Bell represents what may be called a simulacrum of Mexican, and by extension Latin American, food. What is a

simulacrum? According to Jean Baudrilliard, it is "the generation by models of a real without origin or reality: a hyper-real. . . .
It is no longer a question of imitation, nor duplication, nor even
parody. It is a question of substituting the signs of the real for
the real."[33] Taco Bell is neither Tex-Mex, Cal-Mex, nor any other
Mex, but rather the image of Mexican food, the sign of Mexican
food. Regardless of origin, however, Taco Bell's product is generally assumed to be food of some sort. But there is no food in this
ad. When the thwarted Chalupa eater, a reasonably fit American
millennial, complete with game-day stubble, observes dejectedly,
"Dude, it's huge. I can hardly finish it," he has not taken a single
bite. As such, his act represents the image or simulacrum of eating the Chalupa. His fast-food reality is, in fact, a hyper-reality.

Things get even more hyper-real when seemingly out of nowhere,
Girardi appears, fully uniformed, and to the starting Chalupa eater's
protestation, signals for a right hander. From a table in the background, Rivera rises, puts down a cup from which he has just taken
a sip—the only actual consumption in this spot—announcing,
"I'll take it from here, kid," in heavily accented English. The camera closes in, first on the packaging, which reads XXL, then on a
graphic reading XXL, then on the Chalupa, which is shot from
straight on, making it seem as if it is protruding from the screen,
emphasizing its enormity. Clearly, the only one prepared to get
the job done, whatever the actual job is, is Rivera.

To understand the impact of the giant, protruding Chalupa that
only Rivera can finish, it is useful to refer back to Marshall McLuhan's discussion of the magic property of numbers, particularly
as it relates to popular culture. Numbers, in McLuhan's terms, are
extensions of our digits. When used to describe physical objects
numbers can become "sensuously tactile."[34] XXL, however, is not
a number. But it is shorthand for a size, also suggesting an extension of the self, though in this case, not a digit. In these terms, this
portion of the spot calls to mind Rafael Palmeiro's Viagra endorsement, which attempts to quantify the effects of the drug with the
player's statistics. There is no denying that the Taco Bell ad with
its emphasis on size, like the Viagra endorsement, references the

notion of machismo—Latin masculinity, albeit of a kinder, gentler variety. It seems to suggest that only Rivera, with his brown skin, his impossibly wide grin, accented English, and presumed Latino machismo, is the only man for the job, a job he seems to relish, given his self-assurance, his swagger, his cool.

Normally, all this machismo and Chalupa-eating inscrutability might be seen as threatening. But Taco Bell's Rivera counterbalances any threat by performing *Latinidad* as understood by generations of consumers. When Girardi praises the thwarted Chalupa eater, saying, "You chewed a hell of a Chalupa today, kid," Rivera, doing his best Chico Escuela imitation adds, "Yeah, for a rookiieee." In this way, the pitcher tempers his Latino machismo by playing to stereotype. While never as obvious as it is in Sosa's endorsement commercials, Rivera's Taco Bell spot nevertheless displays echoes of the Chico Escuela factor.

Shooting the Moon

In 2005 soft drink manufacturer PepsiCo signed Yankee Alex Rodriguez and Los Angeles Angel Vladimir Guerrero, winners of the 2003 and 2004 American League MVP Awards respectively, to endorse its flagship brand, Pepsi Cola. With many of Pepsi's stable of MLB endorsers, Jason Giambi and Sosa among them, embroiled in the BALCO performance-enhancing drug scandal, Rodriguez, not yet tainted by the PED stain, and Guerrero became the fresh, multicultural, Afro-Latino faces of the established brand. No matter how wrong-headed the choice of Rodriguez may seem in retrospect, at the time, he and Guerrero, now enshrined in the Baseball Hall of Fame, represented a new, positive Pepsi generation of MLB celebrities. That year, Guerrero and Rodriguez appeared in a television spot called "Standoff," dueling against one another in their own private home-run derby. Following a previously established trend, PepsiCo, produced "Standoff" in Spanish as well as English, despite the fact that there is but one word of dialogue.

As the commercial begins, it is night. The camera moves in on a brightly illuminated Pepsi can resting on a small table. The image is accompanied by the sounds of a flamenco guitar playing a paso doble, meant to evoke a bullfight. Beginning with an ominous arpeggio, the music builds as the combatants enter the batter's box, their makeshift bullring. The camera focuses first on their faces, then their eyes, and finally the prize—the can. Then the combat begins. Hitting off a tee in a ballpark, empty save for the contestants, Guerrero sends a ball into the parking lot, the sound of breaking glass followed by a car alarm signaling that the ball has found its unintentional target, a windshield. Next, Rodriguez does his opponent one better, shooting out one of the ballpark lights illuminating the duel. Finally, Guerrero sends a ball deep into the night, shattering the moon. Rodriguez yells "Run!" ("*Corre*" in the Spanish-language version), and they take off, but Rodriguez returns momentarily to grab the prize, though he is the loser.[35]

In many ways, this ad runs counter to the Chico Escuela stereotype. It features grown men displaying tremendous feats of power, on their game when the stakes are high, as they clearly are in this scenario. The music, signifying a type of hypermasculinity associated with Spain and Latin America, serves to reinforce this idea. Nevertheless, "Standoff" still relies on a Latino stereotype, though a more subtle one than Taco Bell's. On the surface, the Pepsi spot emphasizes the dueling batters' machismo. They are big men who swing big bats, powerful enough to shatter windows, lights, and the moon. They take turns enacting the role of the matador, though the ball is always the bull. But closer examination reveals the combatants as resembling small boys, terrified at being caught hitting a ball through the neighbor's window. On balance, "Standoff" not only infantilizes these strong, potent Latino athletes, it also represents them as low-level juvenile delinquents, powerful enough to cause real property damage, unwilling to accept responsibility for their actions. In this way, this ad echoes Taco Bell's "Steal a Base, Steal a Taco" and may even hearken back to the Frito Bandito.

Chillin' with Big Papi

Despite the persistence of the Chico Escuela factor and other forms of ethnic stereotyping in advertising featuring Afro-Latino MLB players, a subtle shift may be under way. In the summer of 2015, David Ortiz, the Boston Red Sox's powerful designated hitter, accompanied by New England Patriots' tight end Rod Gronkowski—Big Papi and Gronk, respectively—teamed up, in what Caroline Sikes of the *Sporting News* calls "a match made in auto-tune heaven," to release four viral videos in support of their "album," "Summer Chill."[36] So popular were these videos that the pair followed up with a fifth in 2016. In reality, "Summer Chill" is a collection of commercials for Dunkin' Donuts Iced Coffee. As advertising, these videos are local in scope. They directly target New Englanders, fans of the Red Sox and Patriots. But because they are viral videos, these ads need not conform to the constraints of traditional broadcast advertising. By virtue of their medium, their reach extends well beyond the northeastern United States to the entire country and even beyond. As such, their representation of David Ortiz, the Afro-Latino ballplayer, has wide implications in terms of effectively countering the Chico Escuela image.

Given his star power both on the diamond and in product endorsement, David Ortiz has been a fixture in advertising practically since joining the Red Sox in 2003, following a less distinguished career with the Minnesota Twins. In addition to Dunkin' Donuts, Ortiz has endorsed the requisite sporting goods and videogames as well as Vitaminwater, Pedigree dog food, JetBlue airlines, and Wise potato chips. His image has appeared on Big Papi En Fuego hot sauces, Vintage Papi wine, and now, Arias by Big Papi. The New England–based D'Angelo Sub Shop chain named a sandwich after him, and the now-defunct Song airline, Delta's attempt to compete with the Papi-endorsed JetBlue brand, went as far as to christen one of its planes bearing Ortiz's likeness in the characteristic pose pointing both index fingers to the sky, "Big Papi." And the list goes on.

But Ortiz has also engendered his share of criticism, not from his failed 2003 drug test, which has been largely overlooked, but from activity connected to his 2014 Samsung endorsement. Just one day before his Red Sox visited the White House to celebrate their 2013 World Series victory according to custom, Ortiz signed a deal with the cell-phone manufacturer that required him to make regular social media posts using his newly released Galaxy Note 3 "phablet."[37] He wasted no time. Seemingly within minutes of his meeting with President Obama, Ortiz's presidential selfie, naturally shot with his Galaxy Note 3, was retweeted more than forty thousand times, most notably by the manufacturer to its 5.2 million followers. The White House was not amused.[38]

Perhaps inevitably, *l'affaire Samsung* led to Ortiz's own SNL "Weekend Update" moment, actually several moments. As any regular viewer of Pedigree's award-winning viral videos in support of shelter dogs or 2017 postseason analysis knows, David Ortiz is bilingual. He speaks fluent though accented English. His public image may be that of a gentle giant, loveable and fun-loving, though not above talking smack when it comes to opponents, but David Ortiz is no buffoon. This appears to have been unimportant to SNL's writers and performers. Of the misguided White House selfie, SNL's David Ortiz, as played by Kenan Thompson, claims ignorance, telling anchor Colin Jost—"El Yost" to the pseudo-Ortiz, recalling Chico Escuela's "Hane"—"I no know is a problem, man. Is a problem? I no know. I talk to Sam's son, I talk to Sam. They tell me is no problem."[39] SNL's Ortiz is totally ignorant of any offense he might have caused. After all, his inappropriate, sponsored, presidential selfie tweet was the result of a misunderstanding caused by his poor comprehension of English and his simple-mindedness.

Thompson reprised his Big Papi impersonation after the real Ortiz announced that he would retire following the 2016 season. This time, Thompson's Ortiz appeared on the satirical news parody segment to discuss his post–baseball endorsement opportunities. Speaking of his sponsorships, Thompson's Ortiz announced he would "sponsor ships": "Ships, if you want to get somewhere slow and soaking wet. It's like a plane, but bad." He also reported on the opening of his new gym—"yim," as pronounced by Thompson's ballplayer—"Iguananox, like a regular yim, but full of lizards."[40]

Though perhaps more articulate than Chico Escuela in this case, Thompson's Ortiz is clearly situated in the Chico Escuela tradition. Embodied by Kenan Thompson, an African American comedian like Morris, this Big Papi speaks heavily accented, broken English. Because he lacks the ability to speak or understand English fluently, he is necessarily a simpleton. After all, only an individual of limited intelligence would mistake an agreement with Sam's son for a large corporate sponsorship deal, and only someone who doesn't speak fluent English could possibly be this gullible. And like all Latino baseball stars, he wants nothing more than to endorse a business type that is obviously common in the Dominican Republic—a facility that combines reptiles and exercise equipment. Although savvy baseball fans would no doubt know that Thompson's impersonation, which Ortiz himself has praised, does not truly represent Big Papi, *SNL's* Ortiz paints a different picture to general audiences, those with only a cursory knowledge of the player and his game. Thus at the same time that "Weekend Update's" Big Papi serves as a twenty-first-century iteration of Chico Escuela, it also serves to brand the real David Ortiz as someone lacking good judgment based on his limited command of English, transferring meaning from pseudo-Ortiz to real Ortiz via Thompson's impersonation.

"Summer Chill" is different. All five "Summer Chill" videos present a Big Papi very different from *SNL*'s iteration, each in its own way. "Turn It Up" is a pop/hip-hop video parody. Playing DJ to his partner's MC at a house party, Ortiz mans the turntables, rapping in unison with Gronkowski. Both also sing vocoder-enhanced solos, as a giant Dunkin' Iced Coffee mascot dances in the background and a smoke machine billows. It is a musical disaster, and intentionally so. Perhaps even worse from a musical standpoint is "Sippin," a jangly, guitar and "cup solo"–driven pop parody that features the two superstar athletes lounging at a pool, riding a tandem bicycle, and in Ortiz's case, making something approximating music with a cup and straw, as the ubiquitous Dunkin' Iced Coffee mascot cleans the pool and plays rhythm. Writing of "Sippin," Hayden Bird opines, "The topic is iced coffee. The result is a setback for the music industry it may take decades to overcome. Dominated by a complete dearth of musical talent is the absolute definition of a systemic failure on the part of Dunkin', whose team

12. David Ortiz, "Big Papi," of the Boston Red Sox, and New England Patriot Rob Gronkowski appeared in four viral music video parodies selling Dunkin' Donuts Iced Coffee in 2015 and another in 2016. "Sippin'," a jangly pop-rock parody, was the second to drop. Courtesy of Dunkin' Donuts.

of producers, apparently at no point thought to say out loud, 'wow, this is an inescapably terrible song.'"[41]

Less than two weeks later, the BostInno sports columnist reassessed his opinion, noting, "To the naked eye (or perhaps judges on *American Idol*), the musical collaboration of two of New England's biggest sports celebrities would appear a horrific flop. But to Dunkin', it's pure gold. And the results are self-evident, since more than a million people have watched the YouTube video."[42] Indeed, the concept behind the campaign, which also features a "making of" video, was to create ads that were "not the best music, but catchy and funny," according to Heather Morin, field marketing manager of Dunkin' Brands.[43] More importantly, the videos proved to be "sticky," garnering millions of social media hits while effectively connecting the product to the idea of summer.

That David Ortiz actively and intentionally clowns in these videos is without question. They are not meant to be taken seriously. But neither, in fact, were Sammy Sosa's High Heat or Luis Tiant's Yankee Frank ads. There is, however, an essential difference. Unlike the earlier endorsement ads, which both contributed to and banked on the Chico Escuela factor, these two Dunkin' videos do not refer in any way to their performers' race or ethnicity. Gronkowski, a white athlete, clowns right along with Ortiz in the videos. Unlike comedy that depends upon an unequal power dynamic, as is so often the case when a duo is involved, the humor and charm of these two videos is entirely dependent upon nothing more than the pair's equal lack of talent and their apparent chemistry. In no way does Ortiz's performance refer to or stem from any ethnic or racial stereotypes. In fact, it is almost deracialized.

While the 2016 viral commercial "Dunkin' Paradise" is essentially a reprise of "Sippin'," the other original videos depart from the established formula. They still play on the celebrity athletes' total lack of musical talent, and they are also music video–genre parodies. But rather than erase racial and ethnic difference, they celebrate them. As its name unequivocally announces, "Me Estoy Enamorando" ("I'm Falling in Love") is a Spanish-language, or at least mostly Spanish-language, video. This ad features Ortiz dressed in a white suit and cap, surrounded by white billowing curtains in a candle-lit, white-and-beige room, singing about Dunkin', the object of his desire. His beloved, as represented by the mascot, frolics outside the window and in the ballplayer's imagination. Here, Gronkowski plays second fiddle, sitting at an easel and inexplicably drawing what appears to be a picture of Ortiz's true love. At first glance, "Me Estoy Enamorando" seems to look backward to embrace a stereotype that the other videos have actively eschewed. But this is not the case. Although the ad actively depends upon Ortiz's Spanish fluency at the same time that it emphasizes his Afro-Latino ethnicity by placing the dark-skinned athlete in a field of white, it does not require him to perform self-parody. Rather, the ad parodies a specific form—the bachata video.

Bachata is a popular music genre originating in the Dominican Republic. Enjoying a twenty-first-century revival, especially among young Latinx audiences in the United States, bachata is always romantic, with lost love and longing its stock-in-trade.[44] Videos of popular bachata artists like Prince Royce and Romeo Santos frequently rely upon the same visual idioms as "Me Estoy Enamorando"—the soft focus, the white-suited singer, the billowy curtains, the candle light, the object of the singer's affection, either imagined or just out of reach. All they are missing is a white, tone-deaf football player with a sketch pad.

Given the purchasing power of Spanish-speaking consumers, it makes sense for Dunkin' Donuts to have released a culturally specific ad as part of its campaign, just as Pepsi did with "Stand-off." But there is only one version of this video, which was released as part of an "album" with the others. As such, it does not target an appreciably different audience than "Sippin'" or "Turn It Up." Rather, it is inclusive. It seems to understand that its target consumers are versed in any number of music genres and will get the joke, whether or not they are Latinx. And just in case English-speaking audiences are unaware of bachata conventions, Gronkowski is there to translate, telling viewers, first, "This is a love song about iced coffee," then clarifying, "That was a love song about iced coffee—in Spanish."[45]

Singing in Spanish rather than in English with a Dominican accent, exaggerated or otherwise, Ortiz has no avenue to invoke Chico Escuela, even accidentally. Instead, his participation in the ad seems to reinforce his *Latinidad*, his sense of Latin-ness, to viewers of the video. More importantly, it speaks directly to his Dominican origins, all for the benefit of an audience that includes Americans of various races and ethnicities as well as a large, culturally diverse Latino viewership. Of course "Weekend Update's" Ortiz is also Dominican. He reiterates this every time he tells "El Yost" that he enjoys a "biiig Dominican lunch" on special occasions. But unlike Thompson's Ortiz, the white-clad, bachata-singing designated hitter puts his heritage on display, celebrating it—though with a wink and a nod—rather than transforming it into an object of derision.

Perhaps even more significant from the point of view of Afro-Latino identity is the final video among the 2015 releases. Unlike the others, "4 Things We Love," actually traffics in stereotypes, but not of Afro-Latino baseball players. Subtly subversive, this country music–video parody—which also parodies the 1974 "Baseball, Hot Dogs, Apple Pie, and Chevrolet" commercial—counters the Chico Escuela image with a message of inclusion even stronger than that of "Me Estoy Enamorando." "4 Things We Love" features Gronkowski playing the part of what might best be described as a redneck, cowboy hat–wearing, pickup-driving, hay-hauling farmer who works out—a lot. Gronkowski is Dunkin' Donuts' answer to Chevrolet's jingle-singing Ed Labunski. As the viral ad begins, he announces in a roughly southern/Texan accent, "Here's a song I wrote about dirt roads, a pickup, and Dunkin' Iced Coffee." In a sense, Gronkowski's buff hayseed/songwriter is the American version of Chico Escuela. After all, the New York State born and raised, Arizona-educated, New England Patriot is no more southern than Garrett Morris and Kenan Thompson are Dominican. But since Gronkowski does not represent all white American football players as a class to an audience unfamiliar with him or his culture, his country singer does not function in the same way as Sammy Sosa's confused baseball player or Mariano Rivera's Chalupa-eating closer do. That he refers obliquely to Labunski also helps to temper the stereotype.

But how does one mild case of stereotyping—though not a terribly offensive one, unless country singers as a group take Gronkowski's vocal stylings into account—serve to counter another, more damaging stereotype? The answer lies in Ortiz's role as Gronkowski's "accompanist" and backup singer and dancer. As the football player sings of his love for the first three things, Ortiz, very much the urban cowboy dressed in a sport jacket, a T-shirt, jeans, sneakers, and a white Stetson, mimes at strumming a guitar. His only solo line is the "fourth thing"—"and America." As he sings, the camera focuses on him. Ortiz is displayed against the central signifier of true American-ness, the flag. More importantly, the word "America," taking up half the screen, is superimposed on the entire image. It is as if the actual message of the video, ostensibly a commercial for iced coffee, is "This is what America looks like—an Afro-Latino baseball player, pretending to strum a guitar." It is reinforced by Ortiz's attempt at line dancing during the chorus, "Those are four things we love."[46] In contrast to Gronkowski, Ortiz is the ideal, knowing, even a little ironic, consumer citizen—the very avatar of American-ness.

In a sense, David Ortiz's participation in the "Summer Chill" campaign, and even his unfortunate tweets from the White House, have helped reframe the image of the Afro-Latino baseball player. Certainly, Ortiz is only one in a long line of talented Afro-Latino players who have excelled on the diamond and continue to do so. But as a product endorser and commercial actor, he represents the new face of the Afro-Latino ballplayer, one who effectively counters the image of Chico Escuela and even Kenan Thompson's Escuela-esque impersonation. Ortiz's ability to shift between languages, between genres, between media, even between skill sets, his singing notwithstanding, may serve as an example of a slow cultural shift.

Yet at the same time, Ortiz may also be seen as a contributor to its slow pace. He may be the very symbol of the new Afro-Latino American in "4 Things We Love," but his 2016 JetBlue retirement commercial tells a different story. Called "charming" by *Adweek*, the forty-five-second spot, "David Ortiz vs. Piñatas" is characterized as a "thank-you" ad from the airline, an official Red Sox sponsor.[47] The spot opens with a head-shot of a papier-mâché dinosaur. In the background, children's voices chant "Go! Go! Go!" Then the camera cuts to the scene of a birthday party. With the celebrant about to be blindfolded in preparation for piñata-busting, the seemingly requisite "Spanish" music begins; this time it is a song by vocalist "El Centauro," Alfredo Lima, accompanied by his Mariachi Mexico Bravia. In steps Ortiz, clearly uninvited, and smashes the piñata with one swing of his bat. He walks away satisfied, leaving terrified children and horrified parents in his wake. And so it goes. Ortiz wrecks a little girl's princess party piñata, grabbing a pink-frosted cupcake and stuffing it in his mouth on the way out.

In his final act of destruction, he smashes a pony piñata, sending the head into the pool of a nearby resident who closely resembles an extra on *The Sopranos*, clearly a *Godfather* reference. The spot ends with Ortiz walking in Fenway Park's outfield with someone who might easily be his agent, lawyer, or accountant, advising his client, "Uh, I'm not sure that's a viable retirement plan." "Just an idea," replies the slugger, as the music swells again. The final frame reads, "Whatever's next for you Big Papi, good luck."[48]

Charming though it may be, "David Ortiz vs. Piñatas" is also problematic. In fact, it shares certain features with "Standoff," the use of music signifying "Spanish" and the Latino power hitter swinging his bat and leaving destruction in his wake, among them. Although the spot is clearly meant to be another example of Ortiz's sense of humor and his skill at not taking himself too seriously, the JetBlue commercial is very different from the Dunkin' Donuts videos. Rather than depict two athletes of different races and ethnicities clowning equally, side by side, "David Ortiz vs. Piñatas" presents the image of a very large, very dark-skinned Afro-Latino, swinging a bat, essentially wielding it as a weapon, striking terror into the hearts of little children, including a group of very little princesses. It seems to suggest that outside the ballpark, David Ortiz is a dangerous man, especially with a bat in his hand. This career move, moreover, is his idea. He does not realize it is a bad one until the authority figure, a short white guy, tells him it is. Looking backward, this ad once again represents the Afro-Latino ballplayer as lacking the intelligence to make an appropriate decision. In this regard, it more closely resembles SNL's Big Papi—the one who relies on Sam and Sam's son for advice and sponsors ships—than the bachata-singing, guitar-strumming, cup-soloing DJ of "Summer Chill."

David Ortiz is not the only highly paid Afro-Latino product endorser on the Major League roster, active or retired. As their individual endorsement earnings in the millions show, Pujols, Cano, and Cabrera are highly compensated for their commercial work, although Cano's bankability has taken a hit as a result of his 2018 PED suspension. In 2017 only Buster Posey made more in advertising.[49] Cano and Pujols have made commercials promoting *SportsCenter*. In keeping with the tone and tenor of the *SportsCenter* campaign, these clever commercials are devoid of any reference to race or ethnicity, no matter how tangential. There are no mariachi horns or flamenco guitar to be heard, although Jose Reyes's 2008 spot "More Hips" does involve salsa dancing. Cabrera's "Tranquilo Yoga with Miggy," advertising MLB's *The Show* videogame for PlayStation, is also intentionally funny and devoid of any real ethnic or racial content, though his yoga practice is "tranquilo." For the most part, however, Cabrera, Cano, and Pujols make the majority of their commercial earnings from contracts with Nike, Adidas, New Balance, and other major sporting-goods manufacturers. They do appear in English-language commercials, but rarely in speaking roles.

At least until he retired at the end of the 2016 postseason, Ortiz remained baseball's biggest endorsement star. More importantly, he continues to serve as the advertising exemplar for all Afro-Latino ballplayers. When Lego sponsored a promotional "day" at Fenway Park on August 31, 2016, it was not longtime team icon Dustin Pedroia or one of Boston's rising stars like Mookie Betts or Xander Bogaerts, but Big Papi who was immortalized in plastic bricks. The Lego Ortiz was highly preferable to a bobble-head giveaway, sponsored by office supply distributor W. B. Mason. Depicting Ortiz with oversized white lips, the doll was reminiscent of nineteenth-century representations of African Americans as watermelon-eating, grinning pickaninnies, an image that was common to the advertising of the era. So insensitive was this representation deemed that the giveaway was actually cancelled.[50]

Inasmuch as representation in advertising affects public perception of any number of racial and ethnic groups, the way in which Ortiz is represented affects the overall perception of his own ethnicity. As "Sippin'," "Turn It Up," and "Dunkin' Paradise" prove, clever, humorous, endorsement advertising need not refer to race or ethnicity, whether positively or negatively. More importantly, "Me Estoy Enamorando" and "4 Things We Love" confront ethnicity and race with humor, one embracing ethnic difference and the other, turning stereotyping on its head. But as "David Ortiz vs. Piñatas" demonstrates, one advertising campaign does not necessarily completely alter commercial rhetoric. Big Papi still stands in Chico Escuela's shadow, though the shadow may be growing faint.

Each baseball season, a new group of young Spanish-speaking, Afro-Latino players enters the public spotlight. With help from interpreters mandated by Major League Baseball and the MLB Players Association, fewer will be faced with the prospects of limiting interaction with the press to a few pat phrases. They will not be forced to revive the oft-returning ghost of Chico Escuela. That is not to say it will disappear altogether from advertising or from the public eye. Given the rise of anti-immigrant sentiment in the United States, which comes and goes in waves as it has always done and will no doubt continue to do, it is questionable whether a few well-placed viral video commercials and product endorsements will really make a difference in the perception of Afro-Latino baseball players and, by extension, Afro-Latinx peoples in general. But a shift in the carefully constructed advertising images of Afro-Latino baseball players may help to normalize the idea that Latin Americans are Americans, as evidenced by "4 Things We Love." Perhaps a change is underway.

CHAPTER EIGHT

"Driven" to "RE2PECT"

Derek Jeter and the (Re)Branding of "All-American"

On September 25, 2014, shortstop Derek Jeter ended his Yankee Stadium career with a flourish, hitting a walk-off home run in front of a wildly cheering sellout crowd. Jeter would go on to play a few more games at Fenway Park, but for the Yankee captain and his fans, this was his valedictory performance. It was also but one event in a season-long series of leave-takings, a farewell tour characterized by widespread media adulation, ceremonial gift giving, and uncharacteristically positive behavior by otherwise unforgiving fans of rival teams and rival players. "It's not just me, it's the whole league," said Boston's second baseman Dustin Pedroia. "This guy has played the game right for a long time. He's a first-ballot Hall of Famer, and when he's done, I don't think there will be a bad thing said about him. He's a first-class guy. He's a winner. The highest praises you could say about a guy is what you would say about Jeter."[1] For a generation of baseball fans, media, players, and executives, Derek Jeter was the face of America's game—the epitome of all that the game symbolized, a grownup version of the All-American Boy for the twenty-first century.

Jeter's final tour around the Major Leagues represented a windfall not only for the Yankees, but also for other teams seeking to boost attendance. MLB also made a tidy profit from the sale of licensed merchandise, as did a bevy of Bronx-based T-shirt vendors selling unofficial Jeter swag. More significantly, the hoopla generated by Jeter's long good-bye afforded a fortunate few advertisers the opportunity to capitalize on the media-generated Jeter-mania. None did so more emphatically than Nike and PepsiCo,

Gatorade's parent company, both of which produced ninety-second national television spots honoring the retiring superstar.

Responsibility for the hoopla surrounding Jeter's farewell tour rested at least in part with the Yankees and the New York sports media. But neither the media nor the Yankees invented this promotional form. This was not the MLB celebrity machine's first farewell tour, nor would it be the last. Cal Ripken Jr. elicited his fair share of encomia and gift giving from his contemporaries on the diamond, in press boxes and broadcast booths, and in the stands after he announced that he planned to retire in 2001. Mariano Rivera, Jeter's longtime teammate and fellow member of the "Core Four"—a designation created by the New York sports writers and broadcasters to distinguish Rivera, Jeter, catcher Jorge Posada, and pitcher Andy Pettitte, all five-time World Series champions, from their teammates following the Yankees' 2009 victory—was similarly feted across Major League ballparks in 2013. And in 2016 David Ortiz, in the midst of a career year at bat, garnered a career's worth of praise as his opponents and their fans bid him adieu. There is no doubt that Jeter-fest 2014 was more than a little over-the-top. Of all the farewell tours, Jeter's received the most publicity, and Jeter, the most praise. Perhaps inevitably, it also received the most criticism from some members of the praise-weary press and public. Still, a little criticism was a small price to pay for the financial benefit his retirement tour yielded for his team, the league, his personal finances, and, above all, advertisers who banked on his image to sell consumer goods.

Brand Jeter

To invoke a classic Yogi-ism, Jeter would not have had to thank his team, the media, the opposition, and his fans for "making this day necessary," or in this case, his entire farewell season necessary, were he not already a household name, an icon off the field as well as on it.[2] Jeter's sterling, virtually spotless reputation was built, first and foremost, on his play. He was, after all, 1996 American League Rookie of the Year. A fourteen-time All-Star, in 2000, Jeter was the first player ever to be named MVP of MLB's midsummer classic and the World Series in the same year. And, of course, he was responsible for one of the most famous plays in MLB postseason history, "the flip," when, seemingly out of nowhere, he corralled a potentially disastrous bad throw near the first-base foul line, saving a run and most likely the game and the 2001 American League Division Series for the Yankees. Most importantly, he was one of only a few marquee players of his era to avoid association with the performance-enhancing drug scandals that rocked the professional baseball world during his tenure. However, he was not the sole great player among his contemporaries. Some had far gaudier statistics; some made even flashier plays. So what was all the fuss about? To a great extent all the praise, all the hero worship, was as much a product of his public image as it was of his considerable athletic prowess. While Jeter's reputation as someone who "played the game right for a long time" yielded multiple endorsement opportunities, the opposite is also true. His widespread stardom, his reputation for excellence, was also grounded upon his work in advertising. The creation of Brand Jeter was in many ways a reciprocal arrangement between advertising and baseball.

Jeter's emergence as a star endorser paralleled his emergence as a star player. At the outset, he lent his name to products of the type most conventionally endorsed by baseball players, including Nike sneakers, Gatorade, and a variety of breakfast and snack foods such as Post cereals, Skippy peanut butter, and Oreo cookies. And as he matured as a player, so did his endorsement portfolio. In addition to a constant stream of regional television spots for Ford, he appeared in national advertising for VISA credit cards and Fleet Bank. He pitched Movado watches and lent his image to Avon men's grooming products. And he told his fans, however indirectly, that a physique like his might be acquired at any time of the day or night at 24 Hour Fitness gyms. Being Derek Jeter paid. All his commercial work contributed to his status as a regular fixture on the *Sports Illustrated Fortunate 50*, the list of America's top athlete-earners. While his salary did not equal that of some of his peers, he led them all in endorsement dollars. Even in 2014, when he finally fell off the list, he remained baseball's top endorser, earning approximately $9 million in his final season for his advertising efforts.[3]

What made Jeter so marketable? According to advertising and branding expert Mark Sanderson (no relationship to Jeter, whose middle name is Sanderson):

> After Derek Jeter's 3,000th hit sailed over the wall and into the cheering stands . . . the Diamond Vision displayed DJ3K merchandise flying off the shelves at Yankee Stadium souvenir shops.
>
> It was a compelling manifestation of Derek Jeter's marketability. In fact, according to USA Today, Derek Jeter is one of the most marketable athletes on the planet. But how can that be? He's not a flashy power hitter and he's not living it up in Hollywood. So, what's his appeal? Simply put, it's his professionalism.[4]

But professionalism, alone, did not make him an endorsement superstar. Major League rosters were replete with players whose professionalism matched Jeter's. But unlike that of his similarly professional peers, Jeter's professionalism was constantly on public display. In this regard, he was peerless. As Howard Smith, MLB's senior vice president of marketing in 2011, told Sanderson, "Look, let's face it. He plays one of the most marketable positions on arguably one of the most marketable sports franchises in the world. He does it quite well and he does it in a manner that makes Yankees fans proud. The fact of the matter is there isn't a product in the mix where Jeter hasn't done pretty well for Major League Baseball." In a survey jointly conducted by E-Poll Market Research and the Nielsen Company at the time of the 2011 All-Star Game, Jeter had an "N-Score" of 165, the highest by far of any player on either roster.[5] An N-Score, according to Nielsen, is a "syndicated solution that assesses the casting and endorsement potential of over a thousand celebrities," aimed at helping "industry players do that very thing."[6] Among the 2011 All-Stars, no one even came close to Jeter. In fact, only two of Jeter's fellow players on the game's roster were also considered by Nielsen to be "endorsement All-Stars"—Alex Rodriguez, with an N-Score of thirty-five, and David Ortiz, whose N-Score was thirty-four.[7]

If their N-Scores made Ortiz and Rodriguez endorsement All-Stars, then Jeter's made him the decade's MVP.

However unwittingly, Jeter assessed his own marketability in 2005, stating, "My Dad is black, my Mom is Irish, and I'm Catholic, so I hear everything. I'm in New York and there are all different people, all races and religions. I can relate to everyone."[8] In terms of celebrity endorsements, the ability to relate to "everyone" and its flipside, "everyone's" ability to relate to a given celebrity, translates into selling to everyone. Although Jeter's allure as a player was not quite universal, it was certainly broad-based enough to earn him the top spot on baseball's advertising roster, with enough crossover appeal to reach outside the diamond and sell to consumers with little emotional connection to the sport. Both on and off the field, Jeter was and has remained a powerful brand, even as he takes up the mantle of the Florida Marlins' most visible new owner.

What is Brand Jeter? One of the most useful ways to look at the construction of product identity is in terms of individual "brand personality." According to Marieke deMooij, "The brand personality model defines the brand as a human personality. Marketers attribute human personality traits (e.g., seriousness, warmth, imagination, sincerity) to a brand as a way to achieve differentiation."[9] In other words, a brand is defined by a collection of extrinsic attributes, which may be expressed in human terms, applied to a consumer product, thereby differentiating it from all of the other products in the same category. There is, however, one problem with defining Jeter in terms of brand personality—he is an actual human being with actual personality traits. But like all celebrities, the public Jeter was and is not the same as the actual person. Jeter the celebrity, like sneakers, sports drinks, and men's grooming products, may be seen as an amalgam of attributes, benefits, and values, as represented by the Yankees organization, the sports media, celebrity gossip sites, social media, and the advertisers with whom he was and continues to be associated. He is, in essence, a product. Certainly, Jeter's actions and attitudes have informed his brand. Were he a known performance-enhancing drug user or, during his on-field career, a married lothario, his actions would have impacted his brand negatively. This is not to say that Jeter's brand personality was always that of a choirboy. As an unmarried player, he was known as something of a Don Juan, a serial dater of supermodels and equally beautiful singers and actresses. In terms of his brand, however, this served as a favorable attribute and played an active role in certain of his product endorsements.

Jeter's reputation as an old-school playboy and lover of the nightlife was foregrounded in a 2003 VISA television spot in which he appears with his boss, the Boss, George Steinbrenner. The commercial played on a dispute between Jeter and his employer, a conflict that might have sullied Brand Jeter with the personality trait "arrogant," had it not been handled properly. In a 2002 interview with Bill Coffey of the *New York Daily News*, Steinbrenner, considering the shortstop for the role of Yankee captain, the first since Don Mattingly's retirement in 1995, had some choice words to say about what he perceived to be Jeter's declining play: "I tell him all the time. I say 'Jetes, you can't be everything to everybody. You've got to be focused on what's important.' When I read in the paper that he's out until 3:00 a.m. in New York City going to a birthday party, I won't lie. That doesn't sit in well with me."[10] Identified as a company man through and through, Jeter was surprisingly unrepentant in the face of Steinbrenner's criticism. Writes the *Daily News'* Roger Rubin, "As he left the Yankees Minor League complex wearing black sweat suit and driving a black SUV yesterday, Jeter was asked if he's going to change anything about his lifestyle. 'I'm not going to change,' Jeter said. 'Not at all.'" Indeed, he seemed to be willing to relinquish any claim on the captaincy if it got in the way of what Rubin called "Jeter's stylish Manhattan living."[11]

The VISA spot effectively encapsulated the conflict. It offered viewers a fly-on-the-wall experience, taking Jeter's fans into Steinbrenner's inner sanctum to witness his opprobrium of his player. "You're our starting shortstop. How can you possibly afford to spend two nights dancing, two nights eating out, and three nights just carousing with your friends?" Steinbrenner asks. Jeter, in turn, raises his eyebrows, and without uttering as much as a peep in response, flashes his VISA card, to which Steinbrenner responds,

"Oh." The spot ends at a nightclub, with Jeter on a conga line. Several spaces behind him, holding the bare midriff of a beautiful female partier is Steinbrenner, dressed in his iconic white turtleneck and sports jacket, waving at the presumed paparazzi.[12] The commercial's denouement, the notion that Jeter is in possession of special knowledge that even the powerful Steinbrenner is unable to access without his help, is what drives the ad. Jeter alone knows that certain New York hotspots accept no other credit card; he alone holds the key. Although Steinbrenner has taken him to task, the gracious Jeter generously shares his special knowledge with Steinbrenner, allowing the Boss to join his party. The ad lets consumers in on Jeter's special wisdom, making them insiders, as well. Ultimately, the spot suggests that Jeter's fans, like Steinbrenner, are but one credit card application away from joining him on that conga line.

As history and hagiography have shown, the very public feud between Jeter and Steinbrenner was patched up and became little more than comic fodder for commercial use. Unspoken in the ad is the fact that in 2001, Jeter signed a contract that would pay him $189 million over ten years, exclusive of endorsement earnings. Theoretically, he did not need the VISA card to pay for his "stylish Manhattan living." Still, the ad was effective. Of the spot, VISA's vice president for advertising, Nancy Friedman, remarked, "It's perfect for what we want to communicate about leadership and acceptance," presumably referring to Steinbrenner's leadership rather than Jeter's acceptance of Steinbrenner's money.[13] In addition to stressing leadership and acceptance, two already strong personality traits of Brand Jeter if not of Brand Steinbrenner, the ad publically signaled an end to the very public conflict between labor and management. This was extremely important to Brand Jeter's continued strength. And it seems to have worked. On June 3, 2003, Steinbrenner did, in fact, name his starting shortstop captain. This, in turn, became another attribute of Brand Jeter.

Although Brand Jeter and Jeter the individual are two different things, they share certain important features, especially as regards identity. As Jeter himself observed in connection to his ability to relate to everyone, he is both biracial and multiethnic. His unwillingness to commit to a single ethnic or racial identity led former teammate Gary Sheffield to assert that Jeter "ain't all the way black."[14] Nevertheless, Jeter was and continues to be a celebrity of color. Historically speaking, prior to 1947, the very existence of MLB's color line severely curtailed opportunities for individuals of Jeter's heritage to play in the Major Leagues at all. And not only were players of color barred from playing organized baseball, de facto Jim Crow standards severely limited their endorsement opportunities. In fact, Jim Crow's tendrils extended into the world of mainstream product endorsement long after the color line was breached.

Gary Sheffield's opinion notwithstanding, Jeter may be defined as African American by virtue of his parentage. During his playing days, Jeter was one of a dwindling number of American-born players of color. Despite MLB's self-congratulatory rhetoric surrounding its own continuing place in the civil rights narrative, there were twice as many African American players on the field when Pumpsie Green desegregated the Red Sox in 1959 than there were in Jeter's final season.[15] In 2014 the percentage of African American players on MLB Jackie Robinson Day rosters, though up slightly from a low in 2012, was but 8.3 percent.[16] Certainly, players of color are still well represented in the professional sport. But the majority of them are Afro-Latinos, like David Ortiz, many of them foreign-born. If they had played before 1947, they, too, would have been subject to Jim Crow's restrictive laws and customs. But by the consensus of twenty-first-century sports media, fans, and their fellow players, Afro-Latinos are perceived differently than African American players and are categorized differently in demographic surveys of baseball rosters. They are also treated differently as product endorsers.[17]

Derek Jeter was by no means the first American sports star with African roots to make a killing in endorsement earnings. His millions paled in comparison to NBA advertising legend Michael Jordan's. In 2016, more than a decade after his retirement as an active player, Jordan was on track to earn roughly $30 million more than any other athlete in the world in any sport, active or retired.[18] Nor was Jeter the first biracial athlete to make a splash on the endorsement scene. Tiger Woods earned as much as five times Jeter's endorsement take, even after his reputation was marred by scandal and the quality of his play fell off considerably.[19] Nor was Jeter the first biracial baseball player to pitch consumer goods. That honor went to Dodgers catcher Roy Campanella, who appeared in a landmark Gillette Blue Razor ad in the mid-1950s. But Jeter was the highest-profile, biracial player-endorser in recent MLB advertising history. When Jeter publically proclaimed that his background bestowed on him a near-universal ability to relate, he made a powerful statement. Indeed, Jeter's racial identity as the product of an African American father and an Irish, and, by extension, white mother is very much a constituent part of his brand.

Driven

In 2006 Avon introduced its new line of men's colognes in an international, integrated campaign that included print ads, an interactive website, and a variety of outdoor signage on New York City buses, taxis, and at the entrances to subway stations. The face that looked out from the ads, greeting readers, web surfers, and commuters, belonged to Derek Jeter. Jeter's image also graced as many as twenty-five million company brochures, distributed by the cosmetic giant's half million sales representatives to potential customers in Canada, Puerto Rico, and Mexico, as well as in their primary market, the United States.[20] At first glance, the commercial marriage between Avon and Jeter appears to be an odd one, but it is not really all that unusual for an athlete of Jeter's stature to have lent his name to cologne. This was hardly a new practice; Michael Jordan had led the way with his own branded scent several years earlier. What made Driven unusual was its target consumer base.

Although Jeter had certainly sold his fair share of breakfast cereal to children and sporting goods and sneakers to amateur athletes and style-conscious teenagers, his primary image as constructed by the media and advertising industry bespoke class. His VISA commercial and his appearances in fashion spreads in upmarket men's magazines like GQ and *Esquire*, as well as his endorsement of high-end Movado 800 series chronograph watches, underscored the meaning of luxury as another constituent part of Brand Jeter. Avon's Driven, in contrast, was by definition a mass-market product. The majority of readers of glossy men's fashion and lifestyle magazines were not among those whom *Sports Illustrated*'s Adam Hoffstetter, with tongue planted firmly in cheek, suggested were "spraying on a little Driven before taking that special someone to the Olive Garden."[21] While this may have been true, it did not stop Avon from placing a Driven print ad in the December 2006 issue of GQ. In doing so, Avon attempted to associate its men's scent with qualities of Brand Jeter's personality, in this case, a taste for the good life. As such, the company seems to have looked to its endorser to elevate its product and its own brand personality.

Avon's public relations rhetoric reinforced the message that Driven was a high-end scent. Announcing Avon's collaboration with Jeter on Driven, the company's executive vice president for North America and global marketing, Liz Smith, enthused, "We are thrilled to be partnering with Derek Jeter—a man whose care and commitment to accomplishments make him an outstanding fit for the brand . . . we have a shared commitment to giving back to society and improving the lives of others. We're impressed with Derek's personal dedication to his Turn 2 Foundation which motivates young people to choose healthy lifestyles."[22] The Driven ad uses similar rhetoric:

> Derek Jeter is . . .
> A four-time World Series Champion, a seven-time All-Star, captain of the most storied baseball team in sports history.
> Derek Jeter is . . .
> A community leader dedicated to helping disadvantaged youth through his Turn 2 Foundation, a role model for our generation.
> Derek Jeter is . . . Driven.[23]

Interestingly, the Jeter-branded Movado ad uses strikingly similar language to sell a different class of product to a different demographic. With a certain economy of language, it reads, "Derek

Jeter—humanitarian, leader, athlete." While both ads make the same basic points as they link their respective products to three very important meanings of Brand Jeter—athleticism, leadership, and good works—the order of the qualities is reversed in the Movado ad. Movado puts the most emphasis on the endorser as humanitarian, while Avon points to his athletic prowess above all else. Although the product, the Movado 800 series chronograph, is a sports watch, and although *Esquire* and its ilk pay some attention to sports, the advertisers seem to assume that humanitarianism would carry more weight with its well-heeled readership, or, more appropriately, with its readership that aspires to be well-heeled, than with readers of mass-circulation sports publications like *Sports Illustrated* or ESPN: *The Magazine*. Those upmarket consumers who cared about sports would already have been acquainted with these aspects of Brand Jeter. For readers of upmarket men's magazines with little or no interest in sports coverage or the lives of athletes, the picture of an extremely handsome celebrity, accompanied by the label "humanitarian," may have had some appeal; a picture of a jock in action, identified as a jock in action, would have none. In the Avon ad, in contrast, Jeter's athletic achievements supersede his community work.

Driven is a product designed for men but marketed to Avon's key consumers, women. Avon, after all, bills itself as *the* company for women.[24] To sell Driven to women, who would presumably order it for the men in their lives, Avon's advertising had to stress the manliness of the product. Hence, Avon's ads trumpet primacy of sports, emphasizing Jeter's leadership in sports terms. Still, the advertising brochure certainly does not overlook Jeter's community leadership, itself a quality that would appeal to Avon's core consumers. Like Movado, Avon transfers goodness and generosity to its product through Jeter. But in this case, Avon narrows its focus to Jeter's well-worn mantle of "role model" to "disadvantaged youth," naming Jeter's foundation and his dedication to working with at-risk children rather than stressing his overall humanitarianism, with its whiff of class consciousness.

Of course, copy alone does not provide meaning to advertising. In both the Avon and Movado ads, copy is subordinate to image.

With a few exceptions, the visual components of the ads mirror one another. In both, Jeter is dressed in a simple pullover, tinted to blend into the ad's background. What he wears, however, is of secondary importance. Of primary significance in both ads is Jeter's face, as it emerges almost symbolically from the shadows, a stark light gray against a black background in the Movado ad, burnt sienna complimenting the smoky blue in the Avon ad. In neither ad does Jeter appear to be passing for white; in neither is he truly black.

First and foremost, Jeter as represented by Avon and Movado is visually attractive. A 1985 study measuring the effect of attractiveness in celebrity endorsements concluded, "Participants were more likely to intend to purchase after exposure to an attractive rather than an unattractive celebrity."[25] When attractiveness is combined with likeability, the resulting icon is practically irresistible. Jeter's status as a mixed-race celebrity, as an icon who is neither black nor white, can "relate to everyone," and who serves his community selflessly, is pretty close to irresistible. Moreover, Jeter's own willingness to situate his racial and ethnic identity squarely with his parents gave him top scores on the likeability scale. After all, Jeter's parents played a central role in his narrative, serving as a constant reminder of his racial identity throughout his career. Seemingly every time he stepped up to bat in a crucial situation, every time he made a splashy play in the field that impacted the outcome of an important game, there were his parents, praying for a clutch hit or cheering for their son's success. As Ed Bradley noted in his 2005 profile of Jeter on *Sixty Minutes*:

> Jeter's parents Charles and Dorothy are his most devoted fans. Dorothy is an accountant, and Charles, a former college shortstop, is now a clinical social worker. Derek never starts a game until he finds where his parents are seated. It's a habit he has had since Little League. And as soon as he spots his mom, he says hi.
>
> "We communicate," says Dorothy Jeter. "Sometimes, you know, he'll just stick up his head and go like that," she says, glancing up. "It means he's going to try to hit a home run. I shouldn't give that away, should I?"[26]

Of course, virtually every time Jeter located his parents in the stands, so, too, did the camera. And who, especially among Avon's target market, does not like a young man who is so close to his parents?

At the same time the camera captured the Jeters' devotion to their son and his to his parents, it also captured their race. Unlike the shortstop, there is nothing racially ambiguous about the very white Dorothy and the clearly African American Charles. But rather than dwell on their racial identity, sports announcers preferred to focus on the Jeters' professions. In fact, over the course of Jeter's career, it became customary for those covering the shortstop to refer to his father as Dr. Charles and his mother, Dorothy, the accountant. This focus on profession, and by extension, class, appears to have been designed to mitigate any discussion of race. The camera may have said, "These are Derek Jeter's parents. His father is black, his mother is white. Derek Jeter is biracial." The announcers, however, countered with, "These are Derek Jeter's parents. His father has a doctorate. His mother is a professional accountant. See how these people are productive, upstanding, upper-middle-class community members. There is nothing here to fear."

Jeter's racial identity may have actually contributed to his marketability. "The fact of his biracial heritage and how he has handled it adds an entirely new dimension to his iconic appeal and potential marketability," writes cultural critic Leon Wynter. "For starters, the camera loves his sharp but racially ambiguous features. Every time it lights on him, the eye wants to linger, not only on the total package of good looks, but on each of the parts, in a vain attempt to calculate the racial whole."[27] Jeter's branding as the biracial, All-American marketing icon may be read as an expression of an important advertising trend. According to advertising executive Ron Berger, "Both in the mainstream and at the high end of the marketplace, what is perceived as good, desirable, successful is often a face whose heritage is hard to pin down."[28] Despite the clear message communicated by the constant presence of Jeter's parents on game broadcasts that their son is biracial, his ethnic ambiguity remains part of his appeal.

The marketability of ethnically and racially ambiguous celebrities like Jeter is the result of several factors. An ever-increasing number of Americans identify themselves as bi- or multiracial. In 2013, according to the U.S. Census Bureau, approximately nine million Americans chose multiple categories when asked about their race. In addition, the number of Americans of mixed black-and-white heritage doubled between 2000 and 2010.[29] Thus, the fact that multiracial Americans, as a growing consumer group, sought to see themselves in advertising no doubt contributed to the trend. But for Wynter, the attractiveness of Jeter and Tiger Woods, who in 2002 exceeded Jeter's marketability, was an expression of something even deeper. He writes, "Being neither and both like Jeter; or none and all three like Woods, is more powerful than just being Black or Hispanic, or Asian American, or more important, just white. It's not just because the mixed-race icon can command the combined loyalties of disparate ethnic audience segments. Mixed-race icons are powerful because their whole beings represent more than the sum of their racial parts. They are the embodiment of the new transracial ideal." Indeed, Jeter, with his self-proclaimed ability to relate to everyone and his refusal to be categorized as belonging to any one race or ethnic group, served as the very exemplar of this transracial ideal both in advertising and in baseball.[30] Of course, this transracial ideal was just that, an ideal, perpetrated by advertising and its sidekick, the fashion industry, rather than a reality. Nevertheless, its impact was undeniable.

Of all Jeter's endorsement advertising, the campaign and the product that made the best use of his position as an expression of the new pop-cultural transracial ideal was Driven. The very notion that Avon, a company selling to the mass-market, chose to build a product line around a nonwhite baseball player, and the very notion that Avon's core customers might just want the men in their lives to splash on a little Derek Jeter, may have pointed to a shift in attitude concerning race—though it proved to be temporary—at least on a personal, individual level. That it may have paved the way for the mass acceptance of an even more important celebrity embodiment of the transracial ideal, President Barak

Obama, is purely speculative. Nevertheless, the mass acceptance of
Jeter as the very image of a nonthreatening, yet purely masculine,
celebrity of color, one who is neither black nor white, but both and
neither, the very avatar of the twenty-first-century All-American
Boy, may very well have served as a bellwether for Obama's ascen-
dance as a national figure.

So what does Derek Jeter smell like? "The fragrance, a Fresh
Fougere, is a blend of chilled grapefruit, clean oak moss and spice,
according to Avon's public relations department."[31] And the original
Driven was not just available as cologne; Avon also marketed a line
of Driven grooming products. As required by the FTC, Jeter was
required to use Driven as long as Avon made it available to consumers. As he told *Women's Wear Daily* in an article entitled "Home-
Run Hottie," "My pregame grooming ritual consists of showering,
shaving, dressing for work and putting on some cologne. . . . You
always find Driven cologne, body lotion, toothpaste, and deodorant in my away-games toiletries kit."[32] His beef with Steinbrenner
commemorated in the VISA spot notwithstanding, Brand Jeter,
the public iteration of the transracial ideal, the ballplayer who
was so fastidious that he showered *before* games, the humanitarian who spent his time and money helping disadvantaged youth,
the athlete who would not raise his bat until he knew where his
parents were sitting, the style-conscious celebrity whose punctu-
ality was assured thanks to his Movado 800 series chronograph,
who smelled of chilled grapefruit, was and continues to be, like
the notes of oak moss in his cologne, nothing if not clean.

Driven Black

Capitalizing on the success of its Brand Jeter cologne, Avon introduced a brand extension, a new fragrance called Driven Black, in
2007. As opposed to the original, blue-bottled, grapefruit-y, clean
oak-mossy scent, Driven Black was described as "a mysterious blend
of exotic saffron, blood orange and precious woods." Its pitchman,
noted Avon's promotional material, was, "Intense, yet approachable.
Determined, yet easy going. He's self-assured, yet humble. Derek
Jeter is back in full force launching his second exclusive fragrance

1 3. Derek Jeter's second scent in Avon's Driven line was Driven Black, represented in 2007 print ads. Courtesy of Avon Products.

with Avon. He is the spirit of DRIVEN BLACK."[33] Avon's introductory ad features Jeter dressed in a black suit, depicted both in profile and in a three-quarters view, his white collar and light brown skin standing out against a black background, accompanied only by the words "Driven Black." The image speaks for itself.

In contrast to the original Driven campaign, both Avon's promotional language and the ad itself remind consumers that Brand Jeter is multifaceted. As such, Driven Black, unlike its predecessor, hearkens back to the Steinbrenner VISA commercial. But Driven Black's Jeter is more mature, more masculine. The Jeter of Avon's second cologne is a connoisseur of the nightlife, but he is also intense and determined. The Jeter of the VISA ad is a cocky kid, but Jeter, the spirit of Driven Black, is also mysterious, precious—as in costly—and exotic. The nocturnal version of Driven's daytime pitchman, Jeter is even a little dangerous. He is, in short, the transracial ideal, driven black.

A 2011 Ford TV commercial that aired repeatedly during the postseason in the New York Metropolitan region also touched upon meanings intertwined with Jeter's racial identity. Compared to Avon's Driven Black advertising, it is actually subtle. The thirty-second spot begins with Jeter—clearly not white, but not quite black, either—emerging from the darkness onto a brightly lit field, holding his signature black bat. He steps up to the plate, facing an unidentified, Caucasian pitcher and launches one into the presumed seats. "It's not just about power; hitting it five hundred feet," Jeter tells consumers via voice-over. "It's where to place it; how to convert it. That's power with efficiency."[34] Here, Jeter's racial identification is not the only thing that is ambiguous. So, too, is the subject of the ad. What is *it*? The intended answer is "power," and by extension, Ford pickup trucks. But throughout the ad, *it* serves as a floating signifier; *it* is an empty vessel waiting to be filled by the viewer with any number of meanings. *It* contains the idea of athletic prowess—the ability not only to hit the ball, but to place it efficiently. *It* contains the ideas of strength and will, as embodied by the celebrity endorser. However obliquely, *it* also contains the idea of sexual potency, reinforced by the way in which Jeter wields his bat. As such, the ad's connotations are dangerous. It is highly unlikely that the Tri State Ford dealers, retailers targeting mainstream consumers via mainstream All-American advertising, featuring the most mainstream All-American of athletes, playing the mainstream, All-American game, intentionally invoked notions of both black power and black potency in this ad. Still, *it* suggests indirectly that to be like Jeter in every way is to be more powerful than the white pitcher. *It* is to be like Derek Jeter, driven black.

RE2PECT

As was expected, an onslaught of video and print ads, billboards, and branded merchandise capitalized upon Jeter's announcement of his pending retirement in 2014. Above all the others, two video commercials captured Brand Jeter as the All-American, transracial warrior, heading home after battle more completely than any others. Nike's "RE2PECT"—the spelling and logo were created by replacing the *S* in respect with Jeter's number, 2—and Gatorade's "Made in New York," elevated the subgenre of tribute advertising to an art form. "RE2PECT" features a series of gestural testimonials by players, fellow celebrities, fans, and the odd team mascot. "Made in New York," depicts the departing player as he exits his limousine two blocks from Yankee Stadium to walk among the common folk, accompanied by the swelling strains of Frank Sinatra's "My Way." With their inflated emotional content and freighted imagery, these spots are so monumental that they, and not Jeter's otherwise mediocre performance during his final season, marked his swan song. If nothing else, they assured that Jeter would retain his prime position in the collective American memory channel, at least for a while.

The elegiac "RE2PECT" begins with a back shot of Jeter advancing to the plate. Taken slightly from below, the image very briefly recalls the famous photograph of Babe Ruth, also shot from behind and below, taken during his final appearance in Yankee uniform shortly before his death. Rather than tying Jeter specifically to the wasted Ruth, the image connects Jeter unambiguously to the Yankees' storied past via his posture and place on the field. By extension, the spot imparts a historic, even mythical significance to the product via Nike's Jordan Brand sports apparel. The sound accompanying the opening underscores Jeter's connection to the Yankee pantheon. As the camera follows Jeter to the plate, the late Yankee Stadium announcer Bob Sheppard proclaims his name

14. Nike's RE2PECT campaign that marked Jeter's retirement featured billboards as well as print ads and a ninety-second viral video. Courtesy of Nike.

and number in thundering tones. Although Sheppard retired in 2007, later passing away in 2010, he continued to announce Jeter's approach to the plate via voice recording. In fact, it seemed during the final season's sentimental outpouring as if Sheppard was calling down to proclaim Jeter's sanctity from the heavens, an effect reinforced by the ad's soundtrack. As the camera follows Jeter to the plate, it focuses on his feet, shod in spikes bearing the familiar Jordan Brand logo. Here is Jeter, the super-consumer, the baseball superstar who knows by wearing Jordan Brand that he is, like the Gatorade drinker in an earlier series of ads, "like Mike." At the same time, he urges consumers to follow his lead, thereby becoming more "like Derek."

Moving around Yankee Stadium, then onto the streets of New York and beyond, "RE2PECT" alternates its focus between images of ordinary people and celebrities. Common folk, such as a stadium vendor and some rather grudging Red Sox fans in a bar, tip their cap to the Yankee captain. So do easily recognizable public figures. On their own, each cap tipper sends the same message— Jeter has earned their respect. In this way, the spot's intent is clear. Several of the images also stand in striking juxtaposition with one another. Such is the case with consecutive shots featuring two iconic New York celebrities whose public personae could not possibly be farther apart. Presumably, no one could be more different than director-writer-actor Spike Lee and former mayor Rudolph Giuliani, who share a love of the Yankees and little else, most notably attitudes toward race. While Lee tips his hat from the left side of the stadium, Giuliani tips his from the right. In fact, it seems almost as if they are tipping their caps to one another in grudging agreement as to Jeter's greatness.

Following two more shots of the ethnically and racially diverse Yankee Stadium crowd, the camera settles on that most familiar of images, Jeter's biracial family. The close proximity of these four images—Lee, Giuliani, the multiethnic crowd, and Jeter's family— serve an essential purpose in this spot. They speak directly to contemporary racial politics, not just in New York, but nationally. They seem to suggest if that if the outspoken Lee, the racially divisive Giuliani, and the "rainbow" crowd and family can all celebrate the same man—one so publically identified as neither black nor white but both and neither—the transracial ideal, within the milieu of America's game, then really, America's racial divide may not be so big, after all.

Of course, all advertising is aspirational, and aspirational is perhaps the best way to define the message of racial healing as personified by a single, retiring baseball player. Nevertheless, the following image further supports this image, as the camera moves into the bedroom of a young fan, one that appears to be bi- or multiracial like his idol. In fact, the boy so closely resembles an eight-to-ten-year-old version of Jeter that the ad almost suggests that the future, not just of the game, but of American civilization, rests upon the shoulders of this child and those like him, a new generation of transracial consumer citizens, ready to lead the country wherever their Jeter-branded Brand Jordan footwear takes them.

Missing amid this commercial celebration of racial diversity is gender diversity. There are women in the crowd scenes, and Jeter's mother and sister are featured, as are a female kitchen worker and a limo passenger. There is, however, only one woman who merits a frame of her own—WNBA star Maya Moore, who tips her hoodie in tribute to Jeter. At first glance, the choice of Maya Moore as the sole representative of female athletes in this video appears to be an unconventional one. Unlike the male celebrities featured in the spot, Billy Crystal, Jay-Z, Red Sox pitcher Jon Lester, Tiger Woods, and David Letterman among them, Maya Moore is hardly a household name. She is, however, one of the few female athletes belonging to the "Jordan Family" of endorsers, supposedly "hand-picked" by the great Jordan, himself, to represent his own brand.

Foregrounded in the commercial, Moore is thereby imbued with some of Jeter's culturally constituted meanings. Offering her RE2PECT, she also earns RE2PECT, by means of the ad. She is, moreover, the only tribute player shrouded in a hoodie. In fact, her attire serves a dual purpose. By donning a hoodie, she rebrands it, replacing its negative connotations with the meanings of Maya Moore, Derek Jeter, and Michael Jordan. The hoodie also sets her apart both from the other women in the commercial and those associated with Brand Jeter's perceptual map—the partying women in the VISA ad and the steady stream of supermodels connected to Jeter at various times. In a sense, the inclusion of Moore in the commercial points to an attempt to disassociate Jeter's bachelor playboy image from the brand, thereby making it more female friendly. Still, the dearth of female fans and celebrities showing Jeter their RE2PECT suggests otherwise.

The final tipped cap, quite naturally, belongs to the epitome of Brand Jordan, Michael Jordan himself. By means of this spot, Jeter is allowed to "Be like Mike" at the same time Jordan takes on the imprimatur of Brand Jeter. Given the immense power of Jordan's own brand, it seems unlikely that he would have anything to gain by assuming meanings associated with Jeter. Although Jordan has contributed his fair share to community organizations and other charities, helping disadvantaged youth is not necessarily an attribute of his personal brand. However obliquely, it is possible that one quality always associated with Jeter—humanitarianism, to borrow from Movado's advertising—may be transferred to Brand Jordan and by extension, to Nike. But the connection between Brand Jeter and Jordan Brand runs even deeper.

Nike was and continues to be the real beneficiary of all this meaning transfer. After all, it was Nike that commissioned the billboards and paid for the ninety-second video. And the company profited handsomely from the sale of RE2PECT-branded apparel that continued to sell well after Jeter's retirement, including but not limited to T-shirts, retailing for forty dollars apiece. So potent a marketing tool was "RE2PECT" that in July 2016, nearly two years after Jeter left the field, Nike announced that it had re-signed the former Yankee captain as "Captain of Jordan Training," according to the corporate website. Given that the RE2PECT apparel line was one of the best-selling for Jordan Brand, the continued relationship makes sense. Of Captain Jeter, the website notes, "The 14-time All-Star will help the brand identify and recruit baseball athletes who embody his values on the field. Jeter will be a key figure working with Jordan Brand Sports Marketing and Michael himself to build the Jordan family of baseball athletes."[35] In this way, Brand Jeter has become an attribute of Jordan Brand, and by extension, Brand Jordan, thereby adding the meaning of the new All-American Boy, the transracial ideal, to Nike's sporting apparel juggernaut.

Made in New York

While "RE2PECT" was constructed to represent the fans' farewell to Jeter, "Made in New York" functioned as Jeter's farewell to his fans. Shot in nostalgic black and white and scored with vocals by Frank Sinatra, the ninety-second spot underscores the idea that the end is, in fact, near. Unlike Nike's Jordan Brand, Gatorade does not employ retired athletes as endorsers. There are no retired Gatorade Brand captains. After the "final curtain," there is no more sweat, so there is no longer any need for sweat replacement. Thus, "Made in New York" really is a farewell of sorts—a brand's farewell to its longtime endorser. Over the course of his almost two-decade-long MLB career, Jeter appeared in countless Gatorade commercials, both alone and along with other sports stars, demonstrating the beverage's magical hydrating power.

Notable among Jeter's Gatorade ads are "Can Jimmy Play?" in

which he stars along with former NBA star Yao Ming and quarterback Peyton Manning, also endorsement superstars. In it, each of the three athletes sequentially visits the eponymous young boy to play backyard versions of their given sports. Notable in this spot is the way in which the product is foregrounded. As in a number of earlier Gatorade ads, in "Can Jimmy Play?" each of the athletes and their pal are associated with Gatorade products of different colors. When they sweat, they sweat in the neon hues of their respective sports drinks. This commercial makes meaning transfer explicit. It suggests that by drinking the same color Gatorade as Jeter and friends, the consumer, in this case Jimmy, literally consumes what makes them great. Jimmy, drinking Gatorade prior to playing with his superstar buddies, is prepared to compete with them on the field of play on their level, since he has already ingested their meanings. Referring once again to the landmark Gatorade ad, the drink allows Jimmy to "be like" Manning, Yao, and, of course, Jeter.

This ad works on a yet another level. Each of its three endorsers represents not only a different sport, but also a different racial or ethnic group. Manning, like Jimmy, is Caucasian, Yao is Chinese, and Jeter, the transracial ideal, "can relate to everybody." The ad differentiates them in terms of color, as well. But in this case, the colors are neon green and blue, thereby replacing ethnic and racial differences with bright food dyes. Gatorade is the great equalizer. The product's slogan, "Is IT in you?" seeks to reinforce the message. Once again *it* has multiple meanings—*it* refers to a competitive drive; *it* refers to athletic ability; *it* refers to Gatorade. Ultimately, *it* refers to all the meanings of all the athletes in this spot—meanings that both include and transcend racial and ethnic difference.

Another notable Jeter Gatorade spot features the shortstop on the base paths. Accompanied by music suggesting mystery and suspense, Jeter contemplates stealing a base, having singled to lead off an inning. As if from nowhere, actor Harvey Keitel appears on the diamond, but only Jeter is aware of his presence. Encouraging Jeter to steal first base on pitcher John Lackey's move, Keitel cues

Jeter into Lackey's intentions, saying, "The thing is, that *schmedrick*, he keeps looking over here." Nodding to the unidentified catcher, Keitel warns, "And that one, he's got a gun. But you gotta do what you gotta do." Naturally, Jeter swipes the bag, leading Keitel to respond "Ah, stealin'. It's a beautiful thing."[36] As in most Gatorade spots, this is followed by a shot of the slogan. In this case, Gatorade's *it* is even more complex. Not only does *it* contain all the other meanings of Derek Jeter, *it* also contains the wherewithal to do whatever is necessary to win, even if it means doing something that in any other circumstance might be considered dishonest. But this is baseball, and this is Derek Jeter. Stealing in this milieu is legal, and only under these circumstances would Jeter listen to the baser part of his conscience—embodied by Keitel—and do *it*. Jeter, the twenty-first-century iteration of the All-American Boy at play, like all boys at play, is not above a little mischief. That is in him, too.

"Made in New York" is fundamentally different from "Stealin'" and "Can Jimmy Play?" In fact, it differs from virtually every other Gatorade commercial, because it does not ask "Is *it* in you?" An almost pure tribute, save a brief shot of the Gatorade logo at the end of the video and a Gatorade cooler in the Yankee dugout—it is an ad, after all—it places Jeter on such a high pedestal that he, alone, has *it*, if only for the video's ninety-second running time. Although the spot was the brainchild of TBWA\Chiat\Day, the Los Angeles–based agency, Jeter was actually responsible for some of the copy as well as the choice of music, leading Michael McCarthy of the trade publication *Adweek* to suggest, "If the retiring Jeter is looking for a new career, he can get a job on Madison Avenue." "It was a true collaboration between Derek and Gatorade," said Molly Carter, Gatorade's senior director of consumer engagement.[37]

In the ad, Jeter strolls the streets around Yankee Stadium and greets his fans in person, something he rarely, if ever, did prior to shooting. To provide verisimilitude, Gatorade hired all the extras, the common folk themselves, but did not inform them as to the nature of the commercial; roping off a stretch of River Avenue outside Yankee Stadium, uncharacteristically empty on a game day.[38] Indeed, the extras seem genuinely excited to rub elbows with their hero. Throughout "Made in New York," it is clear that Jeter is a man of the people, capable of bringing delighted smiles to the faces of small children, thrills to his young female fans—glaringly absent from the Nike "RE2PECT"commercial—and joy to the appropriately licensed T-shirt vendors and denizens of Stan's Sports Bar, a local institution.

Jeter, as he ambles down the street, looms large. Nearly a head taller than the tallest extra, Jeter towers above his admirers both literally and figuratively. In nearly every shot, the sun shines on his face, illuminating his smile, despite the fact that most of the commercial's action takes place in the shadow of elevated subway tracks, creating a dramatic sense of light and dark. Art historians label this effect "tenebrism"—extreme light and dark contrast used to convey a message of spiritual enlightenment.[39] As he moves among his flock, essentially laying on hands each time he makes physical contact with his fans, the light seems to emanate from his face.

Jeter bids farewell to the gathering throng and enters the stadium, paying his respects to his fellow Yankee gods in Monument Park. At once he is transformed into a uniformed player. Heading through the tunnel from the locker room onto the field, he is bathed in a holy, almost blinding light. Luminous, he touches, then passes under a sign emblazoned with Joe DiMaggio's words, "I want to thank the Good Lord for making me a Yankee," as Sinatra belts out the lyrics, "To say the things he truly feels, and not the words of one who stands and kneels."[40] Even if the rest of the ad had not represented Jeter as godlike, this shot makes his divinity explicit. Finally, he steps onto the field, depicted once again from behind and slightly below, waving his cap to the sellout crowd, while they chant in unison "Der-ek Je-ter, Der-ek Je-ter." As in the Nike commercial, this final image recalls Babe Ruth bidding farewell to his adoring public, reinforcing, yet again, the unbreakable link between Jeter and the Yankee pantheon, relying upon tenebristic lighting to reinforce the point. The Jeter "Made in New York" is not a shortstop. Derek Jeter was born in New Jersey and raised in Michigan. Rather, the Jeter made of "Made in New York" is a baseball god. He is Brand Jeter.

Just as Derek Jeter's baseball career is bound to land him in the National Baseball Hall of Fame, so, too, would he be a first-ballot endorsement Hall of Famer, if such a distinction or institution existed. But Brand Jeter is more than just a testimonial advertising giant, more than a mythical New York ballplayer, more than the embodiment of *it*. Jeter, both the perceived individual and the brand, as previously noted, is essentially the early twenty-first-century iteration of the All-American Boy, albeit in the form of a mature adult. He is by no means the first baseball player, nor the first All-Star endorser, to be elevated to the role of exemplar of American manhood and American masculinity. Each era in baseball history has provided an icon for its times; and the advertising of each era has done its job to imbue the icon with meanings and, more importantly, convey meanings from the icon to America's consumer citizens by way of given ads for different products. Just as baseball's first golden age, also the advertising industry's first golden age, gave American consumers Ty Cobb and Babe Ruth, two very different icons with two sets of meanings for changing times and changing attitudes, just as the first golden age of baseball on television gave American consumers Mickey Mantle, Willie Mays, and Yogi Berra, complete with their own meanings, so, too, did baseball's new golden age, ushered in by the late 1990s, give American consumers Derek Jeter.

Over the course of his career, Jeter accrued a series of meanings that went beyond those that came with his professional job description. The majority of these meanings or qualities were expressed in his endorsement advertising. Through Skippy peanut butter and Post cereals, he proved to play an integral part of a tradition more than a century old of associating breakfast with baseball. Through VISA, he expressed his elegance, his savoir faire, and his willingness to question authority—but not too loudly, not too often, and only when he was clearly in the right—and his sense of humor. Through Movado, he indicated his humanitarianism, his leadership, and his athletic ability; through Driven, his athletic ability, his leadership, and his humanitarianism. Through Driven Black, he suggested exotic sex appeal. Through Nike, he demanded respect, and through Ford and, ultimately, Gatorade, he demonstrated that he had *it*. So who is the twenty-first-century version of the All-American Boy grown up? He is tall, handsome, and strong, elegant, and clean smelling. He is someone who devotes himself to disadvantaged youth. He is a leader, a captain. He is an entrepreneur, America's first biracial team owner. And even in an America that is clearly racially and ethnically divided, he is the embodiment of the transracial ideal, the individual everyone can relate to, because he can relate to everyone. He is Brand Jeter.

Epilogue

Pitching in the Future Game

I n 1964 Marshall McLuhan considered the role of advertising in the coming age of global media, writing, "The historians and archeologists will one day discover that the ads of our times are the richest and most faithful daily reflections that any society ever made of its range of activities. The Egyptian hiero-glyph lags far behind in this respect."[1] McLuhan's assessment of baseball was somewhat less on the mark, as he predicted the spec-tator sport's demise, the victim of "the inclusive mesh of the TV image." According to McLuhan:

> Baseball is a game of one-thing-at-a-time, fixed positions and vis-ibly delegated specialist jobs such as belonged to the now passing mechanical age, with its fragmented tasks and its staff and line in management organization. TV, as the very image of the new corporate and participant ways of electronic living, fosters hab-its of unified awareness and social interdependence that alienate us from the peculiar style of baseball, with its specialist and posi-tional stress. When culture changes, so do games. Baseball, that had become the elegant abstract image of an industrial society liv-ing by split-second timing, has in the new TV decade lost its psy-chic and social relevance for our new way of life. The ball game has been dislodged from the social center and been conveyed to the periphery of American life.[2]

Although McLuhan's observation that television would impact the ways in which American consumers consumed the game is on point, his augury only went so far. He clearly did not foresee the advent of the internet, with its interactive fantasy games, multimedia platforms, and social media sites, all of which have already proved to be fertile ground for the game's development. If twenty-first-century baseball-related advertising tells future historians and archeologists anything, it will be that the game, though perhaps no longer occupying its privileged position in the center of American cultural life, has by no means been pushed to the periphery.

MLB Advanced Media

Digital media, rather than banishing Major League Baseball to the edge, is at least partially responsible for MLB's robust health. Baseball's longtime partner, advertising, an industry for the digital age if ever there was one, now so entwined with the game as to be inextricable, certainly remains at the center of American cultural life. Although digital media has reshaped social relations in twenty-first-century America and in the world as a whole, it nevertheless follows the form of the revolutionary media that preceded it. Historically speaking, the baseball-advertising-digital-media nexus resembles nothing so much as the baseball-advertising-radio nexus of the early twentieth century. To a lesser extent, the same may be said of the baseball-advertising-television nexus. Like its predecessors, especially radio, the World Wide Web began life as an experimental, noncommercial medium.[3]

A project of CERN (European Organization for Nuclear Research), led by British scientist Tim Berners-Lee, the web's initial purpose was to serve as a platform by which scientists and research institutions could share information automatically and with ease.[4] When CERN released its technology to the public in 1993, free of licensing fees, it was with scientific collaboration in mind. Given the precedent set by radio, a medium much like the web, initially intended for educational rather than commercial purposes, it should not be at all surprising that within a year, the web was colonized by advertising. In 1994 the first internet ads were placed on *Wired* magazine's website, then called HotWired. "HotWired," writes Ryan Singel, "launched with banner ads from 14 companies including MCI, Volvo, Club Med, 1–800–Collect and Zima, but legend has it that the first HotWired banner ad was from AT&T, prophetically asking, 'Have you ever clicked your mouse right here? You will.'"[5] One product not advertised on the new medium in October 1994 was baseball, since the professional game was in the throes of the worst labor dispute in its history, leading to the cancellation of the World Series. But in the strike's aftermath, the World Wide Web, with its advertising and promotional potential, aided in MLB's recovery perhaps as much as the steroid-fueled, home-run race of 1998.

Flash forward six years—in 2000, all thirty Major League Baseball teams voted to combine their internet rights into a centrally controlled entity, MLB Advanced Media (MLBAM). At the outset, each team contributed $1 million in seed money for the new venture. It was and continues to be fantastically profitable.[6] What is MLBAM? According to its website, "MLBAM is a full service solutions provider delivering world-class digital experiences for over ten years and distributing content through all forms of interactive media. Our digital leadership and capabilities are a direct result of an appreciation for designing dynamic functionality for the web, mobile applications, and connected devices while integrating live and on-demand multimedia, providing valuable products for millions of fans around the globe."

Naturally, by its own estimation, MLBAM is a leader in advertising and sponsorship. It "offers a full suite of partner promotions, provides ad operations and support for all industry standard media and custom executions and video ad serving for pre-roll, post-roll and multi-platform live stream commercial insertion with companion display and banner support."[7] In other words, MLBAM is responsible for all the video advertising that appears before, during, and after live streams and online highlights, as well as on television, on both conventional broadcast networks and on the regional sports networks that have proliferated on cable and satellite TV—all the advertising that has become part of the very fabric of the game.

Pitching to the Bros in Hyperreality

Among the factors behind the creation of MLBAM was the need to appeal to younger viewers. At the turn of the twenty-first century, MLB's primary fan base, its viewing audience, was rapidly graying. Indeed, as Ira Boudway, writing for *Bloomberg News*, noted, baseball was faced with an "Old-People Problem."[8] One of the league's initiatives to grow its fan base was the introduction of the MLB Network, a joint venture between the MLB and a consortium of cable and satellite TV companies. Judging by the list of the network's initial sponsors, the new channel aimed at attracting new, young viewers, as evidenced by deals with Domino's Pizza, Kraft, Sony PlayStation, and 2K Sports, while keeping the older ones, viewers targeted by Geico, Progressive, IBM, and Viagra.

Commenting on MLB Network's potential, media marketing professional Christine Merrifield told the *New York Times*, "It is getting good traction not only from sports advertisers, but also from some nontraditional sports advertisers," credit card companies, banks, and pharmaceutical manufacturers among them.[9] Of course, the new network required content. Since it initially had rights to just twenty-six regular-season games, some spring training contests, and the World Baseball Classic tournament, it was tasked with creating original programming. After all, there were just so many times the network could repeat Ken Burns' *Baseball* documentary series if it hoped to attract new fans to its product and, more importantly, to grow its roster of sponsors.

In an attempt to capitalize on the reality TV trend, the MLB Network created its own series. On March 31, 2011, MLB's Opening Day, Michael O'Hara, a thirty-seven-year-old aspiring actor, and his "wing man," twenty-six-year-old Ryan Wagner, took to the couch in the MLB Fan Cave, the name of both the show and the space in which it was produced. O'Hara and Wagner were reportedly selected from over ten thousand applicants to watch all 2,430 Major League Baseball games from the beginning of the season to its end, not to mention the postseason, live tweeting and blogging their experience as the "Cave Men." According to the *New York Daily News*, the MLB Fan Cave, the studio, featured "a machine to test pitching speed, a fantasy baseball counter, memorabilia museum, a pool table, bar, a '50s diner, ever-changing photos in electronic frames, and a tattoo parlor."[10] In its second season, the

Fan Cave upped the ante by adding an element of competition to the mix. The resulting program, complete with an online component that allowed viewers to vote to determine which contestants would advance from one challenge to the next, was something of a hybrid between *The Amazing Race*, *Survivor*—without the rats—and a hypermasculine, hereto-normative version of *Project Runway*, absent the clothing and Heidi Klum, pitting thirty contestants against one another to see who would be the uber–Cave Man at the postseason's end.

But MLB *Fan Cave* was not only a television program with an online component filmed in an eponymous studio, it was a semipublic space. Housed in a prime piece of commercial real estate, the fifteen-thousand-square-foot former retail venue in the historic Silk Building on East Fourth Street and Broadway in New York City, the Fan Cave closely resembled a store. Most of the Fan Cave's features, most notably its wall of fifteen video monitors, were visible from the street through huge plate-glass windows, seeming to the beckon shoppers, New York University students, and tourists to stop in for peek. The Fan Cave, however, was rarely open to the public. Indeed, during the Fan Cave's tenure on Broadway, the sight of confused passersby attempting to open its doors, only to discover that they were locked, though the storefront seemed to be open for business, was common. This is because, for all intents and purposes, the MLB Fan Cave was not a store, but a three-dimensional billboard. Technically, the Fan Cave was an example of what the advertising industry calls Digital Out-of-Home advertising (DOOH). Now a regular feature of the urban landscape, conventional DOOH displays consist of digital screens installed in public places, mass-transit waiting areas, doctors' offices, New York City's Times Square, and of course, ballparks, which show a series of ads. According to industry expert Blaise Nutter, "Digital OOH ads are, by definition, uninvited and unexpected. They invade a new audience space and are, therefore, surprising."[11]

But the Fan Cave was so much more than a living DOOH display; it was an entire digital out-of-home storefront with interactive elements. Utilizing the Foursquare social media check-in application—now largely irrelevant, but popular at the time—individual pedestrians were able to check into *The Franchise*, a Showtime documentary series that followed the exploits of a single team for a season. The Foursquare users thereby activated the Fan Cave's "intelligent storefront," which rewarded their social media activity with MLB/Showtime's *The Franchise* co-branded baseballs, one per customer.[12]

Nevertheless, the Fan Cave's impact as DOOH advertising was limited. Surprising and interactive as it may have been to those who saw it in person, its reach was limited to actual pedestrians, bus riders, bicyclists, and drivers stuck in Broadway traffic. This, however, was counterbalanced by the Fan Cave's presence in cyberspace, where it was not entirely accurately represented as something of a New York City attraction. According to industry metrics, the Fan Cave was a smashing success, generating hundreds of millions of "earned social media impressions" over four seasons.[13] A Nielsen product, the earned media impression looks at "consumer conversations about and with brands," digital versions of word-of-mouth advertising, the oldest and perhaps most effective form of spreading the message about goods and services. It measures the number of times a given brand is liked, mentioned, or shared on a social media site. Most importantly, it considers conversations that are consumer driven rather than advertiser driven.[14] As such, MLB did not pay for hundreds of millions of consumers to like or share stories about the Fan Cave, the Fan Cave earned the likes and shares by itself.

Clearly, millennials were the MLB *Fan Cave*'s target demographic. Judging by O'Hara, Wagner, and many of the subsequent participants in the reality competition, the *Fan Cave*'s market segment corresponded roughly to the type of young adult men routinely represented in beer ads as needing visual aids to determine whether their beverages are cold—in other words, "bros." According to Canada's *Globe and Mail*, "The bro emerged as a social type in the aughts, shooting to fame thanks to the womanizing Barney Stinson on *How I Met Your Mother*. Ever since, society has struggled to make sense of him. Is he affable and ultimately harmless, perhaps even admirable, like Channing Tatum? Or is he a prime example of white male entitlement?"[15] In fact, bros are a little of both.

According to mlb.com, the participants in the 2012 Fan Cave reality competition included "recent college graduates, journalists, bloggers, actors, musicians, a self-described 'unemployed comedian,' a made-up superhero and a professional wrestler." More than two-thirds of the participants were male. In fact, the idea of bro-hood was suggested by the very name of the promotion, the Fan Cave, alluding, of course, to the "man cave." Essentially, the man cave is an inner sanctum of masculinity within the female-dominated home, a bro refuge. As Mike Yost and Jeff Wilser, the authors of *The Man Cave Book* observe, "The man cave should be originated by men, driven by men, and built by men. But the other gender can visit."[16] As if to counter *Fan Cave's* bro atmosphere, seven women were among the second season's contestants. Rather than serving as threats, intruding on the masculine bro-hood of the Fan Cave, the women were essentially female bros. As such, they tried as hard as possible to act like their male role models. For example, in her introductory interview, contestant Christy McGough ate salsa right from the jar on camera.[17]

With its bar with no patrons, its pool table with no players, its '50s diner with no waitresses named Flo, and its tattoo parlor without ink, the MLB Fan Cave was essentially the simulacrum of a man cave. It was filled not with real furnishings, but images of furnishings, generated to be consumed virtually. As each of the participants posted digital skits, made for consumption on the internet, with the hope that their work would go viral and earning them a simulated space on the simulated Fan Cave couch, each was in essence a simulated bro, actors in a "hyperreality" show. In this regard, the Fan Cave was a twenty-first-century version of Plato's "Allegory of the Cave"—the Allegory of the Fan Cave—consumers never saw the real baseball games or even the real cave dwellers, just their shadows or images projected on their smartphones.

Representation theory aside, the real purpose of the Fan Cave was to extend MLB's brand in an attempt to attract younger viewers. Despite all those social media impressions and early success, the enterprise never really took off. After the second season, the Fan Cave became a part-time concert venue, home to promotional events for sponsors like Budweiser and Scotts lawn care products, and the studio for *Off the Bat from the MLB Fan Cave*, produced by MTV2, another joint venture, which sought to "cover all the bases on the biggest stories in baseball, pop culture and entertainment," from "locker room pranks to hilarious interviews, in-studio games, lifestyle features and much more," according to the network's website.[18] It lasted but one season. In 2015, shortly after Bob Manfred assumed the role of baseball commissioner, the Fan Cave closed its doors permanently, as MLB moved to consolidate its social media presence under the auspices of MLBAM.[19]

MLB at Bat

As recent history has shown, MLB *Fan Cave* was far from a home run. The same cannot be said for MLBAM's mobile application At Bat. First released for iPhones on July 10, 2008, At Bat was one of the original paid apps available for purchase from Apple's iOS App Store, which not so coincidentally launched on the same day. It proved to be a huge hit from the outset. In 2010 MLBAM followed its initial release with versions for the iPad as well as Android and BlackBerry devices and the Windows Phone 7 and webOS.[20] MLB At Bat was lauded by the industry, winning MOBI awards for Best Mobile Video and Best iPad Branded App the same year.[21] At Bat served not only to deliver streaming video, audio, scores, and other information to baseball fans, it also sold iPads, just as iPads sold the MLB brand. Whether the new app had a positive effect on Apple's bottom line is unclear. It did, however, contribute to the coffers of MLBAM. In fact, the release of the next iteration, At Bat 11, set all sorts of records. At Bat 11 became the highest-grossing application for both the iPhone and the iPad on the day of its release in advance of spring training 2011.[22]

And the hits just keep on coming. In October 2016 At Bat was once again named the top mobile sports device by App Annie—not an application groupie, as its name might suggest to baseball fans, but an app tracking site. The top sports league app for both iOS and Android, the 2016 version of At Bat had roughly 12.2 million downloads as the postseason got underway and was expected to surpass the previous year's record of 13.1 million downloads by the year's end. Indeed, MLBAM estimated that approximately 8.5 million fans used the At Bat app every day.

According to the media website CNET, a subsidiary of CBS, "Strengths of the At Bat app include providing continuous live streaming content, allowing users to see multiple scores on screen and picture-in-picture game feeds. . . . Fans can also watch out-of-market games."[23] And, of course, another of At Bat's strengths is its functionality as a fully integrated advertising platform. At first glance, there actually appears to be very little advertising on At Bat, other than promotions for the game itself. But scratch the surface, and the app reveals a wealth of paid promotional content for MLB sponsors, sponsors of individual teams, and for companies that pay individual players for their endorsements. First and foremost, At Bat is a live streaming app. Free with subscriptions to MLB.TV and MLB Gameday Audio, At Bat allows fans to watch out-of-market games on a choice of feeds, usually supplied by both the home team, the away team, and occasionally on an MLB feed, as well. Although many commercials are blacked out, not all are. Streamers are regularly subjected to the same advertising as the more conventional viewers at home. No matter how fans watched the 2016 All-Star Game, they received the message that MasterCard was the official sponsor. And the AT&T Call to the Bullpen was the same whether delivered over the airwaves, via broadcast, or through a mobile device. It was still the AT&T Call to the Bullpen.

Consumers who watch MLB games online are also exposed to one of the oldest forms of baseball-related advertising—ballpark signage. With the advent of conventional DOOH displays, ballpark billboards are no longer limited to a single message. Ads on ballpark walls behind home plate, placed there primarily for the benefit of viewers at home, play on a loop, allowing for multiple sponsors to occupy a single space. Depending upon individual ballpark design, similar DOOH displays rotate on the facings of the stands and pretty much anywhere else physical space is available. Even the old, manual scoreboard at Wrigley Field has been enhanced by a DOOH display along its bottom border. And of course, traditional ballpark signage of the type that paid sponsors once feared would provide free advertising to competitors during the early days of commercial television—painted or printed advertising— also targets online audiences. The smiling Chevron cars on the outfield wall at San Francisco's AT&T Park are every bit as visible to MLB.TV subscribers watching the Giants on their At Bat apps as they are to viewers stretched out on their Barcaloungers in front of their big-screen TVs at home, though the ad is certainly smaller.

Although streaming video, audio, live pitch-by-pitch updates, and real-time scores are At Bat's most important features, the app also includes a news feed. Most of the news deals directly with baseball action, but not all of it. Some is clearly advertising. Amid a slew of stories surrounding the 2016 postseason, a featured item dealing with Chicago Cub Dexter Fowler was posted on the At Bat newsfeed. At first glance, the piece, actually a link to another MLBAM website like all the stories on the newsfeed, appeared to be a standard postseason player profile. But the article told a different story. Correspondent Ben Cosman, writing for Cut 4, reported:

> With the Cubs preparing to take on the Dodgers in the NLCS, Dexter Fowler gifted his teammates their own pairs of Air Jordan 12s. You know, it's probably not a bad idea to wear the sneakers of a certain successful Chicago athlete while trying to win your team's first World Series in 108 years—especially sneakers that would definitely pair well with whatever fashion themes Joe Madden might be cooking up for the end of October. What's for certain: This is just the latest salvo in the increasingly generous game of teammate gift-giving. Christmas is coming, guys.[24]

No doubt, Fowler's teammates appreciated the gesture. But with 2016 MLB minimum salaries set at $505,500, most of the players would not have gone shoeless but for Fowler's heralded generosity. And as a rule, the vast majority of Major Leaguers have their own endorsement deals that provide them with footwear, at the very least. Fowler's deal, not surprisingly, was with Nike. Whether or not MLBAM, Cut 4, or Cosman were compensated by Nike for the article does not really matter. The short piece is essentially a digital version of a reading notice or advertorial. It is, moreover, a classic endorsement ad. By bestowing his magic Jordans upon his teammates, Fowler effectively transfers Jordan's magic to the Cubs. By putting on his charmed shoes, they, too, may wear the sneakers of the most successful of Chicago athletes, thereby potentially putting the goat and its curse to bed. The piece seems to suggest that Fowler's Jordans may have proven to be the key to the Cubs winning their first World Series in 108 years. Of course, superstitious Cubs fans—any Cubs fans or fans of any team, for that matter— might easily share in Fowler's magic with the purchase of Air Jordan 12s. In this regard, At Bat's newsfeed hearkened back to old print media. Just as newspaper readers of Deadball Era newspapers learned that Ty Cobb owed his excellence to regular doses of Nuxated Iron in ads that were all but indistinguishable from other content, At Bat newsfeed aficionados learned that the key to the Cubs' success lay not in great pitching or clutch hitting, but in Fowler's supernatural shoes, via digital "news."

Streaming ads and endorsement news are but a few of the commercial elements of At Bat. Among the others are links to the Esurance-sponsored MLB Awards as well as to a series of games and apps, all bearing the MLB logo. Among them are MLB Clubhouse and Home Run Derby, both of which include embedded advertising. Ballpark, another MLBAM app, which is basically an advertising delivery system for individual parks around the league, is also linked to At Bat. While it is unclear whether MLBAM will attract a younger fan base via such digital media, early returns are promising.

Buster Posey Is a Smart Person

With the proliferation of regional sports networks and the advent of MLBAM's streaming services, viewing opportunities for baseball-related advertising have multiplied with Malthusian vigor. So it would make sense that national endorsement ads for star players would increase geometrically right along with opportunities to disseminate advertising. This, however, has not been the case. MLB's stars lag far behind the NBA's top endorsers. Even Derek Jeter, MLB's most recent brand-name celebrity, who reportedly earned more than $300 million in endorsement deals over the course of his career, could not match the NBA's biggest stars for advertising clout. LeBron James, for example, made $42 million in 2013 alone, more than MLB's top ten endorsers combined. And Kobe Bryant earned $34 million the same year, at a time when his play was in decline.[25] There are a variety of reasons for the disparity. MLB, despite McLuhan's dire prediction, remains healthy. But its reach is limited. Certainly, baseball is the spectator sport of choice in certain international markets. Japan, Korea, Taiwan, Cuba, the Dominican Republic, Puerto Rico, Venezuela, and Mexico share a love of the sport with the U.S. But MLB's international reach does not come near to that of the NBA. Virtually every cab driver in Shanghai, when faced with an American passenger, knows enough English to say, "America, NBA, LeBron, Kobe!"

In fact, baseball remains a fundamentally local sport. As marketing executive Nick Gregorian told *Forbes* in 2015, "Baseball is provincial. Players have access to local deals, but there are few baseball players that resonate across the U.S. and can secure national ad campaigns that pay mid-six figures."[26] This was true even of Jeter, whose multiple Ford endorsement ads played only in the New York metropolitan area. In this regard, practices have not changed significantly from Ty Cobb's day. Although Cobb was in all likelihood never the monster Al Stump made him out to be, he was a polarizing figure in the game. Nevertheless, he was one of baseball's first endorsement stars, pitching a multitude of products, most of them in Detroit or in his native Georgia. Even Babe Ruth, baseball's first media celebrity in the contemporary sense, pitched more products to local New York City consumers than to national audiences, Wheaties and Huskies notwithstanding.

Even so, new stars are constantly vying to fill the vacuum left by MLB's great endorsers as they retire. In May 2016, Washington's Bryce Harper signed a ten-year endorsement deal with Under Armour, reported to be the most lucrative deal ever for an MLB player. Harper, notes the *Washington Post*, "believes in bringing baseball to the forefront of attention and fashion." The young, charismatic player, who also has deals with T-Mobile, Gatorade, and New Era, has considerable social media savvy. As such, he uses twenty-first-century avenues for the purpose of meaning transfer, allowing a new crop of fans to access the qualities that make him great with the purchase of Under Armour Harper One cleats after streaming his viral videos on their T-Mobile smartphones.[27] More deals are sure to be in his future.

San Francisco Giant Buster Posey also became an endorsement star in 2016. In a synergistic move, Esurance, the official MLB auto insurance company, signed Posey to a multiyear deal. Starring in a campaign titled "Smart People Get Esurance," Posey is smart. Therefore, he does not spend the night in his locker, launder his socks in the clubhouse whirlpool, and fill his cap with chicken strips from a luxury suite, all with the aim of saving money. This is because Posey knows that he can save all the money he will ever need on car insurance with the Esurance app. Posey, selected in 2015 by a fan poll as "the face of baseball," according to an Esurance marketing executive, made the perfect brand ambassador, "He has proven to be even stronger than we expected. Everything he stands for and is, is why we've decided to work with him in the first place."[28] Much like Jeter's ability to embody, then transfer *it* to consumers via advertising, Posey seems to be able to bestow a series of undefined and shifting qualities and meanings—everything he stands for and is—to the product simply by not sitting in a locker in a thirty-second spot. And rising to challenge Posey's dominance as the face of baseball may be another young superstar endorser, 2017 Rookie of the Year, New York Yankee Aaron Judge, who has recently signed lucrative deals with Pepsi, JBL audio, Adidas, and Under Armour, among others, no doubt with more to come.

Marshall McLuhan Was Wrong

McLuhan was clearly correct when he asserted that historians and archeologists may one day find the richest and most accurate record of American culture in advertising. Since its birth as a professional industry in the mid-nineteenth century, advertising's job has not only been to hold up the proverbial mirror to American culture, but to create American culture. In its partnership with advertising, professional baseball has also done its fair share to help shape American identity. And the partnership between the two industries has certainly proven to be more than the sum of its parts. MLB's audience may be graying. The NFL may be more popular. NBA stars may earn more money for endorsements. But baseball endures, and advertising's continuing role in the sport's perpetuation is as certain as the sport's role as constant content provider for the industry.

Baseball, though no longer the only important American sport, has not relinquished its place at the center of American life, regardless of how crowded the center has become. Indeed, it has even outlived the type of broadcast television that McLuhan claimed would displace it. After all, regional sports networks and cable sports channels have largely replaced the old broadcast model. Marshall McLuhan was wrong. Going forth into the twenty-first century, chicks still dig the long ball, branded presidential selfies still receive lots of social media play, Wheaties is still the Breakfast of Champions, and the dispute as to whether Miller Lite tastes great or is less filling has not yet been resolved. Ask your doctor if it's right for you.

Notes

Introduction

1. Angell, "Two Strikes on the Image," in *Summer Game*, loc. 1384, Kindle.

2. "When It Was a Game: The Complete Collection," Amazon.com, accessed October 23, 2016, https://www.amazon.com/When-Was-Game-Complete-Collection/dp/B004QRUN8M.

3. McCracken, "Advertising: Meaning or Information," 122.

4. McCracken, "Who Is a Celebrity Endorser?," 317.

1. Hustlers, Hucksters, Snake-Oil Salesmen

1. Fox, *Mirror Makers*, 4. See also Newman "The Pitch," 203–19.

2. "1870 Census," accessed January 26, 2014, http://www.censusrecords.com/content/1870_Census; "1900 Census," accessed January 26, 2014, http://www.censusrecords.com/content/1900_Census.

3. Norris, *Advertising and the Transformation of American Society*, 12. The constant prices per capita in terms of the 1926 dollar were $201 in 1870 and $420 in 1900.

4. Norris, *Advertising and the Transformation of American Society*, 9.

5. Tocker, "Standardized Outdoor Advertising," 16.

6. "History of Outdoor Advertising," accessed January 17, 2014, http://www.billboardconnection-tucson.com/_blog/Billboard_Specialists/post/History_of_outdoor_advertising/.

7. "History of OOH," Out-of-Home Advertising Association of America, accessed January 16, 2014, http://www.oaaa.org/outofhomeadvertising/historyofooh.aspx.

8. The Third Brooklyn ball park of that name, Washington Park (III) opened in 1898 and housed Brooklyn's National League team until the opening of Ebbets Field at the start of the 1913 season. Lowry, *Green Cathedrals*, 36–37.

9. "Pop Bottles Fly in Brooklyn Game," *New York Times*, July 9, 1911, C5. See also Newman, "Now Pitching for the Dodgers," 99.

10. Newman, "The Pitch," 211.

11. "Baseball Player Show Figure," *American Folk Art Museum*, accessed on August 22, 2014, http://folkartmuseum.org/?t=images&id=3503.

12. Baseball Player Show Figure," *American Folk Art Museum*, 212.

13. Dickson, *Dickson Baseball Dictionary*, 144–45.

14. *"Bull" Durham Baseball Guide*, 2.

15. American Tobacco Company, *Sold American*, 21.

16. Porter, "Origins of the American Tobacco Company," 190.

17. Eliasson, "In the Hands of Children," 194.

18. Black, "Corporate Calling Cards," 291.

19. Black, "Corporate Calling Cards," 293.

20. American Tobacco Company, *Sold American*, 20.

21. Black, "Corporate Calling Cards," 299.

22. Frank Ceresi, "Tobacco Baseball Cards and Wagner's Own Wagner Card," *Baseball Almanac*, accessed February 12, 2014, http://www.baseball-almanac.com /treasure/autont005.shtml.

23. Black, "Corporate Calling Cards," 396.

24. "Printing Yesterday and Today," Harry Ransom Center, University of Texas at Austin, accessed January 28, 2014, http://www.hrc.utexas.edu/educator/modules /gutenberg/books/printing/.

25. "Lines of Communication," *Printers' Ink: A Journal for Advertisers* 184 (July 28, 1938): 32.

26. Ads, *Spalding's Official Base Ball Guide*, 137–52

27. Ad, "Syracuse Gun," *Reach's Official 1900 Base Ball Guide*, accessed January 31, 2014, https://archive.org/stream/reachofficialame1900lphil#page/n7/mode/2up.d.

28. Sleight, *Sponsorship*, 4.

29. Chasser, "Historical Perspective," 34.

30. "Spalding," *Legal Force*, accessed on August 27, 2014, http://www.trademarkia .com/trademarks-search.aspx?tn=spalding.

31. Missouri Court of Appeals, *Missouri Appeals Reports* (St. Louis MO: F. W. Stephens, 1911), 412–27

32. McMaster, *McMaster's Commercial Decision*, 412.

33. Batey, *Brand Meaning*, 4.

34. "No Difference in Balls," *New York Tribune*, October 14, 1911, 5.

35. "Newspaper Statistics," in *Publisher's Weekly* 3, no. 52 (November 9, 1983): 30.

36. Erbe, "New Horizons," 10.

37. Erbe, "New Horizons," 10.

38. Ad, *Chicago Daily Tribune*, July 19, 1882, 7. Hugh "One Arm" Daily pitched for the Buffalo Bisons of the National League in 1882, one of many teams for which he played. "Hugh Daily," accessed January 17, 2014, http://espn.go.com/mlb/player /stats/_/id/20699/hugh-daily.

39. Lears, *Fable of Abundance*, 40.

40. Ad, "Yellow Label Cigars," *Atlanta Constitution*, April 10, 1888, 8.

41. Ad, "Old Judge," *Los Angeles Times*, January 17, 1888, 2.

42. Anheuser-Busch, "Our Heritage," accessed December 29, 2014, http://anheuser -busch.com/index.php/our-heritage/history/.

43. An example of this ad may be found in the *New York Times*, May 28, 1910, 5.

44. Ad, "Budweiser," *Washington Post*, April 15, 1910, 8.

45. Ad, "Budweiser," *Washington Post*, April 20, 1910, 9.

46. Marchand, *Advertising the American Dream*, 111.

47. Ad, "E. B. Barnum and Co.," *Washington Post*, July 23, 1887, 4.

48. "Fair Use of Logos," *Houston Chronicle*, accessed December 24, 2014, http://smallbusiness.chron.com/fair-use-logos-2152.html.

49. "E. B. Barnum and Co." 4.

50. Fox, *Mirror Makers*, 16.

51. Fox, *Mirror Makers*, 19.

52. Friedman, *Birth of a Salesman*, 51.

53. Bruns, *Preacher*, 66.

54. Anderson, *Snake Oil, Hustlers and Hambones*, 6.

55. Although these proprietary nostrums were commonly referred to as "patent," they were protected by trademark regulations rather than by patent law. "History of Patent Medicine," Hagley Museum and Library, accessed on December 24, 2014, http://www.hagley.org/online_exhibits/patentmed/history/history.html.

56. Erbe, *Printers' Ink: Fifty Years, 1888–1938*, 18.

57. Ad, *Washington Post*, July 18, 1888, 3.

58. Fox, *Mirror Makers*, 17.

59. Ad, "Dr. Barlow J. Smith's Caloric Vita Oil," *San Francisco Chronicle*, July 10, 1887, 4.

60. Ad, "Dr. Barlow J. Smith's Caloric Vita Oil," *California Rural Press* 20 (September 25, 1880): 206.

61. "Reading Notice," 440.

62. Ad, "Warner's Safe Cure," *Orchard and Garden* 10 (November 1888): 227.

63. Reading Notice, "Benson's Plasters," *Atlanta Constitution*, June 28, 1888, 7.

64. Ads, *Spalding's Official Base Ball Guide*, 147.

65. Ads, *Spalding's Official Base Ball Guide*, 147.

66. Ad, *Sporting Life*, May 4, 1895, 17.

67. Ad, *Sporting Life*, May 4, 1895, 17.

68. Ad, *Sporting Life*, May 18, 1896, 16.

69. Ads, *Sporting Life*, November 9, 1995, 10.

70. "Misbranding of Vita Oil U.S. v. Loring J. Barker (Vita Oil Co.), Plea of guilty. Fine $100. (F.&D. No. 9909. I.S. Nos. 11825–p, 11826–p)," *Notice of Judgment Under the Food and Drugs Act, Issue 11000* (Washington DC: U.S. Department of Agriculture, 1920), 518–519; "Misbranding of 'Collins' Ague Remedy,' 'Swaim's Panacea,' 'Swayne's Panacea.' U.S. v. James F. Ballard. Plea of guilty. Fine $30 and costs (F.&D. No. 6022. I.S. Nos. 8212-e, 8890-e, 8891-e)," *Notices of Judgment Under the Food and Drugs Act, Issue 4001; Issue 5000* (Washington DC: U.S. Department of Agriculture), 550–55.

71. Pendergrast, *For God, Country, and Coca-Cola*, 22.

72. Pendergrast, *For God, Country, and Coca-Cola*, 53–54.

73. Pendergrast, *For God, Country, and Coca-Cola*, 26.

74. Pendergrast, *For God, Country, and Coca-Cola*, 38.

75. The Coca-Cola Company, "125 Years of Sharing Happiness: A Short History of the Coca-Cola Company," accessed December 23, 2014, http://assets.coca -colacompany.com/7b/46/e5be4e7d43488c2ef43ca1120a15/TCCC_125years_Booklet _Spreads_Hi.pdf.

76. Pendergrast, *For God, Country, and Coca-Cola*, 57.

77. James Hamblin, "Why We Took the Cocaine Out of Soda," *Atlantic*, January 31, 2013, accessed January 3, 2013, www.theatlantic.com/health/archive/2013/01/why -we-took-cocaine-out-of-soda/272694/.

78. Newman, "The Pitch," 211.

79. Ritter, *Glory of Their Times*, 88.

80. "Sunday Games to Aid the War," *Christian Science Monitor*, May 24, 1917, 14. See also Newman, "Now Pitching for the Dodgers," 100.

81. "Session Justices Refuse to Drop Sunday Ball Case," *Brooklyn Daily Eagle*, August 28, 1917, 1.

82. "To the Patriotic and Baseball Public of Brooklyn," *Brooklyn Daily Eagle*, September 18, 1917, 3.

83. "To the Patriotic and Baseball Public of Brooklyn," *Brooklyn Daily Eagle*, September 18, 1917, 3.

84. "Coler-Riegelmann Recount Tomorrow; Day-Night Shifts," *Brooklyn Daily Eagle*, October 16, 1917, 1.

2. "It Pays to Be Personal"

1. Fox, *Mirror Makers*, 94.

2. Fox, *Mirror Makers*, 90.

3. Rein, Kotler, and Stoller, *High Visibility*, 17.

4. Seymour and Mills, *Baseball: The Golden Age*, v.

5. Fox, *Mirror Makers*, 78–117.

6. Mrozek, "From National Health to Personal Fulfillment," 25.

7. Mrozek, "From National Health to Personal Fulfillment," 34.

8. Ford, *Case Against the Little White Slaver*, 65.

9. "Haelan Laboratories, Inc. v. Topps Chewing Gum, Inc., F, 2d 866 (2d Cir. 1953)," accessed on 1/8/2015, http://law.justia.com/cases/federal/appellate-courts /F2/202/866/216723/.

10. Ad for "Nuxated Iron," *Hartford Courant*, September 28, 1916, 12.

11. "Nuxated Iron," *Hartford Courant*, September 28, 1916, 12.

12. Ad for "Nuxated Iron," *Hartford Courant*, September 27, 1916, 16.

13. Miller, "Tuning Up the Ball Players of the Big Leagues," 533.

14. See Newman, "Driven," 73–74.

15. McCracken, "Who Is a Celebrity Endorser?," 317.

16. McCracken, "Who Is a Celebrity Endorser?," 315.

17. McCracken, "Who Is a Celebrity Endorser?," 318.

18. Cobb and Stump, *My Life in Baseball*, 280.

19. "Propaganda for Reform: Nuxated Iron," 1244.

20. "Propaganda for Reform: Nuxated Iron," 1245.

21. Fox, *Mirror Makers*, 89.

22. Stump, *Cobb*, 227.

23. Pendergrast, *For God, Country, and Coca-Cola*, 146.

24. Ad "Coca-Cola," The Coca-Cola Company Historical Sports Photo Gallery, accessed 1/16/2015, http://www.coca-colacompany.com/coca-cola-historical-sports -photo-gallery#hv-sports-ty-cobb.

25. Ever the savvy investor, Cobb also held a financial stake in General Motors.

26. Stump, *Cobb*, 243.

27. "In and About the Agencies," *Automotive Industries* 21, no. 15 (October 7, 1909): 624.

28. "New York-Atlanta Good Roads Tour," *The Horseless Age* 24, no. 18 (November 3, 1909): 503–4.

29. "Ty Cobb Will Drive Against Nap Rucker on Speedway," *Atlanta Constitution*, September 25, 1910, A1.

30. Wheeler, preface to *Busting 'Em*, v.

31. Rein, Kotler, and Stoller, *High Visibility*, 80.

32. Rein, Kotler, and Stoller, *High Visibility*, v.

33. Holmes, introduction to *Ty Cobb*, xxi.

34. Holmes, *Ty Cobb*, xxi.

35. Holmes, *Ty Cobb*, 167.

36. Stump, *Cobb*, 278.

37. Stump, *Cobb*, 342.

38. Tygiel, *Past Time*, 77.

39. Ad, "Title & Rich," *Hartford Courant*, June 2, 1920, 13.

40. Marchand, *Advertising the American Dream*, 54.

41. Court of Customs and Patent Appeals, "George H. Ruth Candy v. Curtiss Candy Company," accessed June 6, 2015, https://casetext.com/case/george-h-ruth -candy-co-v-curtiss-candy.

42. See "Fishbein and Blintz on Fame," *Washington Post*, January 29, 1922, 57, and H. I. Phillips, "The Once Over: Those Lady Baseball Fans," *Boston Daily Globe*, September 1, 1925, 14.

43. "George H. Ruth Candy v. Curtiss Candy Company."

44. For a detailed discussion of the dispute, see Poekel, "Babe Ruth vs. Baby Ruth," 225–28.

45. Whether or not the candy bar was named after Ruth, Curtiss Candy, now owned by Nestlé, publically celebrates the connection. See Ira Berkow, "Sports of the Times: A Babe Ruth Myth Is Stirred Up Again," *New York Times*, April 7, 2002, 8.2.

46. Ad, "Babe Ruth Cigars," *Boston Daily Globe*, January 28, 1920, 7.

47. "Babe Ruth Sells His Own Brand to Boston Trade," *United States Tobacco Journal* 93 (February 21, 1920): 14.

48. "Christy Walsh Syndicate," *Motor West: The Motoring Authority of the Pacific Coast* 35, no. 2 (May 1, 1921): 66.

49. "Trade Personals," *The Horseless Age* 42, no. 2 (October 15, 1917): 80.

50. Walsh, *Adios to Ghosts*, 12.

51. Walsh, *Adios to Ghosts*, 13.

52. Creamer, *Babe*.

53. Voigt, *American Baseball*, 237.

54. Gorn and Goldstein, *Brief History of American Sports*, 192.

55. "Rick's Distribution Spectacular," *Automotive Topics* 63, no. 5 (September 17, 1921): 358.

56. Ad, "Blue-jay Corn Plasters," *New York Times*, June 6, 1926, RPA6.

57. Marchand, *Advertising the American Dream*, 150.

58. Melville E. Webb Jr., "Very Pretty Comeback Was That Staged by Jack Scott," *Boston Globe*, April 17, 1925, A22.

59. McGovern, *Secret of Keeping Fit*, 58–59.

60. Ad, "The McGovern System of Health Building," *New York Times*, December 5, 1926, SM15.

61. Ad, "McGovern's Gymnasium," *Wall Street Journal*, March 8, 1927, 14.

62. Ruth's fondness for tobacco has long been linked to his premature cancer death at fifty-three, though recent research has uncovered the fact that he did not, in fact, suffer from throat cancer, as was often assumed. Lawrence K. Altman, MD, "The Doctor's World; Ruth's Other Record: Cancer Pioneer," *New York Times*, December 29, 1998, accessed March 19, 2015, http://www.nytimes.com/1998/12/29/science/the -doctor-s-world-ruth-s-other-record-cancer-pioneer.html.

63. Kanner, "On Madison Avenue," 21.

64. Ward, *Federal Trade Commission*, 6.01.

65. Ad, "Old Gold," *Boston Globe*, July 10, 1928, 20.

66. Kluger, *Ashes to Ashes*, 72.

67. Napier, *Issues in Tobacco*, 3.

68. Brandt, *Cigarette Century*, 56.

69. Brandt, *Cigarette Century*, 59.

70. Dr. William Brady, "Health Talks: Lady Nic versus Goddess Hygeia," *Atlanta Constitution*, January 29, 1928.

71. Brady, "Health Talks," *Atlanta Constitution*, January 29, 1928.

72. Ad, "Equitable Life Assurance Society," *New York Times*, January 6, 1931, 2.

73. "Why Did This Bank Close?" *Washington Post*, December 13, 1930, 6.

74. Gary Richardson, "Banking Panics of 1930 and 1931," *Federal Reserve History*, accessed on June 2, 2015, http://www.federalreservehistory.org/Events/DetailView/20.

75. Markham, *Financial History of the United States*, 248.

76. "Equitable Life's New Business," *New York Times*, January 7, 1931, 51.

77. Will Rogers, "Will Rogers' Dispatch," *Boston Globe*, January 9, 1930, 1.

78. Fox, *Mirror Makers*, 122.

79. *Printer's Ink*, 184, no. 4 (June 28, 1938): 398.

80. Fox, *Mirror Makers*, 118–19

81. Fox, *Mirror Makers*, 151.

82. Ad, "Old Gold," *Bradford Era*, October 10, 1928, 21.

83. "Lou Gehrig," accessed June 9, 2015, http://www.lougehrig.com/business /business.html.

84. "Scorecard," *Sports Illustrated*, May 14, 2001, accessed October 20, 2016, http:// www.si.com/vault/2001/05/14/8096547/scorecard.

85. Fox, *Mirror Makers*, 116.

3. Breakfast of Champions

1. *Printer's Ink*, 184, no. 4 (July 28, 1938): 398.

2. Fox, *Mirror Makers*, 120.

3. Lears, *Fables of Abundance*, 238.

4. Fox, *Mirror Makers*, 120.

5. Tygiel, *Past Time*, 87–88.

6. Tygiel, *Past Time*, 90–91.

7. "Newsroom Archive," United States Census, accessed June 22, 2015, https://www .census.gov/newsroom/releases/archives/census_2000/cb02-cn62.html.

8. J. R. Walker, *Crack of the Bat*, 23.

9. Smulyan, *Selling Radio*, 70.

10. "Advertising through Radio to be Strictly Regulated," *Printers' Ink* 119, no. 5 (May 4, 1922): 10, 12.

11. Marchand, *Advertising the American Dream*, 94.

12. *Printer's Ink*, 184, no. 4 (July 28, 1938): 379.

13. J. R. Walker, *Crack of the Bat*, 117.

14. Ad, "Atwater Kent," *Lost Angeles Times*, October 8, 1925, A11.

15. Ad, "The Broadway Department Store," *Los Angeles Times*, October 4, 1924, A4.

16. J. R. Walker, *Crack of the Bat*, 55.

17. J. R. Walker, *Crack of the Bat*, 7.

18. "The Story of Wrigley: Leadership, Innovation and Integrity," accessed July 15, 2015, http://www.wrigley.com/global/about-us/the-story-of-wrigley.aspx.

19. Cruikshank and Schultz, *Man Who Sold America*, 159.

20. Gunther, *Taken at the Flood*, 96. See also *Newman*, "The Pitch," 217.

21. J. R. Walker, *Crack of the Bat*, 56.

22. J. R. Walker, *Crack of the Bat*, 55.

23. J. R. Walker, *Crack of the Bat*, 56.

24. J. R. Walker, *Crack of the Bat*, 117.

25. D. L. Lewis, *Public Image of Henry Ford*, 314.

26. Ad, "Ford V-8," *Sunday Register* (Beckley, Raleigh County, West Virginia) September 30, 1934, 5. This ad was published nationally in multiple sources.

27. Ad, "Ford," *Atlanta Constitution*, October 4, 1934, 15.

28. "Cards Will Get $5,941 Apiece; Tigers $4,313," *Chicago Tribune*, October 10, 1934, 25.

29. Irving Vaughn, "How Ford Paid $100,000 Not to Air the Series," *Chicago Tribune*, November 4, 1937, 21.

30. Ad, "Davega City Radio," *New York Times*, October 6, 1937, 32.

31. Ciment, "Consumer Debt and Bankruptcy," 422.

32. Carter, *Financing the American Dream*, 276.

33. Ad, "Sterchi's," *Atlanta Constitution*, October 4, 1937, 8.

34. Thorson and Duffy, *Advertising Age*, 21.

35. *Printer's Ink*, July 28, 1938, 242.

36. *Printer's Ink*, July 28, 1938, 411.

37. Gray, *Business Without Boundary*, 141.

38. Bruce and Crawford, *Cerealizing America*, 77.

39. Gray, *Business Without Boundary*, 157.

40. Gray, *Business Without Boundary*, 159.

41. Gray, *Business Without Boundary*, 161.

42. Subject of a long court battle, Percy Crosby's comic strip is probably also the source for the Skippy peanut butter brand name. For a more thorough discussion, see "Skippy v. Skippy: The Great Peanut Butter Trademark Wars," *Trademark & Copyright Law*, accessed on July 23, 2015, http://www.trademarkandcopyrightlawblog.com/2014/03/skippy-v-skippy-the-great-peanut-butter-trademark-wars/.

43. Bruce and Crawford, *Cerealizing America*, 78.

44. Bruce and Crawford, *Cerealizing America*, 89.

45. Bruce and Crawford, *Cerealizing America*, 138.

46. Marchand, *Advertising the American Dream*, 110.

47. Marchand, *Advertising the American Dream*, 112.

48. Ad, "Babe Ruth the Home Run King," *Hartford Courant*, July 30, 1933, G3.

49. Sivrulka, *Soap, Sex, and Cigarettes*, 101.

50. *Printers' Ink*, July 28, 1938, 412.

51. Marchand, *Advertising the American Dream*, 229.

52. Marchand, *Advertising the American Dream*, 232.

53. Ad, "Huskies," *Chicago Tribune*, July 14, 1936, 18.

54. Bruce and Crawford, *Cerealizing America*, 88.

55. "Believe It or Not," *Broadcasting*, August 15, 1937, 32.

56. *Broadcasting*, September 1, 1937, 44.

57. Quoted in Bruce and Crawford, *Cerealizing America*, 89.

58. Gray, *Business Without Boundary*, 168.

59. Bureau of Labor Statistics, "Graph of U.S. Unemployment Rate, 1930–1945," *HERB: Resources for Teachers*, accessed July 24, 2015, http://herb.ashp.cuny.edu/items/show/1510.

60. *Broadcasting*, April 1, 1932, 19.

61. *Broadcasting*, April 1, 1933, 17.

62. *Broadcasting*, August 1, 1932, 19.

63. J. R. Walker, *Crack of the Bat*, 125.

64. Gray, *Business Without Boundary*, 168.

65. "1935–41 Wheaties," accessed July 30, 2015, http://www.oldcardboard.com/f/cereals/wheaties/wheaties.asp?cardsetID=1097.

66. *Broadcasting*, April 15, 1934, 44.

67. "The Wheaties Story," accessed August 4, 2015, http://www.wheaties.com/feature/the-wheaties-story/.

68. "Baseball Trophies Will Be Awarded by General Mills," *Broadcasting*, May 1, 1936, 20.

69. *Broadcasting*, November 15, 1936, 14.

70. Letter to the editor, *Broadcasting*, August 15, 1936, 54.

71. Harold Parrott, "Ebbets Field to Go Radio if MacPhail Gets Job," *Brooklyn Daily Eagle*, January 12, 1938, 14.

72. Tommy Holmes, "MacPhail First Boss Since Ebbets," *Brooklyn Daily Eagle*, January 20, 1938, 16.

73. "Giants and Yanks Complete Arrangements for Broadcasting Their Home Contests," *New York Times*, January 26, 1939, 29. Saucony-Vacuum Oil, a spin-off of the Standard Oil trust, would eventually adopt the name of one of its subsidiaries, Mobil Oil.

74. Jim Thielman, "How General Mills Helped Shape Baseball Broadcasts," accessed August 5, 2015, http://www.blog.generalmills.com/2015/07/how-general-mills-helped-shape-baseball-broadcasts/.

75. "Promotion Methods for Baseball Games Outlined at General Mills Gathering," *Broadcasting*, May 1, 1939, 36.

76. Gray, *Business Without Boundary*, 168.

77. Ad, "Wheaties," *Boston Globe*, August 6, 1939, A11.

78. Bert Keane, "Calling 'Em Right," *Hartford Courant*, July 14, 1938, 15.

79. Bob Ray, "The Sports X-Ray," *Los Angeles Times*, January 29, 1939, A11.

80. Edwin Rumill, "Rumors of Greenberg's Departure Are Prevalent," *Christian Science Monitor*, September 12, 1939, 11.

81. *Broadcasting*, May 15, 1938, 58.

82. "Reverend Charles E. Coughlin," *America and the Holocaust*, accessed July 29, 2015, http://www.pbs.org/wgbh/amex/holocaust/peopleevents/pandeAMEX96.html.

83. For example, see "Editorial Comment," *Oelwein (Iowa) Daily Register*, December 14, 1938, 2, and the letter to the editor published in the "Open Forum," *Manitowoc (Wisconsin) Herald Times*, March 31, 1939, 4, claiming that Coughlin doesn't hate all Jews, just Jewish Communists.

84. A. James Rudin, "A Dark Legacy of Henry Ford's anti-Semitism," *Religion News Service*, accessed July 29, 2015, http://www.religionnews.com/2014/10/10/dark-legacy-henry-fords-anti-semitism-commentary/.

85. "A $100,000 Radio Deal Is Completed: Mutual Gets Air Rights to the World Series," *Chicago Tribune*, August 18, 1939, 21.

86. "Staff for World Series Is Complete; Controversy on Rights Still Simmers," *Broadcasting*, October 1, 1939, 16.

87. J. R. Walker, *Crack of the Bat*, 99.

88. McKibben, *Cutting Edge*, 32.

89. "Gillette Co.," AdAge.com, accessed on July 21, 2015, http://adage.com/article/adage-encyclopedia/gillette/98674/.

90. McKibben, *Cutting Edge*, 37.

91. Ad, Gillette, *Boone (Iowa) News Republican*, October 4, 1939, 5.

92. McKibben, *Cutting Edge*, 37.

93. "Through the Years: World Series Broadcast Rights Fees," *Sports Business Daily Global Journal*, accessed on July 21, 2015, http://m.sportsbusinessdaily.com/Journal/Issues /2003/10/20031013/Media/Through-The-Years-World-Series-Broadcast-Rights-Fees.aspx.

4. Pitching in Black and White

1. Ad, "Lynch Mobs Don't Always Wear Hoods," *New York Times*, May 13, 1947, 19.

2. Walter H. Waggoner, "A. N. Spanel, 83, Philanthropist and Playtex Chief, Dies," *New York Times*, April 2, 1985.

3. Portions of this chapter were published in an earlier form as Newman, "Pitching Behind the Color Line," 81–90. For a thorough examination of the Great Migration, the black press, and the economics of black baseball, see Newman and Rosen, *Black Baseball, Black Business*.

4. Ad, "Amusements," *New York Times*, July 5, 1888, 7.

5. White, *Sol White's History of Colored Base Ball*, 7.

6. Malloy, "Strange Career of Sol White," 64.

7. "Notes of the Game," *New York Times*, July 5, 1888, 3.

8. Jerry Malloy, foreword to *Sol White's History of Colored Base Ball*, 12.

9. White, *Sol White's History of Colored Base Ball*, 24.

10. White, *Sol White's History of Colored Base Ball*, 82–83.

11. Pennsylvania, 1938 *Green Book*, accessed January 22, 2016, https://www.google .com/fusiontables/DataSource?docid=1yV3P2MrKl9wgjH1n4pbkVx8T_aNI8 -LN0E149xWN#rows:id=1.

12. White, *Sol White's History of Colored Base Ball*, 116.

13. White, *Sol White's History of Colored Base Ball*, 7.

14. White, *Sol White's History of Colored Base Ball*, 79.

15. Newman and Rosen, *Black Baseball, Black Business*, 11.

16. DuBoise, *Philadelphia Negro*, accessed January 28, 2016, https://archive.org /stream/philadelphianegr001901mbp/philadelphianegr001901mbp_djvu.txt.

17. "Williams, George Grant," in *Who's Who of the Colored Race*, 286.

18. White, *Sol White's History of Colored Base Ball*, 69.

19. Franklin, "'Voice of the Black Community,'" 264.

20. Aberjhani and West, "The *Chicago Defender*," 61.

21. Newman and Rosen, *Black Baseball, Black Business*, 5.

22. Wilkerson, *Warmth of Other Suns*, 9.

23. Newman and Rosen, *Black Baseball, Black Business*, 6–7.

24. Suzette Hackney, "Big-League Baseball Once Drew Crowds in this Suburb," *Philadelphia Inquirer*, accessed June 3, 2016, http://articles.philly.com/1995–02–12 /news/25704168_1_amateur-teams-delaware-county-black-professional-baseball.

25. Hilldale Club Ledgers, 1921–1922, Cash Thompson Collection, Box 3, African American Museum, Philadelphia PA.

26. Ad, *Philadelphia Tribune*, May 3, 1928, 11.

27. Ads, *Philadelphia Tribune*, May 16, 1925, 10.

28. Undated photograph, Cash Thompson Collection, Box 3, African American Museum, Philadelphia PA.

29. J. E. K. Walker, *History of Black Business*, 238.

30. Newman and Rosen, *Black Baseball, Black Business*, 27.

31. Charles Grutnzer, "Dimes Make Millions for Numbers Racket," *New York Times*, accessed June 6, 2016, http://www.nytimes.com/1964/06/26/dimes-make -millions-for-numbers-racket.html.

32. Lanctot, *Negro League Baseball*, 6.

33. Sundstrom, "Last Hired, First Fired?,"419.

34. Ads, Dream Books, *New York Amsterdam News*, September 23, 1939, 14.

35. Ad, "SWOC," *Baltimore Afro-American*, September 20, 1941, 22.

36. "MLBPA Info: History of the Major League Baseball Players Association," accessed June 6, 2016, http://mlb.mlb.com/pa/info/history.jsp.

37. Skotnes, *New Deal for All?*, 237.

38. Skotnes, *New Deal for All?*, 240.

39. Rudacille, *Roots of Steel*, 82.

40. Spivey, "Satchel Paige's Struggle for Selfhood in the Era of Jim Crow," 107.

41. Ad, "Brown Bomber," *New York Amsterdam News*, April 6, 1930, 12.

42. Drake and Cayton, *Black Metropolis*, 431.

43. Ad, "Bond Bread," *New York Amsterdam News*, August 21, 1943, 3.

44. "'Bricktop' Wright Plea Is Rejected," *New York Amsterdam News*, March 2, 1940, 1.

45. "From the Burning Sands of the Divine Nine," NAACP, accessed June 8, 2016, http://www.naacpconnect.org/blog/entry/from-the-burning-sands-of-the-divine-nine.

46. "'Bricktop' Wright Benefit Stirs Fans," *New York Amsterdam News*, March 30, 1940, 14.

47. Al Moses, "Moses Defends Ball Player's Fiery Actions," *Baltimore Afro-American*, August 14, 1943, 23.

48. Larry Doby, then nineteen years old, also played for the Eagles in 1943. Although he was to become the first African American player to cross the American League color line just a few short weeks after Jackie Robinson's debut, he was hardly a house-hold name in 1943; "1943 Newark Eagles Statistics," accessed June 8, 2016, http://www .baseball-reference.com/register/team.cgi?id=be500516.

49. Moses, "Moses Defends Ball Player's Fiery Actions," *Baltimore Afro-American*, August 14, 1943, 23.

50. David J. Sullivan, "Don't Do This—If You Want to Sell Your Products to Negroes!" quoted in Weems, *Desegregating the Dollar*, 32.

51. Ad, "Silver Rail," *New York Amsterdam News*, August 30, 1947, 15.

52. Ads, "Congratulations Jackie Robinson and the Brooklyn Dodgers," *Pittsburgh Courier*, May 17, 1949, 2.

53. "Picket St. Louis Clothing Store in Effort to Secure More Jobs," *Pittsburgh Courier*, April 23, 1938, 3.

54. Ron Schweiger in Zinn and Zinn, eds., *People Remember Ebbets Field*, 215.

55. Bobrow-Strain, *White Bread*, Kindle edition, loc. 44.

56. Bobrow-Strain, *White Bread*, Kindle edition, loc. 46.

57. Ira Berkow, "Sports of the Times; Dixie Walker Remembers," *New York Times*, December 10, 1981, accessed June 16, 2016, http://www.nytimes.com/1981/12/10/sports /sports-of-the-times-dixie-walker-remembers.html.

58. Ad, "Wonder Bread," *Chicago Tribune*, July 10, 1947, 25.

59. Pollay, Lee, and Carter-Whitney, "Separate, But Not Equal," 46.

60. Pollay, Lee, and Carter-Whitney, "Separate, But Not Equal," 53.

61. Ad, "Old Gold," *Baltimore Afro-American*, May 22, 1948, 3.

62. Pollay, Lee, and Carter-Whitney, "Separate, But Not Equal," 51.

63. Roy Norr, "Cancer by the Carton," *Reader's Digest* (December 1952): 7–8.

64. Norr, "Cancer by the Carton," *Reader's Digest* (December 1952): 55.

65. Ad, "Niagara Mechanical Cushion," *New York Times*, March 29, 1953.

66. Ad, "Rheingold," *New York Amsterdam News*, November 17, 1951, 36.

67. "The Business of Broadcasting," *Broadcasting*, October 1, 1933, 40–41.

68. "Business Briefly," *Broadcasting*, September 15, 1957, 36.

69. Rampersad, *Jackie Robinson*, 336.

70. Linge, *Jackie Robinson*, 122.

71. Ad, *East-West Baseball Classic: Official Souvenir Program*, August 14, 1949, Collection of the National Baseball Hall of Fame Library, Cooperstown NY.

72. Ad, *East-West Baseball Classic: Official Souvenir Program*.

5. Baseball, Hotdogs, Apple Pie, Chevrolet

1. "Watching a Televised Baseball Game," *New York Times*, September 3, 1939, x10.

2. "Watching a Televised Baseball Game," x10.

3. "Baseball Telecast," *Broadcasting*, September 1, 1939, 17.

4. "Watching a Televised Baseball Game," x10.

5. Walker and Bellamy, *Center Field Shot*, 14.

6. "Television Notes," *Broadcasting*, May 1, 1940, 63.

7. Berkman, "Long Before Arledge," 54.

8. Ron Simon, "Fun Facts about Commercial TV's Birth in 1941," The Paley Center for Media, accessed September 6, 2016, https://www.paleycenter.org/p-70-tv-countdown -fun-facts-1941.

9. Samuel, *Brought to You By*, Kindle edition, loc. 349.

10. Walker and Bellamy, *Center Field Shot*, 16.

11. Jeanine Poggi, "Flashback Friday: TV's First Commercial Ran 75 Years Ago Today," *Advertising Age*, July 1, 2016, accessed September 9, 2016, http://adage.com /article/media/flash-back-friday-tv-commercial-ran-75-years-ago-today/304777/.

12. Samuel, *Brought to You By*, Kindle edition, loc. 345.

13. Walker and Bellamy, *Center Field Shot*, 17.

14. Samuel, *Brought to You By*, Kindle edition, loc. 348.

15. Sol Taishoff, "Agencies Ready for Post-War Television," *Broadcasting*, April 17, 1944, 11.

16. Taishoff, "Agencies Ready for Post-War Television," *Broadcasting*, April 17, 1944, 11.

17. "Resumption of Commercial Telecasting at Early Post-War Date Urged by Panel," *Broadcasting*, April 17, 1944, 59; "Average Family Income, By Income Group," http://www.stateofworkingamerica.org/chart/swa-income-table-2-1-average-family-income/.

18. Lawrence E. Davies, "Television Ready, RCA Experts Say," *New York Times*, August 31, 1946, 10.

19. "FCC Licenses 78 Television Stations; 6 in operation," *Wall Street Journal*, October 1, 1946, 2.

20. Walker and Bellamy, *Center Field Shot*, 18.

21. "Programs," *Broadcasting*, November 18, 1946, 72.

22. "Ford and General Foods Sponsor Dodgers Home Game Telecasts," *Broadcasting*, March 3, 1947, 16.

23. "Chesties in Twin TV-Radio Deal for N.Y. Giants," *Billboard*, December 27, 1949, 5.

24. "'Dodgers' Video," *Broadcasting*, February 16, 1948, 19.

25. Walker and Bellamy, *Center Field Shot*, 24.

26. "On the Radio Today—Television," *New York Times*, April 15, 1947, 50.

27. Box Score, "Tuesday, April 15, 1947, Ebbets Field," *Baseball-Reference*, accessed September 8, 2016, http://www.baseball-reference.com/boxes/BRO/BRO194704150.shtml.

28. *Printer's Ink*, quoted in Samuel, *Brought to You By*, Kindle edition, loc. 452.

29. Samuel, *Brought to You By*, Kindle edition, loc. 464.

30. Samuel, *Brought to You By*, Kindle edition, loc. 464.

31. Samuel, *Brought to You By*, Kindle edition, loc. 476.

32. Ad, "Pepco," *Washington Post*, April 14, 1947, 7.

33. Editorial note, *Public Service Management* 33, no. 3 (September 1922): 79.

34. "PUC to Begin Rate Talks with Pepco," *Washington Post*, June 15, 1947.

35. "Pepco Refuses to Place Lines Under Ground," *Washington Post*, June 26, 1947, B1.

36. Ad, "United States Television Mfg. Co.," *New York Times*, April 9, 1947, 17.

37. "Television Price Cut," *Brooklyn Daily Eagle*, September 8, 1947, 10.

38. Ad, "RCA Victor," *Chicago Tribune*, April 21, 1947, 18.

39. Walker and Bellamy, *Center Field Shot*, 25.

40. Ad, "United States Television Mfg. Co.," *New York Times*, April 9, 1947, 17.

41. Ad, "Villanova-Empire," *Hartford Courant*, August 25, 1947, 18.

42. "American Women: Television," *Library of Congress*, accessed September 13, 2016, https://memory.loc.gov/ammem/awhhtml/awmi10/television.html.

43. "Ford Will Telecast Milwaukee Baseball," *Broadcasting*, March 1, 1948, 64.

44. "Chesties in Twin TV-Radio Deal for N.Y. Giants," *Billboard*, December 27, 1949, 5.

45. "New Business," *Broadcasting*, November 29, 1948.

46. "L&M, Ford Sponsor Cubs Game Telecasts," *Broadcasting*, March 15, 1948.

47. Walker and Bellamy, *Center Field Shot*, 27.

48. Samuel, *Brought to You By*, Kindle edition, loc. 667.

49. Keyes, *Quote Verifier*, 1–2.

50. "*Television* Magazine Audience Research," *Television*, June, 1948, 10.

51. "Class 23: Smoking Materials," *Broadcasting*, April 11, 1949.

52. "Laws/Policies," BeTobaccoFree.gov, accessed September 16, 2016, http://betobaccofree.hhs.gov/laws/.

53. "Stanford Research into the Impact of Tobacco Advertising: Marlboro Men," Stanford School of Medicine, accessed September 16, 2016, http://tobacco.stanford.edu/tobacco_main/images.php?token2=fm_st085.php&token1=fm_img2057.php&theme_file=fm_mt006.php&theme_name=Filter%20safety%20Myths&subtheme_name=Marlboro%20Men.

54. "Radio-TV Draw Huge Series Audience," *Broadcasting*, October 6, 1947, 83.

55. J. R. Poppele quoted in "Radio-TV Draw Huge Series Audience," *Broadcasting*, October 6, 1947, 83.

56. John Coe, "3,962,336 Saw Series on Television," *Billboard*, October 18, 1947, 4.

57. Walker and Bellamy, *Center Field Shot*, 68.

58. "Radio-TV Draw Huge Series Audience," *Broadcasting*, October 6, 1947, 83.

59. John Coe, "3,962,336 Saw Series on Television," *Billboard*, October 18, 1947, 4.

60. "Home TV's Series Score," *Billboard*, October 11, 1947, 16.

61. "World Series," *Broadcasting*, September 12, 1949, 58.

62. "Gillette," *Advertising Age*, accessed September 17, 2016, http://adage.com/article/adage-encyclopedia/gillette/98674/.

63. "World Series," *Broadcasting*, October 6, 1962.

64. The Gillette Singing Parrot: "How Are You Fixed for Blades?" YouTube Video, 0:49, posted by Mitch Alan, July 2, 2009.

65. Pee Wee Reese Brooklyn Dodgers Gillette Razor TV Commercial, YouTube Video, 0:55, posted by Jeff Quitney, August 3, 2013.

66. "Gillette," *Advertising Age*, accessed September 17, 2016, http://adage.com/article/adage-encyclopedia/gillette/98674/.

67. Ad, "Gillette," *Life*, April 21, 1952, 92.

68. *Printer's Ink*, quoted in Samuel, *Brought to You By*, Kindle edition, loc. 452.

69. Walker and Bellamy, *Center Field Shot*, 55.

70. "A Little Boy Named Marky!" Homestat Farm, accessed September 22, 2016, http://www.homestatfarm.com/memorylane/thetaleofmarkymaypo/tabid/3083/default.aspx.

71. Mickey Mantle and Willie Mays, Blue Bonnet Commercial, YouTube video, 0:30, published by Club 70, October 15, 2014.

72. Gay Sands Miller, "Change of Pitch: More Food Advertisers Woo the Male Shopper As He Shares the Load," *Wall Street Journal*, August 26, 1980, 1.

73. Claudia H. Deutsch, "The Brouhaha Over Drug Ads," *New York Times*, May 14, 1989, accessed September 22, 2016, http://www.nytimes.com/1989/05/14/business/the-brouhaha-over-drug-ads.html?pagewanted=all. Mantle's Voltaren endorse-

ment and direct-to-consumer drug advertising as relates to baseball are examined in depth in chapter 6.

74. An earlier version of this section was previously published in Newman, "It Pays to Be Personal," 25–42.

75. Rein, Kotler, and Stoller, *High Visibility*, 80.

76. Fox, *Mirror Makers*, 262.

77. "American Airlines, 1955," *George Lois*, accessed September 23, 2016, http://www.georgelois.com/pages/milestones/mile.aa.html.

78. "My First Celebrity Commercial," *George Lois*, accessed September 23, 2016, http://www.georgelois.com/pages/milestones/mile.puss.html.

79. Patricia Winters Lauro, "One of Baseball's Most Colorful Figures Finds He Is in Demand Again," *New York Times*, April 30, 1999, accessed September 23, 2016, http://www.nytimes.com/1999/04/30/business/media-business-advertising-one-baseball-s-most-colorful-figures-finds-he-demand.html?_r=0.

80. Richard Sandomir, "For Yogi and Yoo-Hoo, It's Déjà vu All Over Again," *New York Times*, April 20, 1993, accessed September 23, 2016, http://www.nytimes.com/1993/04/20/business/for-yoo-hoo-and-yogi-it-s-deja-vu-all-over-again.html.

81. Jim Bouton quoted in Richard Sandomir, "For Yogi and Yoo-Hoo, It's Déjà Vu All Over Again."

82. Fox, *Mirror Makers*, 116.

83. Simon, *Public Relations Law*, 416.

84. Richard Sandomir, "For Yogi and Yoo-Hoo, It's Déjà Vu All Over Again."

85. Rein, Kotler, and Stoller, *High Visibility*, 54.

86. Author interview with John Osborn, December 2001.

87. Joshua Johnson, "Greatest Print Campaigns of All Time: Volkswagen, Think Small," *Design Shack*, August 23, 2012, accessed September 24, 2016, https://designshack.net/articles/graphics/the-greatest-print-campaigns-of-all-time-volkswagen-think-small/.

88. Fox, *Mirror Makers*, 257.

89. Briley, *Class at Bat, Gender on Deck, and Race in the Hole*, 212.

90. Kimes and Ackerson, *Chevrolet*, 6.

91. Pelfrey, *Billy, Alfred, and General Motors*, 277.

92. Stuart Elliot, "Ball, Hot Dogs, and Chevy, Redux," *New York Times*, June 30, 2006, accessed October 22, 2016, http://www.nytimes.com/2006/06/30/business/media/30adco.html?_r=0.

93. Chevrolet TV Commercial 1970s—Baseball, Hotdogs, Apple Pie and Chevrolet—Original, YouTube video, 1:00 posted by BENNY sees you, March 3, 2015.

94. Gruesz, "America," e-book, chapter 3.

95. Bradley Johnson, "From 'See the USA in your Chevrolet' to 'Like a Rock,' Chevy Ads Run Deep," *Advertising Age*, October 31, 2011, accessed September 24, 2016, http://adage.com/article/special-report-chevy-100/100-years-chevrolet-advertising-a-timeline/230636/#1950.

96. "Love Affair," YouTube video, 1:01, posted by corporatec, June 30, 2006.

97. "Chevrolet Retail Share Up in August and 7 Out of 8 Months This Year," *General Motors*, September 1, 2016, accessed September 24, 2016, https://www.gm.com/investors/sales/us-sales-production.html.

6. "Let's Just Say It Works for Me"

1. "MLB Announces Commissioner's Initiative on Women and Baseball," accessed July 22, 2016, http://mlb.mlb.com/news/press_releases/press_release.jsp?ymd=20000726&content_id=388145&vkey=pr_mlb&fext=.jsp&c_id=mlb.

2. Jeffrey M. Jones, "Gallup Poll: Nearly Half of Americans Are Baseball Fans," accessed July 22, 2016, http://www.gallup.com/poll/22240/nearly-half-americans-baseball-fans.aspx.

3. Derek Thompson, "Which Sports Have the Whitest/Richest/Oldest Fans?" *Atlantic*, February 10, 1914, accessed July 20, 2016, http://www.theatlantic.com/business/archive/2014/02/which-sports-have-the-whitest-richest-oldest-fans/283626/.

4. Donohue, "History of Drug Advertising," 664.

5. Donohue, "History of Drug Advertising," 665–66.

6. Wallace F. Janssen, "The Story of the Laws Behind the Labels," U.S. Food and Drug Administration, accessed July 22, 2016, http://www.fda.gov/AboutFDA/WhatWeDo/History/Overviews/ucm056044.htm.

7. "The Federal Trade Commission Act of 1938," *Columbia Law Review* 39, no. 2 (February 1939): 259.

8. "The Federal Trade Commission Act of 1938," *Columbia Law Review*, 363–64.

9. Donohue, "History of Drug Advertising," 670.

10. Donohue, "History of Drug Advertising," 667.

11. Rosser Reeves, quoted in Fox, *Mirror Makers*, 188.

12. Fox, *Mirror Makers*, 187.

13. "TV Commercial—Rolaids Tommy Lasorda (1983)," YouTube video, 0:31, posted by JCPro Films, December 15, 2012, https://www.youtube.com/watch?v=XBRzrH6P0ok.

14. Ron Fimrite, "The Bringer of the Big Heat," *Sports Illustrated*, June 16, 1975, accessed July 27, 2016, http://www.si.com/vault/1975/06/16/606641/the-bringer-of-the-big-heat.

15. "Advil Super Bowl XXVI ad feat. Nolan Ryan—It Works (1992)," YouTube video, 0:30, posted by Every Super Bowl Ad, September 2, 2015, https://www.youtube.com/watch?v=JaCOXcfenUI.

16. Ron Fimrite, "The Bringer of the Big Heat," *Sports Illustrated*, June 16, 1975.

17. Morton Mintz, "Lilly Chairman Decided to Sell Oraflex Despite Death Reports," *Washington Post*, accessed August 10, 2016, https://www.washingtonpost.com/archive/business/1983/11/13/lilly-chairman-decided-to-sell-oraflex-despite-death-reports/9a39acd9-0f87-4a1b-b833-271e0ccc8a23/.

18. Donohue, "History of Drug Advertising," 675.

19. Claudia H. Deutsch, "The Brouhaha Over Drug Ads," *New York Times*, May 14, 1989, 8. Oraflex was pulled from the market just a few months after its introduction, the result of serious side effects.

20. Donohue, "History of Drug Advertising," 668.

21. Brian K. Jefferson, MD, "Correspondence," *New England Journal of Medicine* 339 (December 13, 1998): 2024–25, accessed July 28, 2016, DOI: 10.1056/NEJM199812313392715.

22. Louis M. Sherwood, MD, "Correspondence," *New England Journal of Medicine* 339 (December 13, 1998): 2024–25.

23. Portions of an earlier version of this chapter originally appeared in Newman, "It Pays to Be Personal."

24. Ripken and Bryan, *Only Way I Know*, 113.

25. Barbara Martinez, "Here's a Time When Cal Shouldn't Have Shown Up," *Wall Street Journal*, April 7, 1997, accessed July 28, 2016, http://www.wsj.com/articles/SB860357954818919500.

26. Letter to Ellen R. Westrick, Senior Director, Office of Medical and Legal, Merck & Co., Inc. from Victoria J. Babb, Pharm. D., Regulatory Review Officer, Division of Drug Marketing, Advertising, and Communications, FDA, accessed on July 28, 2016, http://www.fda.gov/downloads/Drugs/GuidanceCompliance RegulatoryInformation/EnforcementActivitiesbyFDA/WarningLettersandNoticeof ViolationLetterstoPharmaceuticalCompanies/UCM169313.pdf.

27. Editor's reply, "Correspondence," *New England Journal of Medicine* 339 (December 13, 1998): 2024–25.

28. "FTC Staff Provides FDA with Comments on Direct-to-Consumer Prescription Drug Advertising," Federal Trade Commission, accessed July 29, 2016, https://www.ftc.gov/news-events/press-releases/2003/12/ftc-staff-provides-fda-comments-direct-consumer-prescription-drug.

29. "1999 Claritin Commercial (Baseball)," YouTube video, 0.55, posted by Merck & Co., April 24, 2016, https://www.youtube.com/watch?v=KQ0WHT4KU88.

30. John George, "Claritin Uses MLB to Target Consumer," *Street and Smith's Sports Business Daily Global Journal*, accessed July 29, 2016, http://www.sportsbusinessdaily.com/Journal/Issues/2000/11/20001106/No-Topic-Name/Claritin-Uses-MLB-To-Target-Consumer.aspx.

31. Jonah Freedman, "The Fortunate 50," *Sports Illustrated*, July 4, 2005, 65–69.

32. Fox, *Mirror Makers*, 99.

33. Bob Finnigan and Jose Miguel Romero, "Notebook: Martinez Said No to Viagra," *Seattle Times*, July 1, 2002, accessed on August 1, 2016, http://community.seattletimes.nwsource.com/archive/?date=20020701&slug=mnotes01.

34. Garth Woolsey, "Shirt-peeling Approved But No Ads, Please," *Toronto Star*, March 18, 2002, D12.

35. "macho, n.2 and adj.": *Oxford English Dictionary*, accessed August 1, 2016, http://dictionary.oed.com.

36. Anonymous source, quoted in Margery Eagan, "Sex Enhancer's Competition Gives Rise to Ridicule," *Boston Herald*, May 30, 2002, 12.

37. FTC Guide Concerning Use of Endorsements and Testimonials in Advertising, sec., 255.1(c), accessed August 3, 2016, https://www.ftc.gov/sites/default/files

/attachments/press-releases/ftc-publishes-final-guides-governing-endorsements
-testimonials/091005revisedendorsementguides.pdf.

38. Jim Moore, "Hard Topic, Easy Money; Palmeiro Cashed in on Viagra," *Seattle Post-Intelligencer*, August 1, 2002, accessed on August 3, 2016, http://www.seattlepi
.com/news/article/Hard-topic-easy-money-Palmeiro-cashes-in-on-1092712.php.

39. Garth Woolsey, "Shirt-peeling Approved But No Ads, Please," *Toronto Star*, March 18, 2002, D12.

40. According to reports, Palmeiro was on the 2003 list of players that tested positive for PEDs. That list, however, was meant to remain confidential. Patrick Mauro, "The 103 Who Tested Positive for Steroids in 2003?" *Bleacher Report*, August 1, 2009, accessed August 3, 2016, http://bleacherreport.com/articles/228510-the-103-who
-tested-positive-for-steroids-in-2003.

41. McLuhan, *Understanding Media*, Kindle edition, loc. 1568.

42. FDA, "Prescription Drug Advertising : Questions and Answers," accessed August 3, 2016, http://www.fda.gov/Drugs/ResourcesForYou/Consumers
/PrescriptionDrugAdvertising/ucm076768.htm#non_requirements.

43. "2003 Commercial: Rafael Palmeiro for Viagra," YouTube video, 0:29, posted by CatchTheTaste, October 31, 2014, https://www.youtube.com/watch?v=1-vTJlFUjmY.

44. Ventola, "Direct-to-Consumer Pharmaceutical Advertising," 670.

45. Matthew Harper, "Iron Mike Ditka vs. Erectile Dysfunction," *Forbes*, July 31, 2003, accessed August 4, 2016, http://www.forbes.com/2003/07/31/cx_mh_0731ditka.html.

46. "Principle 16," PhRMA Guiding Principles of Direct to Consumer Advertisements about Prescription Medicines, 7, accessed July 22, 2016, http://phrma.org/sites
/default/files/pdf/phrmaguidingprinciplesdec08final.pdf.

47. "Questions and Answers," PhRMA Guiding Principles of Direct to Consumer Advertisements about Prescription Medicines, 14.

48. Terry Lefton, "ED Era Wanes as Viagra Exits MLB Deal," *Sports Business Daily*, March 12–18, 2007, accessed August 4, 2016, http://www.sportsbusinessdaily.com
/Journal/Issues/2007/03/20070312/This-Weeks-News/ED-Era-Wanes-As-Viagra
-Exits-MLB-Deal.aspx.

49. John Consoli, "A Network Takes Us Out to a Ballgame," *New York Times*, March 24, 2009, B8.

50. Rob Ogden, "Adam Wainwright is Tired of Erectile Dysfunction Commercials," *Chicago Sun Times*, October 8, 2015, accessed October 22, 2016, http://chicago.suntimes
.com/sports/adam-wainwright-is-tired-of-erectile-dysfunction-commercials/.

51. University of North Carolina at Charlotte, "Study Finds that 'Big Pharma' Fails at Self-Policing ED drug Advertising," *Science Newsline: Medicine*, February 15, 2013, accessed on August 4, 2016, http://www.sciencenewsline.com/news
/2013021515000046.html.

52. John Mack, "Use of Celebrities for PR and DTC Advertising," *Pharma Marketing News* 7, no. 1 (2008): 5.

53. Associated Press, "Palmeiro Docked for Steroids," ESPN.com, accessed August 4, 2015, http://www.espn.com/mlb/news/story?id=2121659.

54. Merck & Co., Inc., "Pro Baseball Players Step up to the Plate for Propecia ®," PR Newswire, accessed August 4, 2016, http://www.prnewswire.com/news -releases/pro-baseball-players-step-up-to-the-plate-for-propeciar-john-smoltz-bret -saberhagen-sandy-alomar-jr-and-others-to-participate-in-hats-off-charity-challenge -with-propecia-73561272.html.

55. Merck & Co., Inc., "Atlanta Baseball Pro Walt Weiss Wins Hair Growth Challenge," PR Newswire, accessed August 4, 2016, http://www.prnewswire.com/news -releases/atlanta-baseball-pro-walt-weiss-wins-hair-growth-challenge-pro-baseball -players-tip-their-caps-to-reveal-the-winner-of-the-charity-challenge-with-propecia -72302252.html.

56. Endres, "From 'Lost Manhood' to 'Erectile Dysfunction,'" 91.

7. Four Things We Love

1. Press Release, "Opening Day Rosters Feature 230 Players Born Outside the U.S.," MLB News, accessed August 16, 2016, http://m.mlb.com/news/article/116591920 /opening-daysters-feature-230-players-born-outside-the-us/.

2. Damon Salvadore, "MLB Hispanic Campaign: MLB Looking to Reach Out to Hispanic Baseball Fans," Latin Post, accessed August 17, 2016, http://www.latinpost .com/articles/46707/20150409/mlb-hispanic-campaign-latinworks-agency-hopes -to-reach-out-to-hispanics-baseball-fans.htm.

3. "The World's Highest Paid Athletes, 2017 Rankings," Forbes.com, accessed February 18, 2018, https://www.forbes.com/athletes/#83d535f55ae5.

4. Ben Reiter, "The Big Papi Show: Inside David Ortiz's Transition from Red Sox Hero to World Series Commentator," Sports Illustrated, October 31, 2017, accessed February 18, 2018, https://www.si.com/mlb/2017/10/31/david-ortiz-world-series -commentator-fox.

5. For a historical overview of the ways the different terms have been used, see Arias and Hellmuller, "Hispanics and Latinos and the U.S. Media," 4–21.

6. Jeffery Passel and Paul Taylor, "Who's Hispanic?," Pew Research Center: Hispanic Trends, accessed September 4, 2016, http://www.pewhispanic.org/2009/05 /28/whos-hispanic/.

7. "Who Is Latino?," National Association of Scholars, accessed September 4, 2016, https://www.nas.org/articles/Ask_a_Scholar_What_is_the_True_Definition _of_Latino.

8. "From Ireland to Germany to Italy to Mexico: How America's Source of Immigrants Has Changed in the States, 1850–2013," Pew Research Center: Hispanic Trends, accessed September 4, 2016, http://www.pewhispanic.org/2015/09/28/from-ireland -to-germany-to-italy-to-mexico-how-americas-source-of-immigrants-has-changed -in-the-states-1850-to-2013/.

9. Jeffery Passel and Paul Taylor, "Who's Hispanic?," Pew Research Center: Hispanic Trends.

10. "Race and Hispanic Origin," United States Census Bureau, accessed August 17, 2016, https://www.census.gov/quickfacts/table/RHI125215/00.

11. Renee Stepler and Anna Brown, "Statistical Portrait of Hispanics in the United States," Pew Research Center, accessed August 17, 2016, http://www.pewhispanic.org/2016/04/19/statistical-portrait-of-hispanics-in-the-united-states-key-charts/.

12. Emily Guskin and Amy Mitchell, "Hispanic Media Faring Better than the Mainstream Media," Pew Research Center's Project for Excellence in Journalism: The State of the News Media, 2011, accessed August 17, 2016, http://www.stateofthemedia.org/2011/hispanic-media-fairing-better-than-the-mainstream-media/#television.

13. Laurel Wentz, "Ad Age's 2015 Hispanic Fact Pack is Out Now," *Advertising Age*, August 3, 2015, accessed August 17, 2016, http://adage.com/article/hispanic-marketing/ad-age-s-2015-hispanic-fact-pack/299712/.

14. Fernando Cuza, quoted in Mike Fish, "Advertisers Are Riding the Hispanic Wave," ESPN.com, accessed August 17, 2016, http://www.espn.com/mlb/latinosrise/columns/story?id=2341270.

15. Mike Fish, "Advertisers Are Riding the Hispanic Wave," ESPN.com.

16. Jesse Sanchez, "Beltran's Vision Realized with Translator Program," MLB News, accessed August 16, 2016, http://m.mlb.com/news/article/161857500/carlos-beltran-gets-spanish-translator-program/.

17. Burgos, *Playing America's Game*, 250.

18. Burgos, *Playing America's Game*, 9–10.

19. "Poster Boy of the Week," *Jet*, September 16, 1954, 23.

20. Rampersad, *Jackie Robinson*, 336.

21. "High Heat Baseball—It's So Real," YouTube Video, 0:31, posted by BrandRoyal, July 7, 2011, https://youtu.be/kueCCffiBkY.

22. Burgos, *Playing America's Game*, 251.

23. Burgos, *Playing America's Game*, 252.

24. Chris Isadore, "Sports Biz: No Cork in Sosa's Ad Deals," CNN Money, June 6, 2003, accessed August 18, 2016, http://money.cnn.com/2003/06/06/commentary/column_sportsbiz/sportsbiz/

25. "Schilling, Sosa—Berry, Berry Good," YouTube Video, 0:31, posted by paprinvision, November 25, 2013, https://youtu.be/ewM2Hki9Gv0.

26. Davila, *Latinos, Inc.*, 3.

27. Harvey Araton, "The Understated Elegance of the Yankees' Rivera," *New York Times*, April 26, 2010, D1.

28. Elisabetta Canali, quoted in Harvey Araton, "The Understated Elegance of the Yankees' Rivera," *New York Times*, April 26, 2010.

29. "Arrid Extra Dry Anti-Perspirant Deodorant Partners with 'Cool Under Pressure' Pitcher Mariano Rivera," PR Newswire, September 19, 2011, accessed 8/19/2016, http://www.prnewswire.com/news-releases/arrid-extra-dry-anti-perspirant-deodorant-partners-with-cool-under-pressure-pitcher-mariano-rivera-130163168.html.

30. "Taco Bell Signs on as MLB's National Fast Food Sponsor," *Sports Business Daily*, accessed August 20, 2016, http://www.sportsbusinessdaily.com/Daily/Issues/2004/06/Issue-186/Sponsorships-Advertising-Marketing/Taco-Bell-Signs-On-As-Mlbs-National-Fast-Food-Sponsor.aspx.

31. "Taco Bell Brings Back 'Steal a Base, Steal a Breakfast' World Series Promo," QSRWeb, October 27, 2015, accessed August 25, 2016, http://www.qsrweb.com/news/taco-bell-brings-back-steal-a-base-steal-a-breakfast-world-series-promo/.

32. Noriega, *Shot in America*, 35.

33. Baudrilliard, *Simulation and Simulacra*, 1.

34. McLuhan, *Understanding Media*, Kindle edition, loc. 1567.

35. BBDO New York, "Pepsi—Hitting the Moon," AdForum, accessed August 22, 2016, http://www.adforum.com/creative-work/ad/player/54900/hitting-the-moon/pepsi.

36. Caroline Sikes, "Rob Gronkowski and David Ortiz get auto-tuned for Dunkin' Donuts Single," November 27, 2015, http://www.sportingnews.com/nfl-news/4649188-rob-gronkowski-david-ortiz-dunkin-donuts-commercial-turn-it-up-.

37. Alyssa Newcomb, "Why 'Big Papi' Got Paid to Take Selfie with President Obama," ABC News, accessed August 24, 2016.

38. Lindsay Bever, "After David Ortiz Selfie, White House Draws Red Line," *Washington Post*, April 7, 2014, accessed August 24, 2016, https://www.washingtonpost.com/news/morning-mix/wp/2014/04/07/after-david-ortiz-selfie-white-house-draws-red-line/.

39. "Weekend Update: David Ortiz on his Selfie with President Obama," *Saturday Night Live*, Season 39, April 12, 2014, accessed August 24, 2014, https://www.nbc.com/saturday-night-live/cast/kenan-thompson-15086/impersonation/david-ortiz-81661.

40. "Weekend Update: David Ortiz on Retirement," *Saturday Night Live*, Season 41, November 21, 2015, accessed August 24, 2014, http://www.nbc.com/saturday-night-live/video/weekend-update-david-ortiz-on-retirement/2941772.

41. Hayden Bird, "Here's Dunkin's Diabolical Music Video Featuring Big Papi & Gronk," BostInno, June 8, 2015, accessed August 30, 2016, http://bostinno.streetwise.co/2015/06/08/david-ortiz-rob-gronkowskis-dunkin-donuts-music-video-commercial-is-truly-terrible/.

42. Hayden Bird, "Dunkin', Gronk, Papi, & the Potential of Intentionally Bad . . ." July 7, 2015, accessed August 31, 2016, http://bostinno.streetwise.co/2015/07/07/rob-gronkowski-david-ortiz-dunkin-donuts-turn-it-up-dance-song-in-a-new-commercial-video/.

43. Heather Morin, quoted in Hayden Bird, "Dunkin', Gronk, Papi, & the Potential of Intentionally Bad . . ."

44. "History of Bachata, the Guitar Music of the Dominican Republic," *iASO Records*, accessed August 31, 2016, http://www.iasorecords.com/music/history-of-bachata-the-guitar-music-of-the-dominican-republic.

45. Gronk and Big Papi's "Me Estoy Enamorando," YouTube video, 1:04, posted by Dunkin' Donuts, July 21, 2015.

46. "Summer Chill Single '4 Things We Love,'" YouTube video, 1:06, posted by Dunkin' Donuts, August 4, 2015.

47. Gabriel Beltrone, "David Ortiz Keeps Swinging, Even in Retirement, in JetBlue's Charming Farewell Ad," *AdWeek*, June 7, 2016, accessed September 2, 2016, http://www.adweek.com/adfreak/david-ortiz-keeps-swinging-even-retirement-jetblues-charming-farewell-ad-171849.

48. "David Ortiz vs. Piñatas," YouTube video, 0:45, posted by JetBlue, June 6, 2016.

49. "The World's Highest Paid Athletes, 2017 Rankings," Forbes.com, accessed February 18, 2018.

50. Peter Abraham, "Red Sox Cry Foul at David Ortiz Bobblehead," *Boston Globe*, August 9, 2016, accessed September 5, 2016, https://www.bostonglobe.com/sports /redsox/2016/08/09/red-sox-deem-david-ortiz-bobblehead-racially-insensitive /qwAnoxGz56ov5pxohgrFuM/story.html.

8. "Driven" to "RE2PECT"

1. Joe McDonald, "Red Sox Players Praise Derek Jeter," ESPN.com, July 9, 2011, accessed September 29, 2016, http://www.espn.com/boston/mlb/columns/story?id =6753088&columnist=mcdonald_joe.

2. "Yogisms," *Yogi Berra Museum and Learning Center*, accessed October 4, 2016, http://yogiberramuseum.org/just-for-fun/yogisms/.

3. "The World's Highest-Paid Athletes," Forbes.com, accessed September 29, 2016, http://www.forbes.com/profile/derek-jeter/.

4. Mark Sanderson, "DJ3K and the Marketability of Derek Jeter," *Beneath the Brand*, accessed September 29, 2016, http://www.talentzoo.com/beneath-the-brand /blog_news.php?articleID=10735.

5. Barry Janoff, "Survey, Derek Jeter Tops among MLB Marketing All-Stars," *Big Lead Sports*, July 7, 2011, accessed September 29, 2016, https://epollresearch.com /marketing/biglead_MLB_All_Stars_2011-7-7.pdf.

6. "Deciding Factors: How Analytics Can Help with Talent Decision Making," *Nielsen Insights*, June 22, 2016, accessed September 29, 2016, http://www.nielsen .com/us/en/insights/news/2016/deciding-factors-how-analytics-can-help-with-talent -decision-making.html.

7. Janoff, "Survey, Derek Jeter Tops among MLB Marketing All-Stars," *Big Lead Sports*, July 7, 2011.

8. Maegan Carberry, "Multiculti Chic," *Chicago Tribune*, February 16, 2005, accessed October 1, 2016, http://articles.chicagotribune.com/2005–02–16/news/0502170071_1 _multiracial-people-mixed-race-biracial.

9. De Mooij, *Global Marketing and Advertising*, 29.

10. Bill Hutchinson, "Boss Riding Jeter and Joe," *New York Daily News*, December 29, 2002, accessed October 1, 2016, http://www.nydailynews.com/archives/news/boss -riding-jeter-joe-big-guys-gotta-produce-yankees-owner-warns-article-1.504180.

11. Roger Rubin, "Jeter Fires Back at Boss by George, Won't Change Lifestyle," *New York Daily News*, February 4, 2003, accessed October 1, 2016, http://www.nydailynews .com/archives/sports/jeter-fires-back-boss-george-won-change-lifestyle-article-1.671168.

12. "Jeter-Steinbrenner VISA Commercial," YouTube video, 0:30, posted by Narnia 16, August 6, 2006.

13. Nancy Friedman, quoted in Richard Sandomir, "TV Sports; Echo of '78: Steinbrenner in an Ad," *New York Times*, May 30, 2003, accessed October 1, 2004, http://www .nytimes.com/2003/05/30/sports/tv-sports-echo-of-78-steinbrenner-in-an-ad.html.

14. "Sheffield Calls Out Torre, Jeter, Bonds in an HBO Interview," ESPN.com *News,* July 15, 2007, accessed October 4, 2016, http://www.espn.com/mlb/news/story?id=2935737.

15. "African Americans in MLB: 8%, Lowest Since Integration Era," *USA Today Daily Pitch,* April 15, 2012, accessed October 4, 2016, http://content.usatoday.com /communities/dailypitch/post/2012/04/mlb-jackie-robinson-day-african-american -players/1#.V_QEGPArKUk.

16. Jens Manuel Krogstad, "67 Years after Jackie Robinson Broke the Color Barrier, Major League Baseball Looks Very Different," Pew Research Center, April 16, 2014, accessed October 3, 2016, http://www.pewresearch.org/fact-tank/2014/04/16 /67-years-after-jackie-robinson-broke-the-color-barrier-major-league-baseball-looks -very-different/.

17. For example, see Pew Research Center data in Krogstad, "67 Years after Jackie Robinson Broke the Color Barrier, Major League Baseball Looks Very Different."

18. Kurt Badenhausen, "How Michael Jordan Will Make More than Any Athlete This Year," Forbes.com, March 30, 2016, accessed October 4, 2016, http://www.forbes .com/sites/kurtbadenhausen/2016/03/30/how-michael-jordan-will-make-more-than -any-other-athlete-in-the-world-this-year/#860c14550440.

19. Darren Rovell, "Tiger Woods Made $55M in 2014," ESPN.com, February 6, 2015, accessed October 4, 2016, http://www.espn.com/golf/story/_/id/12288282/tiger -woods-made-55-million-2014-endorsements-comprising-almost-99-percent.

20. "Avon Teams Up with Derek Jeter to Introduce a Signature Men's Fragrance," PR Newswire, July 31, 2006. ProQuest [451135991].

21. Adam Hoffstetter, quoted in Newman, *Driven,* 71.

22. Avon Products, Inc., "Avon Teams Up with Derek Jeter to Introduce a Signature Men's Fragrance," PR Newswire, July 31, 2006.

23. Avon promotional brochure quoted in Newman, "Driven," 74.

24. "Avon: The Company for Women," Avon, accessed October 9, 2016, http:// avoncompany.com/aboutavon/index.html.

25. Kahle and Homer, "Physical Attractiveness of the Celebrity Endorser," 857.

26. "The Captain," *Sixty Minutes,* CBS, September 25, 2005, accessed October 6, 2016, http://www.cbsnews.com/news/derek-jeter-the-captain/2/.

27. Wynter, *American Skin,* 168.

28. Ruth La Ferla, "Generation E.A.: Ethnically Ambiguous," *New York Times,* December 28, 2003.

29. "Multiracial in America," Pew Research Center, June 11, 2015, accessed October 6, 2016, http://www.pewsocialtrends.org/2015/06/11/multiracial-in-america/.

30. Wynter, *American Skin,* 170.

31. Avon Products, Inc., "Avon Teams Up with Derek Jeter to Introduce a Signature Men's Fragrance." PR Newswire, July 31, 2006.

32. "Home Run Hottie," *Women's Wear Daily* 192, no. 50 (September 9, 2006): 5.

33. "Introducing Driven Black by Derek Jeter," Avon Digital Archive, Hagley Museum and Library, accessed October 6, 2016, http://media.avoncompany.com /index.php?s=22969&item=1006.

34. "Jeter Power," YouTube video, 0:30, posted by pbreisch, May 20, 2011.

35. "Derek Jeter to "Captain" Jordan Brand Baseball and Training," July 12, 2016, accessed October 10, 2016, http://news.nike.com/news/derek-jeter-jordan-brand -baseball-captain.

36. "Stealin'," YouTube video, 0:45, posted by Trickyz33, April 20, 2007.

37. Michael McCarthy, "Ad of the Day: Gatorade's Epic Farewell to Derek Jeter Will Be Tough to Beat," AdWeek, September 18, 2014, accessed October 11, 2016, http://www.adweek.com/news/advertising-branding/ad-day-gatorades-epic-farewell -derek-jeter-will-be-tough-beat-160202.

38. John Walters, "How Gatorade Nailed Jeter's 'My Way' Ad," *Newsweek*, September 20, 2014, accessed October 11, 2016, http://www.newsweek.com/how-gatorade -nailed-jeters-my-way-ad-272030.

39. Kleiner, *Gardner's Art Through the Ages*, 683.

40. "Gatorade 'Made in New York' Commercial Featuring Derek Jeter!" YouTube video, 1:30, posted by Cheap Trillz, September 18, 2014.

Epilogue

1. McLuhan, *Understanding Media*, Kindle edition, loc. 3318.

2. McLuhan, *Understanding Media*, Kindle edition, loc. 3412.

3. "World Wide Web Timeline," Pew Research Center, March 11, 2014, accessed October 12, 2016, http://www.pewinternet.org/2014/03/11/world-wide-web-timeline/.

4. "The Birth of the Web," CERN, accessed October 12, 2016, https://home.cern /topics/birth-web.

5. Ryan Singel, "Oct. 27, 1994, Web Gives Birth to Banner Ads," *Wired*, October 27, 2010, accessed October 12, 2016, https://www.wired.com/2010/10/1027hotwired -banner-ads/.

6. Walker and Bellamy, *Center Field Shot*, 315.

7. MLBAM, accessed October 12, 2016, http://www.mlbam.com/.

8. Ira Boudway, "Fixing Baseball's Old-People Problem," *Bloomberg*, April 2, 2014, accessed October 13, 2016, http://www.bloomberg.com/news/articles/2014–04–01 /fixing-baseballs-old-people-problem-with-merchandise-highlights.

9. John Consoli, "A Network Takes Us Out to a Ballgame," *New York Times*, March 24, 2009, B8.

10. Joanna Molloy, "Boys Chill for Summer: MLB Contest Winners to Pass Time Watching and Tweeting on Games," *New York Daily News*, March 30, 2011, 12.

11. Blaise Nutter, "Five Rules for Successful Digital Out-of-Home Advertising," http://www.imediaconnection.com/content/21290.asp.

12. "MLB Fan Cave Debuts Foursquare Vending Experience," *Market Wired*, July 11, 2011, accessed October 13, 2016, http://www.marketwired.com/press-release/mlb -fan-cave-debuts-foursquare-vending-experience-1536578.htm.

13. Eric Fisher, "After 4 Years, MLB Seals the Fan Cave," *Sports Business Daily*, February 9, 2015, accessed October 13, 2016, http://www.sportsbusinessdaily.com/Journal /Issues/2015/02/09/Leagues-and-Governing-Bodies/FanCave.aspx.

14. "Advertising Effectiveness: Understanding the Value of a Social Media Impression," Nielsen Company, accessed October 13, 2016, http://www.nielsen.com/content/dam/corporate/us/en/reports-downloads/SocMediaImpressions_US_rpt_4.19.10.pdf.

15. Dave McGinn, "Everyone Has Their Own Definition of 'Bro.'" *Globe and Mail*, September 17, 2015, accessed October 13, 2016, http://www.theglobeandmail.com/life/relationships/everyone-has-their-own-definition-of-bro-so-what-does-the-term-really-mean/article26393915/.

16. Yost and Wilser, *Man Cave Book*, 9.

17. Mark Newman, "Fab 50: MLB Fan Cave Contestants Selected," MLB.com, February 8, 2012, accessed October 13, 2016, http://mlb.mlb.com/news/print.jsp?ymd=20120208&content_id=26606996&vkey=news_mlb&c_id=mlb.

18. "Off the Bat from the MLB Fan Cave," MTV2, accessed October 13, 2016, http://www.mtv.com/shows/off-the-bat-from-the-mlb-fan-cave.

19. Eric Fisher, "After 4 Years, MLB Seals the Fan Cave," *Sports Business Daily*, February 9, 2015.

20. Josh Catone, "Baseball Everywhere: How MLB is Innovating with Digital Media," Mashable, August 26, 2011, accessed October 15, 2016, http://mashable.com/2011/08/26/mlb-digital-media/#nqqvrOx_Ekqt.

21. "MLB.com Captures Multiple Awards for its Mobile Technology Offerings," *Entertainment Newsweekly*, October 1, 2010, 129.

22. "MLB.com At Bat 11: A Record Setting Debut," PR Newswire, February 25, 2011, ProQuest [853739851].

23. Terry Collins, "MLB.com's At Bat App Topps List of Best Sports App," C-NET, October 7, 2016, accessed October 15, 2016, https://www.cnet.com/news/mlb-dot-com-at-bat-app-best-sports-app-major-league-baseball-nfl-nba-nhl-hbo/.

24. Ben Cosman, "Dexter Fowler Gave His NLCS-bound Cubs Teammates Their Own Pairs of Jordans," Cut4, October 14, 2016, accessed October 15, 2016, http://m.mlb.com/cutfour/2016/10/14/206099478/dexter-fowler-gives-cubs-teammates-jordans.

25. Zach Bergson, "Why Baseball Players Can't Land Big Endorsements," Donald W. Reynolds National Center for Business Journalism, March 31, 2015, accessed October 16, 2016, http://businessjournalism.org/2015/03/sports-and-money-why-baseball-players-cant-land-big-endorsements/.

26. Sam Weber, "The Hunt for Baseball's Endorsement MVP," Opendorse, accessed October 16, 2016, http://opendorse.com/blog/mlb-endorsement-mvp/.

27. James Wagner, "Bryce Harper Signs Extension with Under Armour Believed to be Largest for MLB Player," *Washington Post*, May 3, 2016, accessed October 16, 2016, https://www.washingtonpost.com/news/nationals-journal/wp/2016/05/03/bryce-harper-signs-extension-with-under-armour-believed-to-be-largest-for-mlb-player/.

28. John Ellett, "Esurance Launches New Campaign with Buster Posey as Its Pitchman," *Forbes*, May 17, 2016, accessed October 16, 2016, http://www.forbes.com/sites/johnellett/2016/05/17/esurance-launches-new-campaign-with-buster-posey-as-its-pitchman/#5f439c674c8f.

Bibliography

Aberjhani, and Sandra L. West. "The *Chicago Defender*." In *Encyclopedia of the Harlem Renaissance*, edited by Aberjhani and Sandra L. West. New York: Facts on File, 2003.

Aberjhani, and Sandra L. West, eds. *Encyclopedia of the Harlem Renaissance*. New York: Facts on File, 2003.

American Tobacco Company. *Sold American: The First Fifty Years*. Durham NC: American Tobacco Company, 1954.

Anderson, Ann. *Snake Oil, Hustlers and Hambones: The American Medicine Show*. Jefferson NC: McFarland, 2004.

Angell, Roger. *The Summer Game*. New York: Open Road Media, 2013. Kindle edition.

Arias, Santiago, and Lea Hellmuller. "Hispanics and Latinos and the U.S. Media: New Issues for Future Research." *Communications Research Trends* 35, no. 2 (2016): 4–21.

Batey, Mark. *Brand Meaning*. New York: Routledge, 2008.

Baudrillard, Jean. *Simulation and Simulacra*. Translated by Sheila Faria Glaser. Ann Arbor: University of Michigan Press, 1994.

Beard, Fred, K. *Humor in the Advertising Business: Theory, Practice, and Wit*. Lanham MD: Rowman and Littlefield, 2008.

Berger, Peter, and Thomas Luckmann. *The Social Construction of Reality: A Treatise in the Sociology of Knowledge*. New York: Open Road Media, 2011. Kindle edition. Originally published 1966.

Berkman, Dave. "Long Before Arledge: Sports and TV, the Earliest Years, 1937–1947, as Seen by the Contemporary Press." *Journal of Popular Culture* 22, no. 2 (Fall 1988).

Black, Jennifer M. "Corporate Calling Cards: Advertising Trade Cards and Logos in the United States, 1876–1890." *Journal of American Culture* 32 (December 2009).

Blanchard, Margaret A., ed. *History of Mass Media in America*. New York: Routledge, 2013.

Bobrow-Strain, Aaron. *White Bread: The Social History of the Store-Bought Loaf*. Boston: Beacon Press, 2013.

Brandt, Allan. *The Cigarette Century: The Rise, Fall, and Deadly Persistence of the Product that Defined America*. New York: Basic Books, 2009.

Briley, Ron. *Class at Bat, Gender on Deck, and Race in the Hole: A Line-up of Essays on Twentieth-Century Culture and America's Game.* Jefferson NC: McFarland, 2003.

Bruce, Scott, and Bill Crawford. *Cerealizing America: The Unsweetened Story of American Breakfast Cereal.* Boston: Faber and Faber, 1995.

Bruns, Roger. *Preacher: Billy Sunday and Big-time American Evangelism.* Champaign: University of Illinois Press, 1992.

The "Bull" Durham Baseball Guide. Boston: Baseball Publishing Company, 1911.

Burgos, Adrian, Jr. *Playing America's Game: Baseball, Latinos, and the Color Line.* Berkeley: University of California Press, 2007.

Carroll, Carroll. *None of Your Business: Or, My Life with J. Walter Thompson (Confessions of a Renegade Radio Writer).* New York: Cowles, 1970.

Carter, Lendol. *Financing the American Dream: A Cultural History of Consumer Credit.* Princeton NJ: Princeton University Press, 2009.

Chasser, Anne H. "A Historical Perspective: The International Trademark Association and the United States Patent and Trademark Office." *The Trademark Reporter: Official Journal of the International Trademark Association* 93 (January–February 2003).

Ciment, James. "Consumer Debt and Bankruptcy." In vol. 2 of *Social Issues in America: An Encyclopedia*, edited by James Ciment. New York: Routledge, 2006.

———, ed. *Social Issues in America: An Encyclopedia.* New York: Routledge, 2006.

Cobb, Tyrus Raymond. *Busting 'Em: And Other Big League Stories.* New York: E. J. Clode, 1914.

Cobb, Ty, and Al Stump, *My Life in Baseball: The True Record.* Lincoln: University of Nebraska Press, 1961.

Cox, Jim. *Sold on the Radio: Advertising in the Golden Age of Broadcasting.* Jefferson NC: McFarland, 2008.

Cramp, Arthur J. *Nostrums and Quackery: Articles on the Nostrum Evil and Quackery Reprinted from the* Journal of the American Medical Association. Chicago: Press of the American Medical Association, 1912.

Creamer, Robert W. *Babe: The Legend Comes to Life.* Harmondsworth UK: Penguin, 1983.

Cruikshank, Jeffrey L., and Arthur W. Schultz. *The Man Who Sold America: The Amazing (but True!) Story of Albert D. Lasker and the Creation of the Advertising Century.* Cambridge MA: Harvard Business Press, 2010.

Davila, Arlene M. *Latinos, Inc.: The Marketing and Making of a People.* Berkeley: University of California Press, 2001.

de Mooij, Marieke. *Global Marketing and Advertising: Understanding Cultural Paradoxes.* Thousand Oaks CA: SAGE Publications, 2013.

Dickson, Paul. *The Dickson Baseball Dictionary.* New York: W.W. Norton.

Donohue, Julie. "A History of Drug Advertising: The Evolving Roles of Consumers and Consumer Protection." *Millbank Quarterly* 84, no. 4 (December 2006).

Drake, St. Clair, and Horace R. Cayton. *Black Metropolis: A Study of Negro Life in a Northern City.* Chicago: University of Chicago Press, 1945, 1970.

Drowne, Kathleen Morgan, and Patrick Huber. *The 1920s*. Westport CT: Greenwood, 2004.

Du Bois, W. E. B. *The Philadelphia Negro: A Social Study*. New York: Shocken Books, 1967.

Edgerton, Gary. *The Columbia History of American Television*. New York: Columbia University Press, 2001.

Eig, Jonathan. *Luckiest Man: The Life and Death of Lou Gehrig*. New York: Simon and Schuster, 2005.

Elliason, Meredith. "In the Hands of Children." In *The Scrapbook in American Life*, edited by Susan Tucker, Katherine Ott, and Patricia Buckler. Philadelphia: Temple University Press, 2006.

Endres, Kathleen L. "From 'Lost Manhood' to 'Erectile Dysfunction': The Commercialization of Impotence." In vol. 3 of *We Are What We Sell: How Advertising Shapes American Life . . . And Always Has*, edited by Danielle Sarver Coombs and Bob Batchelor. New York: ABC-CLIO, 2014.

Erbe, P. H., Jr. "New Horizons." In *Printer's Ink: Fifty Years, 1888-1938*. New York: Garland, 1986.

Ford, Henry. *The Case Against the Little White Slaver*. Detroit: Henry Ford, 1914.

Fox, Stephen R. *The Mirror Makers: A History of American Advertising and Its Creators*. Urbana: University of Illinois Press, 1984.

Franklin, V. P. "'Voice of the Black Community': The *Philadelphia Tribune*, 1912–41." *Pennsylvania History: A Journal of Mid-Atlantic Studies* 52, no. 4 (October 1984).

Friedman, Walter A. *Birth of a Salesman: The Transformation of Selling in Modern America*. Cambridge MA: Harvard University Press, 2009.

Garvey, Ellen Gruber. *Adman in the Parlor: Magazines and the Gendering of Consumer Culture, 1880s to 1910s*. New York: Oxford University Press, 1996.

Gorn, Elliott J., and Warren Hay Goldstein. *A Brief History of American Sports*. New York: Hill and Wang, 1993.

Gray, James. *Business Without Boundary: The Story of General Mills*. Minneapolis: University of Minnesota Press, 1964.

Grover, Kathryn, ed. *Images of Health, Sport, and the Body, 1830–1940*. Amherst: University of Massachusetts Press, 1989.

Gruesz, Kirsten Silva. "America." In *Key Words for American Cultural Studies*, edited by Bruce Burgett and Glenn Hendler. New York: New York University Press, 2014.

Gunter, Barrie. *Celebrity Capital: Assessing the Value of Fame*. New York: Bloomsbury, 2014.

Gunther, John. *Taken at the Flood: The Story of Albert D. Lasker*. New York: Harper, 1960.

Habell-Pallan, Michelle, and Mary Romero. *Latino/a Popular Culture*. New York: New York University Press, 2003.

Holden, Perry Greeley, Edmund John McFadden, and Orville T. Bright, eds. *Practical Education: A Home Library of Fourteen Books in One*, Book 12. Chicago: W. E. Richardson Company, 1917.

Holmes, Dan. *Ty Cobb: A Biography*. Westport CT: Greenwood Press, 2004.

Houk, John, ed. *Outdoor Advertising: History and Regulation.* Notre Dame: University of Notre Dame Press, 1969.

Kahle, Lynn R., and Pamela M. Homer. "Physical Attractiveness of the Celebrity Endorser: A Social Adaptation Perspective." *Journal of Consumer Research* 11, no. 4 (1985).

Kanner, Bernice. "On Madison Avenue: Coke vs. Pepsi: the Battle of the Bubbles." *New York* 14, no. 39 (October 5, 1981).

Keyes, Ralph. *The Quote Verifier: Who Said What, Where, and When.* New York: St. Martin's, 2006.

Kimes, Beverly Rae, and Robert C. Ackerson. *Chevrolet: A History from 1911.* New Albany IN: Automobile Heritage Publishing, 1986.

Kleiner, Fred S. *Gardner's Art Through the Ages: A Global History.* Boston: Cengage, 2014.

Kluger, Richard. *Ashes to Ashes: America's Hundred-Year Cigarette War, the Public Health, and the Unabashed Triumph of Philip Morris.* New York: Knopf, 2010.

Knoedelseder, William. *Bitter Brew: The Rise and Fall of Anheuser-Busch and America's Kings of Beer.* New York: HarperCollins, 2012.

Kushner, David. *Levittown: Two Families, One Tycoon, and the Fight for Civil Rights in America's Legendary Suburb.* New York: Bloomsbury, 2009.

Lanctot, Neil. *Negro League Baseball: The Rise and Ruin of a Black Institution.* Philadelphia: University of Pennsylvania Press, 2004.

Lears, Jackson. *Fable of Abundance: A Cultural History of Advertising in America.* New York: Basic Books, 1994.

Lewis, David Lanier. *The Public Image of Henry Ford: An American Folk Hero and His Company.* Detroit: Wayne State University Press, 1976.

Lewis, Robert F. II. *Smart Ball: Marketing the Myth and Managing the Reality of Major League Baseball.* Jackson: University Press of Mississippi, 2001.

Linge, Mary Kay. *Jackie Robinson: A Biography.* Westport CT: Greenwood, 2007.

Lowry, Philip. *Green Cathedrals.* New York: Bloomsbury, 2006.

Malloy, Jerry. "The Strange Career of Sol White." In *Out of the Shadows: African American Baseball from the Cuban Giants to Jackie Robinson,* edited by Bill Kirwin. Lincoln: University of Nebraska Press, 2005.

Marchand, Roland. *Advertising the American Dream: Making Way for Modernity, 1920–1945.* Berkeley: University of California Press, 1985.

Markham, Jerry W. *A Financial History of the United States.* Armonk NY: M. E. Sharpe, 2002.

McCracken, Grant. "Advertising: Meaning or Information." *Advances in Consumer Research* 14 (1987).

——. "Who Is a Celebrity Endorser? Cultural Foundations of the Endorsement Process." *Journal of Consumer Research* 16, no. 3 (1989).

McCue, Andy. *Mover and Shaker: Walter O'Malley, the Dodgers, and Baseball's Westward Expansion.* Lincoln: University of Nebraska Press, 2014.

McGovern, Artie. *The Secret of Keeping Fit.* New York: Simon and Schuster, 1935.

McKibben, Gordon. *Cutting Edge: Gillette's Journey to Global Leadership*. Cambridge MA: Harvard Business Press, 1998.

McLuhan, Marshall. *Understanding Media: The Cultural Extensions of Man*. Berkeley CA: Gingko Press, 2013. Kindle edition.

McMaster, James Smith. *McMaster's Commercial Decision Affecting the Banker and Merchant*. Vol. 15. New York: Commercial Book Company, 1912.

Miller, Sam. "Tuning Up the Ball Players of the Big Leagues." *Physical Culture* 23, no. 6 (June 1910).

Montville, Leigh, *The Big Bam: The Life and Times of Babe Ruth*. New York: Doubleday, 2006.

Mrozek, Donald J. "From National Health to Personal Fulfillment, 1890–1940." In *Images of Health, Sport, and the Body, 1830–1940*, edited by Kathryn Grover. Amherst: University of Massachusetts Press, 1989.

Napier, Kristine M. *Issues in Tobacco*. New York: American Council on Science and Health, 1992.

Newman, Roberta. "Driven: Branding Derek Jeter, Redefining Race." *NINE: A Journal of Baseball History and Culture* 17, no. 2 (Spring 2009): 70–79.

———. "It Pays to Be Personal," *NINE: A Journal of Baseball History and Culture* 12, no. 1 (Fall 2003): 25–42.

———. "Now Pitching for the Dodgers." In *The Cooperstown Symposium on Baseball and American Culture, 2001*, edited by William M. Simons. Jefferson NC: McFarland, 2002.

———. "The Pitch: Baseball and Advertising." In *The Cooperstown Symposium on Baseball and American Culture, 2001*, 203–19, edited by William M. Simons. Jefferson NC: McFarland, 2002.

———. "Pitching Behind the Color Line: Baseball, Advertising, and Race." *Baseball Research Journal* SABR no. 36 (2007): 81–90.

Newman, Roberta, and Joel Nathan Rosen. *Black Baseball, Black Business: Race Enterprise and the Fate of the Segregated Dollar*. Jackson: University Press of Mississippi, 2014.

Noriega, Chon A. *Shot in America: Television, the State, and the Rise of Chicano Cinema*. Minneapolis: University of Minnesota Press, 2000.

Norris, James D. *Advertising and the Transformation of American Society, 1865–1920*. New York: Greenwood, 1990.

O'Neal, Bill. *The American Association: A Baseball History, 1902–1991*. Austin TX: Eakins Press, 1991.

Pelfrey, William. *Billy, Alfred, and General Motors: The Story of Two Unique Men, a Legendary Company, and a Remarkable Time in America*. New York: AMACOM, 2006.

Pendergrast, Mark. *For God, Country, and Coca-Cola: The Definitive History of the Great American Soft Drink and the Company that Makes It*. New York: Basic Books, 2013.

Pennock, Pamela E. *Advertising Sin and Sickness: The Politics of Alcohol and Tobacco Marketing, 1950–1990*. DeKalb: Northern Illinois University Press, 2007.

Poekel, Charles A., Jr. "Babe Ruth vs. Baby Ruth: The Quest for a Candy Bar." In *The Cooperstown Symposium on Baseball and American Culture, 2009–2010*, edited by William M. Simons. Jefferson NC: McFarland, 2011.

Pollay, R. W., J. S. Lee, and D. Carter-Whitney. "Separate, But Not Equal: Racial Segmentation in Cigarette Advertising." *Journal of Advertising* 21, no. 1 (1992).

Porter, Patrick C. "Origins of the American Tobacco Company." In *American Economic Growth: The Historic Challenge*, edited by William F. Donnelly. New York: MSS Information, 1993.

Pracejus, John W. "Seven Psychological Mechanisms through Which Sponsorship Can Influence Consumers." In *Sports Marketing and the Psychology of Marketing Communication*, edited by Lynn Kahle and Chris Riley. Mahwah NJ: Lawrence Erlbaum Associates, 2004.

Printer's Ink: Fifty Years, 1888-1938. New York: Garland, 1986.

"The Propaganda for Reform: Nuxated Iron." *Journal of the American Medical Association* 67, no. 7 (October 21, 1916).

Rampersad, Arnold. *Jackie Robinson: A Biography*. New York: Random House, 2011.

"Reading Notice." In *Encyclopedia of American Journalism*, edited by Stephen L. Vaughn, 440. New York: Routledge, 2008.

Rein, Irving, Philip Kotler, and Martin Stoller. *High Visibility: The Making and Marketing of Professionals into Celebrities*. Chicago: NTC Business Books, 1997.

Ripken, Cal, Jr., and Mike Bryan. *The Only Way I Know*. New York: Viking Penguin, 1997.

Ritter, Lawrence S. *The Glory of Their Times*. New York: William Morrow, 1985.

Rudacille, Deborah. *Roots of Steel: Boom and Bust in an American Mill Town*. New York: Knopf Doubleday, 2010.

Ruth, George Herman. *Babe Ruth's Own Book of Baseball*. Lincoln NE: Bison Books, 1992.

———. *Playing the Game: My Early Years in Baseball*. Edited by William R. Cobb. Mineola NY: Dover, 2011.

Samuel, Lawrence R. *Brought to You By: Postwar Television Advertising and the American Dream*. Austin: University of Texas Press, 2001.

Segrave, Kerry. *Endorsements in Advertising*. Jefferson NC: McFarland, 2005.

Seymour, Harold, and Dorothy Seymour Mills. *Baseball: The Early Years*. New York: Oxford University Press, 1960.

———. *Baseball: The Golden Age*. New York: Oxford University Press, 1971.

Shapiro, Michael. *The Last Good Season*. New York: Broadway Books, 2003.

Shiffert, John. *Base Ball in Philadelphia: A History of the Early Game 1831–1900*. Jefferson NC: McFarland, 2006.

Simon, Morton J. *Public Relations Law*. New York: Appleton, Century, Crofts, 1969.

Sivrulka, Juliann. *Soap, Sex, and Cigarettes: A Cultural History of American Advertising*. Boston: Cengage, 2012.

Skotnes, Andor. *A New Deal for All?: Race and Class Struggles in Depression-Era Baltimore*. Durham NC: Duke University Press, 2012.

Sleight, Steve. *Sponsorship: What It Is and How to Use It.* Maidenhead UK: McGraw Hill UK, 1989.

Smulyan, Susan. *Selling Radio: The Commercialization of American Broadcasting, 1920–1934.* Washington DC: Smithsonian Institution Press, 1994.

Spalding's Official Base Ball Guide, 1889. Chicago: A. G. Spalding and Brothers, 1889.

Spivey, Donald. "Satchel Paige's Struggle for Selfhood in the Era of Jim Crow." In *Out of the Shadows: A Biographical History of African American Athletes,* edited by David K. Wiggins. Fayetteville: University of Arkansas Press, 2006.

Stump, Al. *Cobb.* Chapel Hill NC: Algonquin, 1994.

Sundstrom, William A. "Last Hired, First Fired? Unemployment and Urban Black Workers during the Great Depression." *Journal of Economic History* 52, no. 2 (June 1992).

Thorson, Esther, and Margaret Duffy. *Advertising Age: The Principles of Advertising and Marketing Communication at Work.* Mason OH: Cengage, 2012.

Tocker, Philip. "Standardized Outdoor Advertising: History, Economics, Self-Regulation." In *Outdoor Advertising: History and Regulation,* edited by John W. Houk. Notre Dame: University of Notre Dame Press, 1969.

Tygiel, Jules. *Past Time: Baseball as History.* New York: Oxford University Press, 2001.

Van Munching, Philip. *Beer Blast.* New York: Random House, 1997.

Vaughn, Stephen L., ed. *Encyclopedia of American Journalism.* New York: Routledge, 2008.

Ventola, C. Lee. "Direct-to-Consumer Pharmaceutical Advertising: Therapeutic or Toxic?" *Pharmacy and Therapeutics* 36, no. 10 (October 2011).

Voigt, David Quentin. *American Baseball.* In vol. 2 of *From the Commissioners to Continental Expansion.* University Park PA: Penn State Press, 1992.

Walker, James R. *Crack of the Bat: A History of Baseball on the Radio.* Lincoln: University of Nebraska Press, 2015.

Walker, James R., and Robert V. Bellamy. *Center Field Shot: A History of Baseball on Television.* Lincoln: University of Nebraska Press, 2008.

Walker, Juliet E. K. *The History of Black Business in America: Capitalism, Race, Entrepreneurship.* New York: Macmillan, 1998.

Walsh, Christy. *Adios to Ghosts.* New York: Christy Walsh, 1937.

Ward, Peter C. *Federal Trade Commission: Law, Practice, and Procedure.* New York: ALM Properties.

Watkins, Julian. *The 100 Greatest Advertisements 1852–1958: Who Wrote Them and What They Did.* New York: Dover, 2012.

Weems, Robert E. *Desegregating the Dollar: African American Consumerism in the Twentieth Century.* New York: New York University Press, 1998.

Wheeler, John N. Preface to *Busting 'Em: And Other Big League Stories* by Tyrus Raymond Cobb. New York: E. J. Clode, 1914.

White, Sol. *Sol White's History of Colored Baseball with Other Documents on the Early Black Game, 1886–1936.* Lincoln: University of Nebraska Press, 1995.

Wiggins, David K., ed. *Out of the Shadows: A Biographical History of African American Athletes.* Fayetteville: University of Arkansas Press, 2006.

Wilkerson, Isabel. *The Warmth of Other Suns: The Epic Story of America's Great Migration*. New York: Vintage, 2011.

"Williams, George Grant." In vol. 1 of *Who's Who of the Colored Race: A General Biographical Dictionary of Men and Women of African Descent*, edited by Frank Lincoln Mather. Chicago: Frank Lincoln Mather, 1915.

Wynter, Leon E. *American Skin: Pop Culture, Big Business, and the End of White America*. New York: Crown, 2002.

Yost, Mike, and Jeff Wilser. *The Man Cave Book*. New York: Harper Collins, 2011.

Zinn, John G., and Paul G. Zinn, eds. *The People Remember Ebbets Field: Essays and Memories of Brooklyn's Historic Ballpark, 1913–1960*. Jefferson NC: McFarland, 2012.

Index